Economic Soci

STUDIES IN SOCIAL DISCONTINUITY

Under the Consulting Editorship of:

CHARLES TILLY
University of Michigan

EDWARD SHORTER
University of Toronto

In preparation

Manuel Gottlieb. A Theory of Economic Systems

Robert Max Jackson. The Formation of Craft Labor Markets

Published

Michael B. Katz. Poverty and Policy in American History

Arthur L. Stinchcombe. Economic Sociology

Jill S. Quadagno. Aging in Early Industrial Society: Work, Family, and Social Policy in Nineteenth-Century England

J. Dennis Willigan and Katherine A. Lynch. Sources and Methods of Historical Demography

Dietrich Gerhard. Old Europe: A Study of Continuity, 1000-1800

Charles Tilly. As Sociology Meets History

Maris A. Vinovskis. Fertility in Massachusetts from the Revolution to the Civil War

Juan G. Espinosa and Andrew S. Zimbalist. Economic Democracy: Workers' Participation in Chilean Industry 1970-1973: Updated Student Edition

Alejandro Portes and John Walton. Labor, Class, and the International System

James H. Mittelman. Underdevelopment and the Transition to Socialism: Mozambique and Tanzania

John R. Gillis. Youth and History: Tradition and Change in European Age Relations, 1770—Present: Expanded Student Edition

Samuel Kline Cohn, Jr. The Laboring Classes in Renaissance Florence

Richard C. Trexler. Public Life in Renaissance Florence

Paul Oquist. Violence, Conflict, and Politics in Colombia

Fred Weinstein. The Dynamics of Nazism: Leadership, Ideology, and the Holocaust

John R. Hanson II. Trade in Transition: Exports from the Third World, 1840—1900

Evelyne Huber Stephens. The Politics of Workers' Participation: The Peruvian Approach in Comparative Perspective

Albert Bergesen (Ed.). Studies of the Modern World-System

The list of titles in this series continues on the last page of this volume

ECONOMIC SOCIOLOGY

Arthur L. Stinchcombe

Department of Sociology
University of Arizona
Tucson, Arizona

and

Graduate School of Business
Stanford University
Stanford, California

1983

ACADEMIC PRESS, INC.

(Harcourt Brace Jovanovich, Publishers)

Orlando   San Diego   San Francisco   New York   London
Toronto   Montreal   Sydney   Tokyo   São Paulo

ACADEMIC PRESS, INC.
Orlando, Florida 32887

United Kingdom Edition published by
ACADEMIC PRESS, INC. (LONDON) LTD.
24/28 Oval Road, London NW1 7DX

Library of Congress Cataloging in Publication Data

Main entry under title:

Economic sociology.

   (Studies in social discontinuity)
   Bibliography: p.
   Includes index.
   1. Sociology. 2. Marxian Economics. 3. Human
ecology. 4. Technology--Social aspects. 5. Population.
6. Production (Economic theory) I. Stinchcombe,
Arthur L. II. Series.
HM35.E246 1982   306'.3   82-13717
ISBN 0-12-671380-4 (hardcover)
ISBN 0-12-671382-0 (paperback)

PRINTED IN THE UNITED STATES OF AMERICA

84 85 86   9 8 7 6 5 4 3 2

Contents

v

Preface

When I began this work a decade ago my intent was to provide a basis in economic sociology for a much larger book on comparative macrosociology. Recently, when faced with what I had actually produced, my editor at Academic Press said he felt like an Eskimo confronted with a beached whale: perhaps there was a good deal of value in it, but as it was, it was quite unmanageable. In any case, by the time my tome was finished, comparative sociology had largely given way to the historical study of particular societies, or systems of societies, work usually based on broadly "materialist" conceptions of history.

Since there now seemed to be no interest in the kind of tome I had written, I looked around in sociology to see which parts of what I had said still needed to be said, given that sociology had moved on to a new conception of how macrosociology should be done. It seemed to me that the material basis itself was the worst understood part of macrosociology, even when it was informed by Marxist thought. I therefore decided to turn the economic part of the book into an introduction to economic sociology that would also be a critique of the analysis of the material basis of societies in the recent "neo-Marxist" literature.

I hope, therefore, that this book can serve as theoretical background to a specific analysis of modern economic institutions, as in stratification courses, industrial or economic sociology courses, and organization theory courses that deal with the population of organizations in the economy. (Roughly two-thirds of formal organizational life is now lived in the economic sector of society, narrowly defined.) But, I also hope to address the theoretical needs of the historical branches of the theoretical social sciences (especially historical sociology and economic history) and of the more theoretically oriented historians. Although comparative sociologists are a vanishing breed, except perhaps in social anthropology, I hope the book will be of interest to them, since I still count myself as one of them.

The history of this book shows how fragile cooperative ventures are when history changes the bases and assumptions of cooperation. When it started, it had two coauthors—the anthropologist Neville Dyson-Hudson and the historical sociologist Sasha Weitman—and a textbook publishing house, Harcourt Brace and World. Without the coauthors' contributions to my knowledge of, respectively, the Karimojong and eighteenth-century France, the book's illustrative material would have been much poorer. Without the fantasy of getting rich by writing a textbook, I might never have tried to outline the basic elements of economic sociology. Although the coauthors never put pen to paper and although the publisher, now named Harcourt Brace Jovanovich, made no blue pencil marks in the manuscript, they are all in a very real sense cooriginators of the book. I am sure it would have ended up a better book if the cooperation could have been sustained—the whale might have blown and sounded.

Charles Tilly and Carol Heimer are more nearly coproducers of the book. Tilly saved me from many factual errors on eighteenth-century France and suggested much of the final shape of the book. Carol Heimer gave me much of the notion of how to form the mass of material into this book, and most of the motivation. A penetrating critique of the beached whale by Walter Godlfrank helped strengthen my resolve for the hardest decision, to cut the manuscript by about two-thirds. That decision still hurts, even as I write this preface.

I can no longer remember all the people who provided critical comments, listened to me teach while I was struggling with the ideas, or encouraged me (often with bewildered expressions they did not quite manage to conceal). It therefore seems somewhat unfair to pick out those who made comments on semifinal draft manuscripts. However, that at least is concrete volunteer work for which I can point to specific improved pages. I therefore name Judith Blake Davis, Beverley Duncan, Michael Hout, Nancy Howell, Stanley Lieberson, William Sewell, Jr., and Theda Skocpol. I appreciate their commitment to my scholarship, however tentative that commitment sometimes was.

It will be obvious from what I have said that the process of writing this book was often uncomfortable, and that it is not at all what I started out to write. Nevertheless, when I read it over I get flashes of pleasure. I believe those flashes are more frequent because many people have helped me in one way or another. The fact that the pleasure is compounded with vanity makes it clear I accept responsibility for the book.

In the old days, authors used to commend a book to the reader's attention. In doing that, I earnestly hope, and almost honestly believe, that the reader will benefit by paying attention.

Bergen, Norway
July 1982

1

The Economic Sociology of Neo-Marxism

This book has three somewhat contradictory purposes. Its major purpose is to introduce the student to the main conceptions of economic sociology. In particular, I want to introduce the sociology of the economy in such a way that it can be used to analyze the macroscopic structure of whole societies. The main use of economic sociology in current sociology is as a basis for explaining stratification and class conflict, or for explaining the long-term developments of a society's politics. Economic sociology should in part be shaped so as to be fit for such a job.

The second purpose is to illustrate the application of the concepts and theories of economic sociology by analyzing three societies at different levels of development: a primitive herding society, a late feudal or early capitalist society, and a modern society. I believe people will remember the principles better if they carry the principles around in the form of concrete images of particular societies, as well as in the form of theories, and those images should be of societies that are as diverse as possible.

The third purpose is a critique of the growing literature that uses economic sociology in the explanation of macroscopic social phenomena, mostly deriving from the Marxist tradition. I argue that because neo-Marxists are less interested in economic phenomena than in their effects, they leave major gaps in their analysis. The shaping of society and politics by the economy cannot be properly analyzed without a good analysis of the economy.

In this introductory chapter I try to show the core of Karl Marx's contribution to the analysis of the economy, and how the stunted development of that contribution in modern literature of neo-Marxism has led to theoretical difficulties. I will analyze Jeffery Paige's *Agrarian Revolution* (I will cite books by short titles; the complete citations will be found in the bibliography), Theda Skocpol's *States and Social Revolutions*, Immanuel Wallerstein's *The Modern World System*, and Erik Olin Wright's *Class Structure and Income Inequality*. Then I explain briefly the organization of the chapters of the rest of the book.

THE SOCIOLOGY OF THE
ENTERPRISE IN MARX

The general strategy of Marxist thought is to relate aggregate movements of economic life (e.g., a falling rate of profit) to the pressures on an individual or firm (e.g., pressure to substitute machinery for labor) by using *a theory of the economic enterprise* (e.g., of capitalist extraction of surplus value through hiring labor). That is, *economic sociology* connects great movements of economic forces to behavior of individuals by an examination of the institutional forms and technical constraints in which a society produces its livelihood.

The originality of Marx in his economic determinism was to describe the capitalist industrial enterprise in a two-sided way: on the one side how society-wide or worldwide movements of wages, prices, and profit affect the incentives of capitalists and workers in particular enterprises (these structures of incentives constitute the "relations of production"); and on the other side how these incentives and pressures combine with social and technical arrangements of production itself ("forces of production") to produce the social and economic structure of the economy. In place of the fictional economic man of classical economic theory, Marx placed the capitalist factory as a social unit.

This realism about the institutional units of the economy had many advantages for connecting the economic dynamics to the class struggle, which was probably Marx's main reason for developing the strategy. Only by knowing what incentives and open options faced the capitalists could Marx predict where they would dig in their heels in the struggle. Only by knowing what pressures capitalists would put on workers and what opportunities for factory worker organization were produced by the technology could Marx predict the political organization of the proletariat. The fact that Marx predicted wrongly where the capitalists would dig in (or that Lenin afterward predicted that capitalist governments would hold their colonies to the bitter end) does not invalidate Marx's central insights, namely, that it is the institutional structure of the economic enterprise that translates the great swings of the economy into incentives and pressures on individuals in different economic roles.

By defining class interests in this way Marx can derive the class-specific motivations for changing the institutional order from its operation at the level of the enterprise. For example, when Austrian nobles in the first half of the nineteenth century conducted "studies" of the efficiency of coerced traditional labor (*robot*) versus wage labor, and found that wage labor produces about two to two and one-half times as much, this creates pressure to reorganize labor relations on farms from feudal to capitalist, from "serfdom" to "wage labor." This is because technically efficient cooperative production is much more easily organized with a wage incentive system than with legal coercion (see Jerome Blum, *Noble Landowners and Agriculture in Austria, 1815-1840*, pp. 192–202). That is, *at the level of the enterprise* the "fetters" that feudal labor relations put on productive efficiency produce forces among landowners favorable to a "bourgeois revolution." But it is only when markets give clear prices of labor and agricultural produce that such calculations can be made, and only where free wage labor in agriculture is institutionally possible that the experiment could be made at all. That is, only under the historical circumstances of a world capitalist system can pressures be generated *within feudally organized enterprises* to change the structure of class relations *in the society as a whole* and in the enterprises themselves to a capitalist form. The overall generalization, then, is that when there are free markets in capital, labor, and commodities produced, most feudal enterprises with coerced labor will generate internal incentives and pressures to transform themselves into capitalist enterprises with free tenants or wage laborers. As Marx puts it, feudal labor relations become "fetters" on the progress of the forces of production and tend to be swept away to be replaced by capitalist forms.

In particular, if Austrian nobles can make more money with wage labor, they will put pressure on the government to remove the feudal ties that obligate them to their serfs (as well as obligate their serfs to them). Institutional structures are transformed because they give rise to incentives and pressures to change them. But the theory of how movements of the economy as a whole give rise to such incentives for changing the form of class relations is a theory of the enterprise in a capitalist market. Thus, the connection of economic forces to forces for change in the economic institutional order run through the theory of the enterprise—in particular, a theory of the conditions under which feudal labor relations are "fetters." But also it is the enterprise which works on, creates, modifies, or trains, the "forces of production" (i.e., the technical and organizational way the society's work gets done). The substitution of machinery for labor (i.e., the substitution of last year's labor in a machine shop for this year's labor on the factory floor) is not carried out by "the economy," but by particular factory managers and the workers they hire. The "falling rate of profit" cannot result in increased capitalization of enterprises (as Marx predicted it would) unless particular capitalists have incentives to buy machines. And factories cannot increase in scale or divide labor more finely (thus providing a basis for working-class organization), unless particular capitalists are motivated and able to do so. The social and technical organization of production is therefore created by enterprises that are shaped by the institutional order. The kinds of productive systems the enterprises can create are limited by the possibilities inherent in those institutions, as we pointed out for Austria. But possibilities for new productive activities, from cultivation of the common in new crop rotation schemes to spinning jennies, create pressures to develop institutions that can exploit them effectively. The enclosure movement and factory legislation created new forms of capitalist enterprise, with new forms of class relations, to exploit the new technical possibilities.

It is these two-sided links between the enterprise and economic forces on the one hand, and between the enterprise and the forces of production on the other hand, that make the sociology of the enterprise central to Marx's sociology. The theoretical power he obtained by this strategic innovation has entranced social scientists and historians ever since. It is a great temptation to a theorist to have long economic swings, incentives for the class struggle, incentives for technical and organizational progress, and pressures to reorganize the economic institutions, all in the same neat theoretical package. This in turn means we must examine the places where Marx went wrong, to try to save the main structure while discarding the mistakes.

It is clear that Marx went wrong (among other places) exactly in the center, in his theory of pressures on the capitalist enterprise. For example, he predicted a pressure to increase the ratio of capital to labor, which (given his analysis of what capital is) must mean an increase in the ratio of work in machine shops and other capital-producing enterprises to work in factories producing consumption commodities. But since about 1900 it has been true that it would take roughly three years of the output of the private sector to replace all the private business capital in the economy, and there has been no general tendency for that "capital–labor ratio" to increase. Another way to put this is that the increase in the efficiency of the capital-producing industries has been at least as fast as the increased efficiency of the consumer goods industries; thus, each worker can have more machinery *without* the implication that more labor went into producing those machines. As a consequence, there has been no general tendency for the profit rate per unit of labor to decline as predicted by Marx, and no pressure from this source on capitalists to increase the "rate of exploitation," that is, the ratio of profits to wages. It is true, however, that this rate of exploitation is higher in very capital-intensive industries such as the oil or chemical industries. So clearly Marx's theory of the capitalist enterprise was empirically wrong. (It also did not follow from Marx's own arguments—see Jon Elster, *Logic and Society*, pp. 113–118.) This means, of course, that Marx's predictions about class conflict that are derived from the changes in the "organic composition of capital," (or the capital–labor ratio), cannot be derived from his theory.

Yet Marx was right about what the theory should look like. It should have the institutional structure of the productive enterprise at its theoretical core to translate aggregate economic pressures and opportunities into pressures and incentives that bear on the individual. The idea that those incentives can create class conflict, and an evolutionary succession of enterprise forms ("modes of production"), is clearly right—Austrian noblemen can see that new enterprise forms will pay but that a wage-earning proletariat may be hard to control. New technical possibilities affect first the activities and social organization of production, for example producing pressures toward factory organization of production. Then factories affect the larger institutional order and the prevalence of class conflict. The new Marxism is an attempt to patch up Marxian theory by reanalyzing the relations between aggregate movements of the political economy and pressures on the behavior of individuals.

My general argument in this book is that most of the new Marxists, most of the time, have gone about this job of reconstruction in the wrong way. They have usually taken the tack that Marx's theory was "too economic," and so have tried to add a theory of politics, rather than to repair the core of Marxist theory, the theory of the enterprise. They are right in that it certainly is true that political forces respond directly to economic swings in quite a different way than do individual capitalists. It is also true that the political forms within which capitalism has grown have often been imposed against the will of the capitalists as a class: by feudal forces in late feudal times, by trade unions and socialist parties

in the twentieth century, and by the military requirements and aims of
national governments at all times (see especially Joseph A. Schumpeter,
Capitalism, Socialism, and Democracy and "Imperialism" in *Imperialism and
Social Classes* for an early treatment of both these problems). Although
we certainly need a theory of the response of political forces to economic
conditions, this cannot substitute for a workable theory of economic
enterprises. The fact that Marx got it wrong means that such a theory
will not be easy. To rescue the central valid vision of Marxism, we need
to repair its economic sociology, rather than to patch onto it a theory of
politics operating by quite different principles.

PAIGE AND AGRICULTURAL ENTERPRISE

The central systematic work on the new Marxist theory of the enterprise itself (as opposed to work that adds on politics) is Jeffery Paige's
Agrarian Revolution. He classified types of agrarian systems in the export
sectors of poorer countries by what the income of the various classes
depends on, with the three main alternatives being land, labor, and
capital. For example, coastal Peruvian plantations are distinguished from
traditional highland haciendas by the fact that upper-class income on
plantations is more a return from capital than from land, while on haciendas the reverse is true. Plantation labor is paid directly in wages,
while hacienda workers get to use a plot of hacienda land to raise their
own subsistence. Paige shows that the political behavior of the workers
in export agriculture can be very well predicted by a combination of
three factors: (1) the workers' own source of income, (2) what kind of
upper class they confront (i.e., what the landlords' source of income is),
and (3) the level of repressiveness versus reformism of the government.

What makes this analytical system go is therefore a categorization of
income by its "source." But, of course, it is the agricultural enterprise,
an integrated pattern of activity, done by labor with tools and motive
power applied to land, that produces all the income. The income from
selling cotton from the plantation does not come divided into labor,
land, and capital shares, nor does the wool harvest from a highland
hacienda.

When Paige says that capital, for example, is more important on the
plantation, he means two things: (1) that the *overall returns* to the enterprise depend in a crucial way on the amount of capital supplied, so
that, for example, dividing the land among the workers without supplying them with capital would greatly decrease production; and (2) that
within the enterprise the supplier of capital (in modern times the planter

is almost invariably a corporation rather than an individual) can claim a part of the income stream, given the means to enforce such claims provided to suppliers of capital in the political system and the land tenure system. The first of these, the dependence of production on a factor of production, is largely a technical matter, a matter of the shape of the "production function" that tells how much cotton will be produced at different levels of input of land, labor, and capital. But the second, the determination of the claims on the resulting income, the division of risks and returns among the participants, is clearly an aspect of the social structure. The claims are made valid by practical power, derived from a combination of how essential one's resources are to the enterprise, and of legal guarantees of those claims by the larger political system.

An example from quite far afield clarifies this distinction between the two senses of dependence of income on technology and dependence of income on the legal structure of claims. For a lot of small and medium-sized family-owned farms in the United States, the primary determinant of the total family income of the owner is whether or not the wife works in town. Many marginal farm enterprises would disappear if farm women could not work in the urban economy. This *factual* dependence of the total enterprise on the wife's work is usually not, however, reflected in the formal legal arrangements of the farm as an enterprise, for example, in the ownership of the livestock or the farm machinery. The arrangement of ownership claims to correspond to the female contribution usually comes about only at the death of the male farmer, and not as an incident of the ongoing enterprise that depends on female contributions. This shows that the dependence of the total enterprise income on specific contributions *may or may not* be reflected in corresponding claims on that income: the dependence of the hacienda on labor inputs is often reflected in increased *coercion* of laborers, not their increased income (see Wallerstein, *Modern World System II*, pp. 138–141 and 226–235 for examples of such increases in Europe).

What this means is that Paige's classification is not so purely "economic" as it appears at first glance. If plantation laborers reliably organize trade unions, this is a product of the way the *socially instituted* legal structure of the enterprise constitutes a system of economic incentives for the upper classes and the workers. The result of this is that the plantation owners resist worker organization less violently than do hacienda owners, and workers pursue higher wages rather than claims of landownership and land tenure reform. This structure of incentives gets its *power* to shape the form of conflict from the fact that the rewards it distributes are economic and are what the people have to live on. But it gets its *form*, which determines the direction in which behavior is shaped by the economic power, from the social structure of the enterprise.

This form of the enterprise has two aspects: a technical aspect of activities that plant, cultivate, and harvest crops, or breed, feed, and slaughter livestock, and a claims and rights aspect that divides up costs, risks, and benefits between the various participants and owners. One can have a similar technical form, say large-scale cultivation of cotton by gangs of workers on irrigated land; but in one society (e.g., Egypt during the Nasser regime) the claims may be divided in a socialist enterprise so that workers have claims to a permanent position and a share of the profits, while in another society (e.g., Peru) a capitalist corporation pays taxes to the government and wages to a work force that has fairly high turnover. Furthermore, a rather similar technology (without irrigation) in the American South once divided benefits between a planter family, a credit-providing "factor" who was also the broker for the crop, and a slave labor force. There can also be similar structures of claims (such as sharecropping between a landlord and a non-owning tenant) in radically different technical systems (such as Japanese irrigated "paddy" rice before World War II in less commercialized districts, and American corn belt farms with 100 times as much land and no irrigation).

The technical aspect of the organization of activities to produce goods is generally summed up in the Marxist concept of "the forces of production." The structure of claims on the flow of goods produced, or on the money they are sold for, are summed up as "the relations of production." A general Marxist postulate (cf. G. Cohen, *Karl Marx's Theory of History: A Defense*) is that there is a long-run tendency for the relations of production to assume a form in which the activities of production are efficiently and effectively done; thus, we expect to find that capital-intensive technical structures, such as irrigated cotton production, will assume a "capitalist" (or sometimes a "socialist") form of relations of production because those relations "fit" the technical form. On the other hand, largely subsistence grain and cattle haciendas with low capital intensity in the interior of Peru assume a more "feudal" form in which workers are paid by being allowed to be subsistence tenants on small plots. In Peru when capitalist organization becomes a more efficient way of organizing the forces of production on the coast, a pressure to break up the feudal "fetters" on the forces of production will be created. Among those forces are, of course, the political activities of agricultural workers that Paige is trying to explain, trade union activity on the coast, and sporadic land disputes and land invasions in the interior.

For Paige's purposes of predicting the form of worker political activity, all he has to do is to observe those features of the agricultural enterprise that predict, say, trade unions versus land invasions. For this purpose it may be sufficient to classify together as "plantations" all capital-intensive enterprises that hire large crews of wage laborers, so that a class whose claims on the product are based on capital confronts a class whose claims are based on labor time. But clearly to understand how cotton "plantations" in Egypt became government enterprises or how the subsistence of slaves on southern United States "plantations" was determined, something more is required than a scheme that would correctly reclassify them so that one will not predict, for example, slave trade unions. What one needs for this larger purpose is *a theory of alternative (social) ways to run a given type of technical system*. Such a theory should help us with the problem of whether workers on a socialist cooperative or black slaves derive their income from land, labor, or some third alternative not included in Paige's system.

We will hope that a theory of the alternative ways to run a given type of technical system will include the classical observation that set Marx off along this line, that it is very hard to organize factory production by feudal relations of production, for example by making a worker pay rent on his or her machine. In the piece of history Marx analyzed, a central place must be given to the invention, institutionalization, and further development of the social form of the capitalist factory. Only once that form exists does Paige's generalization become relevant, i.e., that factories or plantations set up like factories will probably generate trade unions rather than other forms of worker protest.

If we examine carefully what it is about the capital intensity of plantations that produces the moderation of landlord behavior, it turns out not to have anything to do with the capital used in agriculture itself. In Peru the irrigation system is the most capital-intensive part of cotton or sugar cultivation. Large plantation owners such as Casa Grace and Gildemeister make money in cotton and sugar mills and in commercial enterprises such as warehousing in the United States and shipping. What they need from the plantations is a regular supply of raw material at the world market price, not large profits in agriculture as such. That regular supply may be furnished by a factory-in-the-field with union labor, or by detailed contracts providing schedules of delivery between the processing factory and independent farmers (as is found in the frozen vegetable industry in the United States), or by many other alternatives. So it is the structure of this kind of capitalist enterprise, not the amount of capital in agriculture, that makes the plantation owner willing to bargain and compromise. Paige (1975) gives as the first reason Grace and Gildemeister had "little to fear" from unionization, that they "are diversified enterprises, and agriculture does not represent their total livelihood. In fact, given the small importance of cane growing to their total profits, the loss of cane lands . . . is not the total tragedy that it is for a small estate owner [p. 145]."

In Viet Nam heavy capital investment in agricultural production in paddy rice did not produce the willingness to compromise, and the result was revolution rather than the formation of trade unions, despite the fact that both the amount and kind of investment was similar to that of Peru (i.e., in some kind of irrigation facilities).

When we turn to the workers who are "paid" in land rather than wages, we find again that it is the structure of the enterprise that shapes cultivator claims. The sharecropper in the delta in Viet Nam and the cash tenant on a 1000-acre North Dakota wheat farm (also in an export enclave) both have precarious tenure on the land and get their "wages" from what remains from the crop after the landlord gets his or her share. To call the North American a smallholder and to predict that he or she will participate in agitation for parity prices and sales to the USSR, while the other is called a wage worker (really) and predicted to be a socialist revolutionary does indeed get their politics right. But it turns out that many Vietnamese tenants had fixed rents rather than the share rents that Paige takes to be a sign of proletarianization, and that landlords tried to find "solvent" tenants (Paige, 1975, p. 305), and that the upper classes in Mekong Delta used credit, marketing, milling, and commercialization profits for a large share of their income (pp. 306–307), just like Casa Grace, and more importantly, just like the upper classes in country towns in North Dakota as described by Veblen (Paige, 1975, p. 29).[1] What is crucial instead is that the North Dakota farmer believes that he or she is on the way to developing "a competence" of agricultural property, and his or her landlord is probably a farmer's widow living off such an accumulated competence inherited from her husband. Obviously this would not be believable to the North Dakota tenant unless in fact the rent was low enough so that he or she had money left over to save, to buy some new land or a piece of farm machinery. The structure of claims based on land is therefore not different; but the quantities of landlord claims turns one cultivator into a socialist revolutionary and the other into a member of the American Farm Bureau Federation (though earlier they voted populist).

---

[1]Paige quotes this from Lipset; the Veblen essay is reprinted in *The Viking Portable Veblen*.

In short, Paige's own classificatory principles do not distinguish his cases. The reason is that they are not sufficiently complete as theories of the enterprises and of the nature of claims on the flow of income produced. It is a testimony to Paige's thoroughness as a scholar that one can use his own data on agricultural enterprises to show that his own classificatory principles will not produce the classifications he uses. But what this means is that his descriptions of agricultural enterprises are more adequate than his theory of them. His economic sociology is not sturdy enough to generate his independent variables. Since his independent variables predict cultivators' political behavior better than any other theory of agrarian movements, it would be worthwhile to develop economic sociology far enough to generate those independent variables.

The core difficulty in Paige's theory has to do with the problem that will occupy us in Chapter 4, specifically, the exact structure of the incentive system. There are specific features of the incentive system used in the delta for the cultivators that the Vietnamese landlords got to set up by virtue of their ownership of the land: the Vietnamese landlords in the delta sought out cultivators who had some capital and good credit rather than hiring the cheapest agricultural labor; the landlords negotiated individual tenancies to specific plots of land, rather than imposing a uniform wage rate for laborers; the owners did not supply supervision of cultivation in the form of a permanent staff of foremen and crew bosses; the landlords' commercial enterprises were small individually owned firms rather than sprawling corporate giants; and few of the tenants had a chance to become smallholders or landlords themselves. In each of these respects, except the lack of opportunity to become smallholders, the incentive system was different for the workers on the Casa Grace plantations in Peru.

Many of these differences in the wage versus tenancy system have very little to do with how much of the profit comes from land versus capital (the Mekong Delta, like the Peruvian coastal desert, is completely unproductive without very substantial investments in water management). Instead they derive from the greater requirements of skill and care in wet rice cultivation than in sugar cane cultivation. The reason that Paige's theory of sources of landlord income (capital versus land) and sources of cultivation income (wages versus land) is not sufficient to distinguish between the systems of the Mekong Delta and the Peruvian coast is that the differences in the economic institutions in the two are traceable in large measure to technical requirements. Corporations with a uniform schedule of wages produce trade unions and individual landlords with individualized tenancy arrangements tend to produce revolutions, whether or not the corporations have low capital investments and the landlords' income is derived from extensive investment in expensive irrigation and drainage work. The core of Paige's classification is thus his implicit theory of incentive structures, a theory we will try to make explicit in Chapter 4, rather than his explicit theory of sources of income.

SKOCPOL AND POLITICAL COMPONENTS
OF MODES OF PRODUCTION

In her *States and Social Revolutions* Skocpol diagnosed the difficulty with Paige's book as inattention to politics (1979: p. 319, note 11). This has two components. The most important, which we will slight here, is that reasonably strong political systems easily resist agrarian revolts so that revolutions cannot really be explained without explaining the weakness of the states in which they occur. Paige may be able to explain why cultivators will, or will not, revolt when they have a chance, but he cannot explain the political circumstances under which they will have a chance. For example, it turns out that the central variable in Paige explaining land invasions and other "agrarian events" (e.g., in highland Peru) is an interaction term, commercial haciendas that pay cultivators in land, multiplied by the presence of a reform or socialist party in government (Paige, 1975: p. 110). Clearly the presence of socialist or reform parties in the government is a political condition of the revolts separate from the land tenure system. So the theory of sources of income in Paige needs a theory of socialist and reform parties to be a complete explanation. Paige's calling such socialist and reform parties "conservative" in the theoretical introduction (1975, p. 29) will not do the theoretical job, because their conservatism does not explain land invasions. Again Paige's empirical scholarship is good enough to provide the basis of its own critique in Skocpol.

Skocpol's second objection is more important from the point of view of our task here. She points out, for example, that if one analyzes the French peasantry as typical individualistic landowners, without noting their extensive village organization for the regulation of three-field agriculture, management of forests and pasture, and for legal disputes with seigneurs, one underestimates how much capacity for collective action the peasantry would show in the Revolution of 1789 (1979, p. 116, 320, note 15; actually as we will see in Chapter 2, it is mainly the peasantry of the Seine and Loire valleys that was organized the way Skocpol says all French peasants were organized).

The objection here is that in the organization of both the technical and the legal aspects of the northern plains French peasant enterprise, the village plays a role that is not captured by pointing out that they were smallholders paying rents and seigneurial dues, extensively involved in commercial production. The village then is a part of the mode of production, *both* of the forces of production in the technical activities of agriculture *and* of the relations of production as an active unit in the land tenure system, a unit run mainly by peasants. (The "villages" in Brittany and in the Massif Central were run much more by landlords and had little legal role in tenure or technical role in cultivation, which according to Skocpol's argument should lead to less revolutionary peasant activity there.)

Skocpol's argument, then, is that neither aspect of the agricultural enterprise, its technical organization of productive activities or its organization of claims on the benefits, can be described without including village politics. Furthermore, this village organization was crucial in determining the massive refusal of French peasants to continue paying feudal seigneurial dues during the Revolution.

Skocpol does not, however, provide an analysis of what exactly the village did in three-field agriculture (three-field agriculture means that each field lies fallow with no crops every third year), or of what was happening to the cultivation of fodder crops, manuring, animal traction, and so forth, that tended at this time to reorganize the village system. Using Skocpol's analysis, the isolated farms of Brittany would be lumped together with the village system. In Brittany the farmhouses were not built in villages and the fields of each farmer were separate from those of others rather than being a piece of each of three big fields. These farmers rotated crops every two years and cultivated few fodder crops. Thus, the relation of the village to the mode of production was radically different, and the cultivation of fodder crops on the common in Brittany was impossible (because the pastures were too hilly and rocky) and so the common was not a subject of dispute between villages and landlords. If one does not have an analysis of what productive activities are done jointly by the village in some places, which may not be done jointly elsewhere, or what opportunities to introduce fodder crops that challenge existing tenure patterns defended by the village do not exist in rocky areas, one will not know how to predict where the village is, or is not, built into the mode of production. We will see that the village was much more built into the mode of production in the Seine and Loire valleys than in Brittany and the Massif Central. For this, a complete analysis of the mode of production and of the structure of the agricultural enterprise in it is necessary. If Skocpol is right that village organization played a crucial role in the Revolution, then one needs a more complete economic sociology than Skocpol's to explain the Revolution.

The analysis of agricultural rebellion in the French Revolution is a very small part of Skocpol's argument, not the core of the analysis as in Paige's. Skocpol's difficulty in analyzing the agrarian rebellion brings out very clearly the ecological aspect of defining a mode of production, even when one uses it for explaining political behavior.

Agriculture is a transaction with nature, as every mode of production ultimately is. But nature varies over France in a way crucial for how cultivation is organized.

We will analyze in Chapter 2 why a map showing where deposits of limestone were exploited outlines quite clearly the areas of the Seine, Loire, and Acquitaine basins where peasants lived in villages, where crop rotations were organized on a village basis, where peasants were relatively literate and engaged in frequent commerce with the cities, and where the Revolution made its deepest penetration into rural areas. Skocpol's analysis of the incentive system in one of the varieties of agricultural production in France is very sensitive. But by failure to complete the analysis of this mode of production by specifying its ecological components, she has failed to specify where the agrarian revolt was most intense and long lasting. We try to show in Chapter 2 how this should be done.

IMMANUEL WALLERSTEIN
AND THE WORLD SYSTEM

Although most of the features of Marxist analysis have disappeared from Wallerstein's work (1974, 1980), the mood that says that the economic dynamics of capitalism explains the political system (somehow or other) pervades that work. He argues that from about the sixteenth century onward the growing edges of all important national economies were producing for a world market. This, in turn, means that the political institutions guiding them were also oriented to the control of opportunities to sell and buy abroad, and to those productive enterprises inside the country that had a competitive advantage in international markets.

Thus, if 4% of the population (say 8% of the labor force) of Mexico in the sixteenth century was occupied in the export sector (mainly silver and gold mines), this does not mean that only 8% of the economy's impact on the government (the King of Spain) was the impact of precious metals mining. Instead the *main* interest of the Spanish regime was to produce precious metals for Spain to use in its international trade and in paying mercenary sailors and soldiers for its foreign policy.

Thus Marx's original materialist argument, that modes of production are the way people produce their livelihood, is substantially modified in Wallerstein. The politically crucial part of the gross product is exactly that *not* consumed in the society that produces it. Both money and political influence come to those sectors (and to the social arrangements of production of those sectors) that produce comparative advantage in the international market. For example, what made textiles crucial for the English Industrial Revolution was not that English people could wear more clothes, but that the cheaper grades of English textiles generated British commercial advantage in Asia, Africa, South and North America, and eastern Europe. What made Dutch shipping central to the Dutch economy and polity in the sixteenth century was not so much that the average Dutchman bought a lot of shipping services, but the fact that the Dutch shippers could ship more tons of goods more miles with one sailor year than could other countries' shippers, which gave the Netherlands and her commerce an advantage throughout the Baltic (Wallerstein 1980: pp. 91–92).

Wallerstein's (1980) argument about the way politics is organized around a country's export industries is not very explicit, but it takes roughly the following form. Export industries in a given country can either be in the control of the importers, as Mexican or Peruvian silver was in the control of Spain, or in control of the exporters, as French wine was in control of the French. These extreme alternative situations tend to be self-confirming, because control of silver strengthens Spain and gives it motives for continuing to control Mexico and Peru, while dependence on French wine subordinates the French colony in Haiti and makes Dutch and English importers pliable. Thus, if we distinguish the *periphery* as countries whose exports are controlled by the importers and the *core* as countries *with valuable exports that are controlled by themselves*, the core–periphery structure will tend to reproduce itself.

But before we can elaborate this analysis, or go on to Wallerstein's elaboration of the apparatus with the concept "semi-periphery," we have to look in more detail at the concept of "control." Clearly, in order for this concept to operate the way it has to (in order to make the concepts of "periphery" and "core" work), it has to confer on the core a self-perpetuating advantage, and on the periphery a self-perpetuating disadvantage. This advantage must involve at least the transfer of some of the "profits" or "surplus" to the core countries. The concept must also outline the processes by which sufficient political support for core rights in peripheral countries are created, so that the Creoles (or in the case of Haiti, the proletariat of the colony) are kept from forming a local government that can take control of the lucrative trade. In other words, colonialism and core dominance must be able to generate the conditions of continued metropolitan control of the colonies.

Note that except for the export sector itself, the peripheral population can be allowed to govern themselves, perhaps after the fashion of the African Local Government (ALG) of British Africa. But it is crucial in order to make Wallerstein's theoretical system work that core countries can reproduce the conditions of their control of the export sector in peripheral countries.

Finally, the concept of control must describe processes that generate strength in the world system for core countries, based on their export industries. That is, the prosperity of English textile manufacturers in the early 1800s or of Dutch shipbuilders and shippers in the 1500s and 1600s have to contribute to the political capacity of England and Holland to prevent domination of their exports. The Dutch had just shaken off a Spanish king during the time of their hegemony; hence the question of control in the Netherlands was obvious and pressing—part of the cause of the rebellion was the control of Dutch exports by the Spanish government. There was no obvious threat comparable to the Spanish crown for the control of English textile exports, but home control of cheap cottons clearly advantaged the British Empire.

Thus, in order to work the way they are supposed to, the concepts of control of exports, and the derived concepts of core and periphery, necessarily involve four subsidiary elements: (1) the idea of a comparative market advantage in the world system for some subsection of a country's economy; (2) the notion of the control of claims by members of one nation on the profits of that sector at the enterprise level, specifically, whether these are members of the local nation or members of an importing nation; (3) the idea of the contribution of the export sector to the creation of the political power (*either* locally by industries in core countries *or* in the mother country for peripheral or colonial countries) that maintains the relations of production in the international arena over time; and (4) the idea of national policy in core countries being directed toward the preservation of the political and economic requisites of a core position.

A systematic development of such a theory (which Wallerstein does not pretend to provide) would require specifying the elements of each of its four main components, and developing a theory of each. For example, a theory of comparative advantage at least requires specification of the causes of differentials between countries in labor productivity, wage rates, productive technology, financial organization, business tax rates and subsidies, transportation costs, power to avoid the imposition of tariffs by importing countries, trustworthy exchange between national currencies (which involves supplies of gold and silver in the times Wallerstein deals with), and so on. A theory of the contribution of an export sector to political power would probably branch into two components, namely, how healthy exports *from a core country's colonies* contribute to that country's power on the one side and how exports *from domestic exporting industries* contribute to a core country's power. The first branch will involve at least the economic causes and consequences of military effectiveness in defending one's ships, collecting taxes on exporting enterprises in the colonies, maintaining core control of the general government apparatus of the colonies, and the like. The theory of domestic industries' contribution to a core country's international power would have to specify the causes and consequences of taxes on and subsidies to exporting industries, the role of commercial advantages in diplomacy, the impact of trade generated in a particular sector on the general health of a country's currency, the acuteness of class conflict in an industry that might divert military and other resources from international arenas, and so on.

The general point here is that a sector of the economy is a subsystem of one or more larger societies. That subsystem creates inputs of different kinds and amounts to other parts of that larger society and in particular to its international relations (or colonial relations) subsystem. Furthermore, it makes unique demands on that international relations subsystem, depending on its own requirements, competitive advantages, and vulnerabilities. What Wallerstein needs to complete his theory, then, is a theory of the dynamics of industrial sectors, especially sectors producing exports or using imports.

A detailed analysis of the shortcomings of Wallerstein's theory requires too much infusion of politics to be appropriate in a book with as narrow a focus as this book has. Further none of the societies we have chosen to analyze is really a colonized or peripheral society, though the Karimojong at the time of the "anthropological present" as described in Dyson-Hudson's *Karimojong Politics* were formally subject to the British imperial government in Uganda. The British did not, however, have control over any central aspect of the Karimojong economy.

We will, however, deal with one aspect of this problem in the conclusion, where we consider the eighteenth-century French military systems' economic requirements, and extend the analysis briefly to the other revolutions considered by Skocpol. Briefly, our argument will be that, considered as an economic enterprise, the military systems of eighteenth-century France and early twentieth-century Russia and China made money in the interior by being the coercive basis of taxation systems on productive agriculture and efficient transportation systems. But in all three societies armies lost money on the frontiers, because in their international environment, conquest or even defense did not generate enough taxation or booty income to pay for itself. The balance of the economic accounts of the French royal government, the Tsarist government, and various Chinese governments thus depended intimately on the relation between taxation of areas securely within the empires, and military conflicts on their borders. By applying some of the concepts developed in the body of the book to the armies of agrarian empires as economic enterprises, we can cast some light on the world system aspects of Skocpol's and Wallerstein's analyses.

ROLES IN THE ENTERPRISE
AND SOCIAL CLASS

In the work of Erik Wright, *Class Structure and Income Inequality*, the definition of social classes is a central concern. Marx's innovation in stratification theory was to base predictions of the behavior of social strata on their position or role in the enterprise. In this way, strata were not merely "layers" of different wealth, prestige, and power, but were instead social classes with different interests derived from the way the rewards of their roles are shaped by market forces. What determines the conflicting interests of capitalists and proletarians is that they have opposite interests in the price of labor, capitalists needing cheap labor to compete successfully and proletarians needing high-priced labor to live in a market economy. But it has always been difficult to analyze the behavior and rewards of the employed middle class using Marx's scheme.

Wright is particularly interested in one peculiarity of the role of employed managers, that they are paid much more than their "labor" is worth—more, that is, than it would cost to hire a comparable person on the labor market. He asks what role in the capitalist enterprise would justify such a premium for managers. He argues that one cannot hire a manager to minimize labor cost per unit of output when the manager's reward goes down as labor costs are minimized. Consequently it is essential to the owners that the level of managers' rewards should clearly be part of the profits picture (to be maximized) rather than part of the labor cost picture (to be minimized).

If this is the explanation of higher managerial rewards, then it should be exactly those managers who control employee rewards who should be overrewarded. Consequently one could define *supervisors* as those who do not control promotion, demotion, wage levels, and productivity measurement, and *managers* as those who do. We would expect supervisors to have rewards that depend on the wages of their subordinates, and managers to have salaries and bonuses that depend instead on their distance from the board of directors and on their role in cost minimization and profit maximization. In Lenin's terms, supervisors are "administrators of things" who require very little extra compensation, whereas managers have to be "lackeys of the capitalist class" who require extra rewards to buy their loyalties. For managers, then, predictors of distance from the top (especially age, education, and specialization in finance) should be more important determinants of reward, while for supervisors the wages of subordinates (e.g., as determined by sex and skill level of subordinates) should be the main determinant.

Wright's own work is mainly directed toward demonstrating the connections between the authority of managers and their reward. But from a larger point of view, we need to know when enterprises require "managers" to participate in profits and to reduce labor costs, and when they need "supervisors" to train workers, to coordinate activities, and "to administer things." It is clear that in some sense "monopoly capitalism" needs more managers, as some of Wright's incidental comments imply. (See also C. Wright Mills and H. H. Gerth, "A Marx for Managers," in R. K. Merton and others, *Reader in Bureaucracy*). But unless a theory of the enterprise of "monopoly capitalism" specifies why it needs managers, not supervisors, we have only the empirical observation that there are more managers in recent times. It takes the classes produced by a system of enterprises as an unexamined fact.

In the section of the American economy in Chapter 4, we will develop a typology of technical systems in the American productive system that can help locate the demand for managers. Then in Chapter 5 we will analyze the creation of managerial roles and the recruitment of people to them, in a way that casts light on the overall place in the mode of production of managers with career incentives that bring their wages above the competitive level.

AN ASSESSMENT OF NEO-MARXISM

The variety and vigor of the scholarly tradition exemplified by Paige, Skocpol, Wallerstein, and Wright shows that there is a good deal of meat left on the Marxist bones. The incompleteness of the explanations shows that the present state of Marxist theory is not adequate to the burdens that have been placed on it. The core of that theory, as exemplified by Marx's own writings, ought to be the connections between the general ecology and technology of a society and the resultant productive activities carried on in the enterprises of the society, the "forces of production," on the one hand, and the claims on the flows of goods and values produced in the enterprises—and the required political supports of those claims—the "relations of production."

The general purpose of this book is to outline and illustrate the economic sociology required to complete and unify the Neo-Marxist tradition.

OUTLINE

In Chapter 2, we will take up the ecological analysis of societies, the natural forces that go to make up a part of the forces of production. But these natural forces have to be analyzed from the point of view of the productive activities they make possible. Thus, for example, one can describe a geographical area by the resources it provides (e.g., rainfall), but this only becomes interesting when activities are described by their resource requirements (e.g., rainfall in hilly country can create power to run mills and hence determined the location of factories up to about 1850; on the plains rainfall can produce food and slow rivers for inland navigation to carry that food but in general cannot run mills). Ecological theory formulates the forces of nature in such a way as to facilitate analysis of productive activities, and hence of what kinds of enterprises will be found in a given place.

As illustrations of the application of such ecological theory, we will analyze ecological aspects of three illustrative economies: a primitive herding ecology with a close dependence on variations in natural conditions among the Karimojong, as described by Dyson-Hudson, *Karimojong Politics*; an intermediate level agrarian ecology in eighteenth-century France, where natural differences produce differences in the mode of production between the regions of France; and a modern industrial economy, the United States, in which almost all activities are carried out in environments especially shaped by people to facilitate the activities and vary very little between seasons or between regions of the country.

Chapter 3 on technology analyzes how economic objectives get translated into requirements on social relations. If one wants to produce automobiles with modern technology, it is efficient to have large assembly plants in which partially assembled cars are moved from one work station to the next mechanically, for example by conveyor belts. The people at the work stations do the same work repetitively on a series of cars. The sizes of the crews at work stations can be larger or smaller and more or less cooperative or individualistic. Volvo in Sweden, for instance, has larger crews at each work station and more cooperative work than the typical American automobile work station. When Henry Ford started working in the automobile industry, craftsmen assembled cars, doing the successive steps one after another on a stationary car. Ford's change of technology to the assembly line changed social relations "required" for producing cars from small firms hiring craftsmen (machinists) to large firms hiring assembly line workers. All the consequences of assembly line organization, repetitive boring work, sharpened class antagonisms, concentration of capital, separation of parts production from assembly in different firms, nationwide standardization of automobiles, are the result of the same economic objectives of making cars for sale as the consequences of craft organization are. One cannot tell what kind of social structure will be produced by a given economic purpose in a given ecological environment unless one also knows the technology available at the time.

The technology of a given time therefore determines how pressures are generated in social relations from economic objectives people have. The "materialism" part of Marx's historical materialism not only says that people's material production of the means of existence is fundamental; it also says that whatever is materially required to produce those means of existence at a given stage of technological development is also fundamental in shaping economic life. The technology of Karimojong herding and horticulture, eighteenth-century French commercialized agrarian society with a bit of rural putting-out industry, and twentieth-century American industrial society are analyzed as illustrations.

In Chapter 4 we move on to the basic structure of claims on the flow of benefits from economic enterprises, the core of the "relations of production" of Marxist theory. The division of income (or of goods in noncommercialized societies) is clearly the main form of incentive system that persuades people to carry out the activities made "necessary" by the technology. Even when some of the activities are motivated by coercion, as in the slave economy of cotton growing in the American South before 1860, those who organize the coercion are motivated by their share of the benefits. Thus one question we always must ask about the division of benefits is how it creates an *administrative apparatus* motivated to carry out the technically necessary activities. This apparatus has to be created by motivating particular people to be attached to the enterprise, and so is a problem of labor supply.

In addition, it is fundamental to modern technologies that a large part of the work required to produce, say, gasoline, is the work of drilling the wells, building the pipelines and tankers to move crude oil to the refineries, building the refineries, then building the delivery vehicles, the gas stations, etc., for distributing gasoline. In the private economy as a whole there are about three years of "frozen labor" in buildings, machines, and inventory used by each worker (about half of all capital in the business economy is buildings and half is machines and inventory). In the oil industry this ratio is very much higher, so that somewhere near half of oil industry labor (including contractors the oil companies hire) in any given year goes into building capital equipment. The requirement for paying labor to build capital equipment whose "product" will be distributed over 20 or 30 years is translated then into a requirement of a flow of "investment" in buildings and equipment. Social separation of "investment" from "labor" and of the returns on investment (profits, rents, and interest) from wages is at the core of the social institutions of capitalism. The relationship between property ownership, investment, and the division of benefits into profits versus wages, is therefore at the core of the "relations of production" of the modern world.

These three topics, the structure of claims on income and resources, how these claims are used to motivate decisions and activities in an administrative apparatus that controls the resources, and the overall resulting structure of flows of income and goods, are illustrated for the Karimojong, for eighteenth-century France, and for the modern United States.

In Chapter 5 we turn to the reproduction of relations of production. The basic problem of reproduction comes from the fact that couples only by accident produce exactly one son and one daughter who come into adulthood just when the father and mother die, so even a fictional unchanging society which emphasizes inheritance needs to adjust the supply of maturing children to the roles they must occupy, and the roles to the supply of children.

In actual societies with social changes, drought, famine and plague, boom and depression, military victory and defeat, roles have to be created and destroyed, and populations have to be recruited to this shifting mix of roles. This process is shaped by technical requirements (e.g., it takes a minimum of about five males of different ages to manage a Karimojong herd successfully), by legal ideas (e.g., in the eighteenth-century French motto *nulle terre sans seigneur*—all lands must have a lord—which created vacancies for nobles), and by requirements of the incentive system (e.g., in a bureaucracy if people are to be motivated by careers with promotions, they must not be hired at the top).

Chapter 5 analyzes the general problem of creating a set of roles for new generations to occupy in such a way as to reproduce the basic structure of the economic system, and the shaping of the flow of children's socialization and placement and of adult careers so that the roles will be filled. The process is illustrated especially sharply in the contrast between the Karimojong, who conceive of role creation as merely reproducing the past structure among the new generation, and the United States with extensive devices for producing social structures that never before existed to make hand-held calculators or to sell money market shares. In eighteenth-century France the matching of the number of viable farms and the number of married sons whose families would occupy them was the core of the problem of reproducing French rural society (see especially E. Le Roy Ladurie, *The Peasants of Languedoc*, for the long-term nature of this problem). Both the nobility and the peasantry had difficulty matching the number of married sons with the number of vacancies on their estates.

Chapter 6 is the conclusion, where we will try to use what we have learned in the body of the book to clarify some of the problems raised in the introduction.

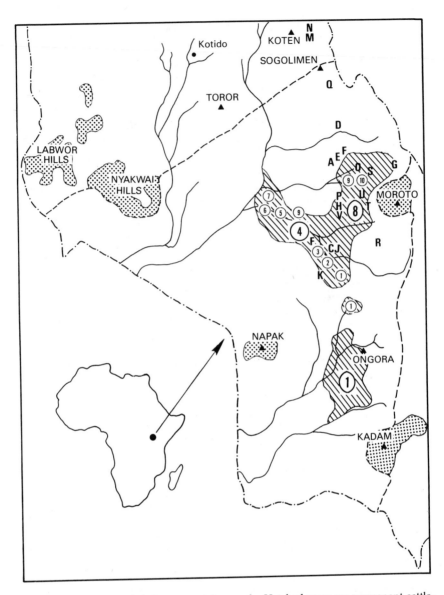

Karimojong sections and their ceremonial grounds. Hatched areas are permanent settlements,——Karimojong tribal boundaries. The distance between Mt. Moroto and Mt. Kadam is about 50 miles. 1, Ngipian; 2, Ngitome; 3, Ngimosingo; 4, Ngibokora; 5, Ngikosowa; 6, Ngikaleeso; 7, Ngipei; 8, Ngimaseniko; 9, Ngimuno; 10, Ngimogwos. **A,** Poro; **B,** Ateleng; **C,** Angaro; **D,** Kadokoyank; **E,** Lokapel; **F,** Napetet; **G,** Kanukurikori; **H,** Kwarikwar; **J,** Akwapua; **K,** Akwapua; **L,** Namatual; **M,** Lomuriamal; **N,** Nakwanga; **O,** Lokal; **P,** Lokitela a ngigete; **Q,** Morv a ngicoma; **R,** Nakadonya; **S,** Nakaruan; **T,** Nabokot; **U,** Kadilakeng; **V,** Nasvgurv. From Dyson-Hudson, *Karimojong Politics.*

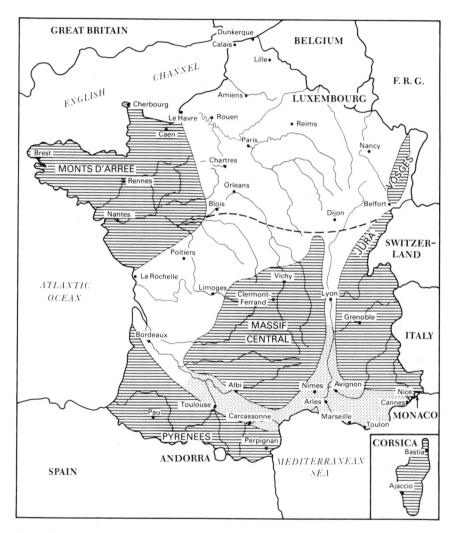

Physical map of France. Stippled areas are the Midi; Mediterranean agriculture. Hatched areas are mountainous or ancient granite highlands, *bocage*, and pasturage. Open areas are ancient sea bottom, clay and limestone plain.– – –Approximate lower boundary of open field agriculture.

Map of the United States.

2

Ecology

ENVIRONMENT AND SOCIETY

The core idea of ecological analysis of social activities is that of resources. Resources are characteristics of environments that can be used in human activities to produce something valuable. Thus, soil fertility is a resource, because food and other plant products are better produced on fertile soil. Water is a resource because of its uses in growing crops, swimming, skiing, washing, drinking, cooling, floating boats, and so on.

But clearly what parts of an environment are useful depends on what activities one wants to carry on. Further given that one wants to raise cattle, for example, one can use grasses in a particular area only if disease germs can be controlled in that area by insecticides, inoculation, or resistant breeds. Thus, what activities can use what resources depends on the technology of those activities.

Generally speaking, the advance of technology multiplies the uses to which a given environment can be put, and so increases the value of the resources. But then it quite often happens that a new use, a new activity, crowds out the old activity or use because it produces more of value than did the old activity. For example, in the eighteenth century in France, cultivated meadows were replacing fallow in the crop rotation system. This crowded out the less productive use of the land as occasional pasturage. Likewise, in some areas of southern France, vines began to be cultivated more extensively and replaced wheat.

Perhaps the most useful concepts that ecologists have developed to analyze such varieties of uses of an environment are *cycle* concepts. The logic of such analyses is a bit tricky, so I will start with an illustration, which plays a crucial role in the analysis of Karimojong ecology: the food chain (see E. P. Odum, *Ecology*, 37–64).

The basic idea of a food chain is that the total biological productivity of a given area is more or less fixed by environmental parameters. These are such things as the quantity of sunlight, temperature, availability of water, and so on. These resources or environmental characteristics determine the total production of biological matter by the growth of a biological substrate—that part of the food chain that converts solar energy into organic compounds. For instance, these variables determine the amount of growth of grass or scrub in the Karimojong tribal area, or alternatively, the growth of sorghum in their garden plots.

Other species live off this biological substrate. Cattle and sheep can live off grass, goats off woody scrub, and cattle, sheep, goats, and human beings off sorghum. The next species in the food chain, let us suppose, is cattle. The proportion of the biological substrate that they can convert into animal flesh and animal products, multiplied by the amount of substrate available to them, determines the amount of animal products and the weight of live animals the area can produce.

The next step up the food chain are the animals that eat cattle, namely, people and predators. The total weight of cattle in the environment will tend to increase as long as cattle produce more weight from grass than they lose to humans and predators. If humans and predators take off more than cattle build up from eating, the total weight of cattle on the land will tend to decrease.

Thus, the weight of cattle carried on the land will increase with any of the following: (1) an increase in the biological substrate, (2) an increase in the efficiency of cattle in finding, eating, or digesting the substrate, or (3) any protective measures against predation, with a consequent decrease in flesh lost to the next higher link in the food chain.

Thus, for example, overgrazing tends to decrease the weight of grass on the land, without increasing the resources to grow grass. Plants less subject to predation by cattle (e.g., thorn scrub) then tend to propagate faster than grass and to crowd it out as a substrate. Overgrazing by sheep, who eat grass roots as well as growth above the ground, increases the predation, and so results in ecological succession (replacement of grass by scrub) at a higher rate.

When people intervene in a natural ecological system to turn it more to their own benefit, they attempt to manipulate the variables above. For example, to increase the weight of cattle carried on the land, the

Karimojong burn the old dried growth of grass, so that any growth will be succulent new growth. This is eaten with much more efficiency by cattle, for several physical reasons. Thus, the proportion of the substrate biological growth used to support the next higher link in the food chain is increased. Predators of cattle are killed off, or chased away by men and dogs, and diseased areas are avoided.

The key to the productive use of this whole set of ecological ideas has to do with the specifying of the biological substrate, and describing it in quantitative terms. Then the efficiency of each of the species at the next stage (e.g., cattle) in converting substrate to flesh can be computed. Rates of predation that this cattle population can then support without declining can be computed from the above two parameters, and so on up the line. Thus, we could estimate the equilibrium weight of biological matter (at different degrees of efficiency) that could be supported at each level of the food chain.

But what does this have to do with cycles? As we trace the vegetable matter produced by the substrate up the food chain, some portion of it is not used at the first stage (e.g., leaf mold and peat) and is returned to the soil, some portion escapes from the environment, and some remains in the environment in the transformed state of animal flesh (e.g., beef) or products (e.g., milk). When the animal dies, some portion of the stored materials returns to the soil, some portion leaves the environment, and some is transformed into the flesh of predators. When the predator dies, the same division takes place. Each link in the food chain after the first is thus a transformation of the resources provided at the next lower level.

The materials and energy produced by the substrate in the environment go through longer or shorter cycles before they return to supply inputs for the substrate again. Different materials have different rates of loss from the environment over the course of the cycle. But many of the crucial resources for any given stage are available mostly from previous stages in the cycle.

Stability of Resources

For the species composition of an environment to remain stable, the accounts of all the essential resources for each species have to balance in each time period. For example, when water is lost by evaporation either it must be replaced by rain or running water; if it is not replaced, species that use little water will survive, and those that use more will die. If the cycles of crucial resources have little loss, then these accounts are balanced internally. The parts of the ecosystem that are vulnerable

to variations in the environment (e.g., to variations in rainfall) are therefore the parts in which the cycles have the highest rates of loss.

Thus, the way one species changes the environment for others is by
taking part in a cycle that retains more (or less) of the scarce resources
of that environment and returns it to further use in the cycle. If a previous
stage returns more resources to the environment, then the species that
use those returned resources are less vulnerable to variations in the
environment, and this stabilizes the species composition. Thus, many
species can live in given environments only if other species that retain
resources they use in the cycle are prevalent in the environment.

When people intervene in an environment, we have to ask whether
the change they have brought about is stable or not. The change will
not be stable if people unbalance the accounts of the various crucial
resources. Generally stabilizing the new ecosystem involves importing
new materials into the environment to balance the new net losses. For
instance, if evaporation rates increase because of cultivation, then irrigation is often required to create a stable system. Mineral loss from the
soil by cultivation often requires fertilization, letting the land lie fallow,
or other periodic balancing of the mineral cycle to be stable. The higher
the rate of loss from the cycle that is established by human intervention,
the higher will be the rate of succession of species in the environment.

The resources available at a given place for human use are, in the long
run, limited by the ecosystems that can be balanced at that place. The
value of the resources at that place depends on the cost, in human
energy and other valuable things, of bringing about that new balance.
That is, if one has to irrigate in order to carry out agriculture, for example,
then the value of the land has to be calculated as the crops minus the
cost of irrigation. Technology increases the variety of ecosystems that
can be made to balance by facilitating imports into the environment, by
providing means for reducing the outflow of crucial resources (e.g., by
reducing predation by insects), or in other ways by increasing the
amount that can be extracted from the ecosystem without causing its
permanent decay into a nonproductive system.

Thus, we can give a formal, ecological definition of what a resource
is. A resource is the set of ecosystems that can be stable in a given
environment, with their associated rates of return of things valuable to
people and the associated costs of maintaining the variant ecosystem.
These determine the possible rates of exploitation of the environment
under a given technology. No activity requiring a different rate of exploitation outside this set of possible ecosystems can be stable in the
environment. Technical change has its impact by increasing the possible

ecosystems, thus extending the range of rates of exploitation, and therefore making possible activities requiring those new rates.

When we say that environment "limits but does not determine" the
activities that can go on at a given place, what we mean is that there are
almost always alternative ecosystems that could be stable in the environment. These alternatives ordinarily have different rates of return. If
an environment is exploited less efficiently; of course, then it will support
fewer humans. The principle of social evolution, a central Marxist postulate, says that more efficient modes of exploitation tend to succeed
less efficient ones. If the principle of evolution works perfectly, then
there is usually a unique exploitative system determined by a given
technology and a given environment.

EXTERNAL ECONOMIES OF ACTIVITIES

The concept of external economies is used to explain why two activities
tend to be done together in the same environment. The concept is intimately related to the idea of cycles in an ecological system. If one
activity or species in an environment uses input that would be valuable
for another activity, or if it produces materials that damage the other
activity, then the two activities are diseconomies for each other. That is,
the more prevalent one activity or species is in an environment, the less
of a competitive species can be sustained by that environment. Those
activities will tend to be done in different environments. But if an activity
uses materials that would damage another (e.g., birds eat insects that
damage crops), or if it produces materials that are resources for another
activity (e.g., cows' manure provides available minerals and partially
rotted vegetable particles for plants), then the two activities are connected by external economies. Those activities will tend to be done in
the same environments.

Thus, when a first species or activity changes a microenvironment to
make it more propitious for a second species or activity, the first activity
is a resource for the second one. When activities or species are mutually
external economies for each other, we speak of *symbiosis*. When the
second species or activity grows at the expense of the first (i.e., takes
up resources which might be used by the first), we speak of *parasitism*.
Either parasitism or symbiosis involves the change of a microenvironment by the host species in a way that makes it more favorable to the
parasite or symbiote. Parasites and symbiotes tend to be found together
in the environments populated by species or activities they feed off of.

Cattle and grass are symbiotic in the sense that cattle dung is good for grass and grass is good for cattle. Rinderpest germs are parasites on cattle, in the sense that cattle are good for the germs but the germs are bad for cattle. In both cases, the effect on the distribution of species is the same: cattle, grass, and rinderpest germs occur in the same environments.

Another way of saying this is that the rate of return for products of the symbiote or parasite activity or species in an environment depends on the prevalence of the first activity or species. The more the species composition of an area is changed to plants that provide usable food for cattle, the higher the rate of return of cattle in that environment. Growing clover is thus an external economy of an obvious kind for obtaining increased cattle products from the land. This made England and France, where clover could be grown, more favorable environments for the growth of activities that use animal inputs, such as woolens manufacture.

ACCESS TO AN ENVIRONMENT

A given environment can support a larger variety of ecosystems when deficits in its accounts under a given ecosystem can be supplied from outside. Thus, the resources available at a place are determined not only by what is there, but also by what is nearby. A place surrounded by rich environments with high productivities of a variety of resources can support (with minor costs) a much wider variety of activities than can an isolated place that is equally endowed. Thus, for example, the variety of activities that are viable in a metropolis is much larger than the variety in a mountainous region, because there are many other things produced in or near a metropolis.

To describe the viable activities in a place, then, we need to specify the costs at that place of supplying the deficits of those activities. Activities can be stable if there is a stable flow of their requisites into the environment, as well as if there is stable production of their requisites in the local ecological cycle.

The resources at nearby places will be available if there are developed channels of transfer. Part of the resources will be used up in the transfer activity. Thus, one multiplies the potential ecosystems of a place by decreasing the cost of transport to it, especially if the new channel provides access to valuable resources. In order to compute the value of a road or harbor for a place, we need to know three things: (1) What are the deficits that various activities would produce in the local system?

(2) What is the productivity of the areas to which a road gives access, specifically productivity of these deficit materials? and (3) How much of those materials is used up in the transportation process? The account of deficits gives an estimate of the rate of *benefits* to be achieved by transporting inputs. The account of accessible resources gives an estimate of the *quantity* of those benefits that can be had. The materials used in transit give an estimate of the *costs* of those benefits.

ECOLOGICAL ANALYSIS OF ACTIVITIES

We start an ecological analysis of the distribution of activities by describing the activity by a set of inputs it requires and a set of outputs it produces. For that activity to be stable in the environment, the accounts for those inputs must be balanced. An imbalance in one of the accounts requires the activity to decrease to a level that balances the system. The productivity of an innovation that balances the accounts is the rate of return of the activity multiplied by the amount of decrease of the activity caused by the imbalance. In linear programming terminology, this gives us the *shadow price* of the resource not in balance.

This imbalance may be corrected by intervening in a different place in the cycle in that environment, so that another activity having the deficit inputs as its outputs is created. For example, finding an iron ore body in an area that also has coal is likely, in the long run, to produce in that area a coke plant to produce coke for refining the iron and for producing steel. This encourages people to introduce into an area activities that are external economies for each other. There is, as economists say, a derived demand for one activity (coke production) due to its value in producing inputs. Conversely, the outputs of an activity may provide inputs for another or otherwise make the environment favorable for its growth. A coke plant may produce ancillary industries to produce coal tar dyes. Symbiotic or parasitic activities will tend to agglomerate together with their hosts. The net imbalance of the account of an environment is reduced by this agglomeration, making the complex of mutually supportive activities less vulnerable to environmental variation than each of them alone.

The net imbalance in the accounts of an area in turn generates a derived demand for imports and hence for transportation. It also makes environments nearby to sources of the goods in deficit more valuable than isolated environments.

The favorableness of a place for a given activity is therefore determined by the resources of the place, the other activities of the place, and access of the place to further resources. By the resources of a place for an activity, we mean the set of materials of which the ecosystem of the area provides a steady supply. This determines the set of activities that are viable in the system, in the sense that their requisites will be steadily supplied. The more activities that are viable, the greater the choice of the society of what to do, and the greater we can expect the rate of return to be.

The other activities at a place change the composition of inputs available, and hence increase the number of activities that are viable in the environment. They provide external economies for new activities in the sense that they change the rate of return for those activities.

Finally, the access of a place to other places determines which deficits in the local accounts can be made up by imports. This again increases the number of activities that are viable in the environment and decreases the constraints of the environment on activities. It increases the expected rate of return of the environment.

If we say, then, that the location of the machine-building industry (automobiles, pumps, tractors, electricity generators, etc.) in the great industrial cities of the American Mid-Atlantic and Midwest has ecological causes, we mean that the environment there makes it easy to balance the material accounts of those activities. It does so because there is a steady supply of resources such as iron and coal in the area, because the presence of the steel industry there provides inputs for that industry, and because the conditions of access in the area make it easy to balance Detroit's or Toledo's deficit of steel from Pittsburgh's production.

When we say that the herding nomadic patterns of the Karimojong have ecological causes, what we mean is that these practices are attempts to balance the accounts of cattle herds. The resources of the area in grass and water make cattle raising a viable activity. The combination of those activities with women's agriculture makes it possible to balance the human food accounts in more years, which in turn provides inputs of human energy to keep the herds going. The mutual access of humans to cattle achieved by herding movements allows the product of grass and water of one area to supply the deficits in animal food products of the settlement area.

In each case, then, we discuss the relation of an activity to an environment by asking what has to be done to balance the accounts of that activity in that environment. Then we ask what the rate of return of that activity is, in the sense of what benefits humans receive from that exploitation. If that rate of return pays the cost of balancing the accounts by human effort, the activity will tend to be found in that area.

ECOLOGICAL ORGANIZATION
AND STRATIFICATION

The fundamental relationship that creates stratification systems is the appropriation by one person or group of an economic opportunity on which other people are dependent. This is how economic relations create power relations, relations of recognized inequality in the worth of people and inequality of their decisions. Economic opportunities are normally appropriated and defended by solidary groups of people who are involved together in the activities of an ecosystem. A solidary group that appropriates economic opportunities and with those establishes a socially recognized inequality between itself and other groups is called a *status group.*

Status groups are powerful social causes because the energy of economic interest is multiplied by the energy of maintaining the honor of the group. Racial conflicts are usually more severe than class conflicts of the same economic magnitude because they add indignation over dishonor and over the violation of honorable ordering of social relations to the frustrations of economic deprivation.

Ecologically differentiated groups (e.g., traders versus local people) are especially likely to establish themselves as status groups. Their common ecological range brings traders into solidary contact with each other. This solidary group has common interests in the economic opportunities on which locals are dependent. The establishment of socially recognized inequality between traders and locals reinforces and legitimates the economic exploitation of local groups by traders. In particular, ecologically differentiated economic groups are likely to become status groups and to add the fuel of social estrangement to economic competition.

The Karimojong, for example, want to appropriate the resources of the highlands between themselves and the Turkana. They compete among themselves about who exactly should get the resources, but unite to establish firmly the inequality of access of Turkana and Karimojong to those resources. The fights between Karimojong are restricted to sticks; they fight the Turkana with spears. Among themselves, they resolve disputes by legal means; the Turkana are considered without rights, and their appropriation of the resources in dispute provokes indignation as well as competition. The same objective competition has different consequences because of the solidarity among the Karimojong. This solidarity is created and maintained by the multiple ecological relations that Karimojong hold in common. Thus, one Karimojong now in competition with another remembers and anticipates being in situations in which he depends on and is helped by the other. He less easily hates the Karimojong than he hates a Turkana who will never be of any use.

We want to note here that solidarity and enmity are strongly shaped by ecological forces. It is not quite true that wars only take place between ecologically organized status groups over geographical resources, but the error in that statement is less important than the truth in it. Likewise, it is not true that *pogroms* only take place against religious groups occupying a distinct ecological niche, for example, as traders. But again the error is less important than the truth. Warfare is extensively ecologically organized with respect to resources and repetitive relations of mutual usefulness. Groups carrying on activities having extensive mutual external economies make war together, against similarly organized groups, to control resources on which they are dependent. Geopolitics is at the core of the sociology of war.

ECOLOGY OF KARIMOJONG SOCIETY

Forms of Energy Transfer among the Karimojong

The crucial variable that affects the relation of Karimojong society to its environment is the food supply, particularly in the dry season. Physical and biological features of the landscape become resources for the Karimojong when they affect food supply. It is convenient to divide Karimojong methods of exploiting the environment into four groups, because the variables and physical features that affect production of food are different for each of the four (see Dyson-Hudson, *Karimojong Politics*, pp. 22–80). These are (1) the camp herd of cattle, made up of bulls, oxen, heifers (young cows who do not give milk), pregnant cows, and a few cows in milk with their calves; (2) the settlement or milch herd, mainly of cows with their calves; (3) the herd of small stock, especially goats, also more often kept at the settlement; and (4) agriculture, especially of sorghum (a grain crop).

Normally Karimojong do not slaughter cattle except for sacrifice on ritual occasions. The camp herd produces a much lower food yield each day per animal than does the settlement or milch herd because of the composition of the herd (see above). A normal animal in the camp herd occasionally is bled by piercing the jugular. (This is discussed in greater detail later in this chapter.) The current product of blood is mixed with milk and used mainly to support the camp population of mature men and herd boys. The periodic product of a newly freshened cow and its new calf is often detached from the camp herd to join the milch herd.

This camp herd is highly mobile, and in the dry season often has at least part of the milch herd reattached to it.

The settlement or milch herd ideally is sufficiently large to supply the humans in the settlement, and the calves, with a supply of milk, but no larger. It makes use of the scarce grazing resources near the settlement and supplies animal products, especially milk, to the women and children who live at the settlement and the men who visit. The settlement herd has a much larger ratio of food supplied to grass eaten than does the camp herd. It is consistantly replenished with newly freshened milch cows and their calves, when the cows in the settlement herd run dry.

The herd of goats and sheep is also often kept at the settlement because goats can browse on the shrubs in the overgrazed central area of the settlements, and sheep can use overgrazed pasture. They can turn a different set of vegetation resources into a small quantity of animal foods, especially goat's milk and meat, than can cattle.

Agriculture is carried on at the settlement. The Karimojong use the special wet season water resources to produce vegetable foods for humans. They use the power of oxen during a brief plowing period and considerable human energy to change the species composition of the vegetation of limited garden areas in a direction that provide a higher yield of human foods per acre than does animal exploitation. This new ecosystem is not stable, however, and land has to be left fallow for long periods after it has been exhausted.

The crucial resources from the point of view of the camp herd, and consequently indirectly of the milch herd, are dry season water, the right species of grass, and protection from raids. The crucial resources for the milch herd are grass near the settlement and water, which are, generally speaking, only available in the wet season. The crucial resource for the goats is thorn scrub. The crucial resources for agriculture are access to the settlement, fertile soil, and wet season rains.

The ecological problem for which the camp herd is designed and managed is that the water and grass in the dry season are scarce, distributed widely, unpredictable, and located in dangerous areas. Dry season rains, or "grass rains" as the Karimojong call them, are much smaller and more irregular than wet season rains. They tend to occur more often in the highlands and headwaters to the east of the settlement area, but they run off quicky because of rocky, steep stream beds, and water remains only in a few rocky pools for parts of the season.

The grass in this eastern district is of species that can maintain cattle in good condition. The grass rains occur sporadically; since the water runs off rapidly, there are few meadows regularly watered by flooding.

As the streams flow toward the west, the slope of the streambeds is reduced. Alluvial deposits build up on the meanders, producing fertile fields near the streambeds. The streambeds are typically sand, and much of the water soaks in to become groundwater, reducing the rate of evaporation and runoff. Reliable wells can be dug that supply enough water in the dry season for humans and small stock, but usually not enough for cattle.

As the streams continue to the west, the slope is further reduced and the ground is more impermeable so that seasonal marshes, or in some places permanent swamps, develop. These relatively reliable water supplies are near to relatively reliable grass sources, but the grass is of species that do not maintain cattle in good condition.

Thus, it requires a favorable conjunction of circumstances for the herds to maintain good condition throughout the dry season. In seven years out of 30 cattle starvation is reported in the district records; in most of the other years some periods of shortage of grazing and water were reported. We find notations such as, "Famine averted by November–December rains which improved grazing" for 1957. In four of the years in which cattle died of starvation and lack of water, the agricultural crops were fair to good, indicating the partial autonomy of agricultural and cattle resources. (This is a summary of the year by year reports presented more completely in Dyson-Hudson's *Karimojong Politics,* at p. 80.)

Since the water and grass resources tend to be concentrated near the periphery of the Karimojong area, they are more exposed to raiding by neighboring tribes. Consequently, the camp is also a military unit, and the herding group needs to be militarily effective as well as effective as a herding enterprise. The presence of women, children, calves, and animals in poor condition is therefore a disadvantage. A large complement of male herders is an advantage. The advantage of dispersion to find irregularly distributed small patches of resources has to be balanced against the social and military advantages of larger concentrations of people at the camp.

The milch herd tends to be kept near the settlement during the rainy season when there is plenty of water and grass, while the camp herd does not have to move as far in search of grazing and water. Thus, the accessibility between the settlement and the camp herds tends to increase during the wet season and to decrease again in the dry season. The milch herd may graze separately from the camp herd in the dry season to make use of small pastures near the settlement, but most often it too must take full advantage of the dry season resources far from the settlements.

The departure of the milch herd from the settlements leaves only the goats and agricultural resources there. During the dry season these typically decrease in quality, because the goats give less milk and the stored grain or beer is consumed by pests. The stored groundwater is farther below the sandy riverbeds, requiring deeper wells to get it. The growth of thorn shrub decreases with decreasing water, though the effect is not as great as it is with grass. As the dry season advances, there is less and less reason to stay in the settlement.

Agricultural resources are nearly as variable as grass and water for cattle. In seven out of 29 years, there has been total crop failure, and in three more there have been poor yields. There are two sources of poor crop yields—too much rain and too little. Too much rain swells the rivers and washes away the alluvial banks on which crops are grown. Too little rain causes the plants to wither, hardens the ground to a hard adobe, and increases the speed of runoff when the rains do come. Probably over half of the settlement's subsistence comes from agriculture. Since agriculture depends on different resources, it provides an insurance against bad luck with the cattle and vice versa. But in roughly one year out of ten, the Karimojong can expect to have neither animal products nor vegetable produce. Both cattle and people have higher death rates in such years.

Land is not a scarce resource among the Karimojong, and they freely leave garden plots fallow for many years until the soil grows a lush set of weeds. The Karimojong have a rich vocabulary describing the agricultural characteristics of different soils. With the introduction of the ox-drawn plow, they have increased the area under cultivation by about four times. But the agricultural production in a bad year still goes to zero, while even starving animals from the herd can provide some food. Consequently, agriculture does not play the central role in Karimojong psychic economy that it plays in the caloric economy.

The Temporal and Spatial Distribution of Resources

The main characteristic of Karimojong physical and biological resources is *unpredictability*. A Karimojong herder must examine his environment to decide what to do. A Karimojong woman must examine the plants to tell whether to plant again, or whether to weed and scare off birds. A Karimojong boy must take the milch herd where nearby grass and water exist, which is likely to be different than last year. A

Karimojong warrior must sleep light to catch the raiders before they get away with his cattle. Karimojong decision structures must therefore be organized into small units, of a minimum size to handle a herd, so that opportunities should not be lost.

This imposes on the society a family-centered economic decision structure, in which only a few crucial decisions (warfare, ritual supplication, and marriage bargaining) require suprafamilial structures. This is not, perhaps, a very strict determination of social structure by environment, in the sense that if the Karimojong made some choices very differently they might organize differently. The Masai and some Central Asian herders rely strictly on cattle (or in some Bedouin tribes, strictly on camels), and trade for agricultural produce. (Some peoples depend entirely on cultivation in marginal and unsteady climates.) A much smaller population might live off hunting. (In fact, when a series of disasters toward the end of the nineteenth century reduced populations in the area to about a fourth, the Karimojong lived from hunting elephants. There now are no more elephants there.)

But given a combined cattle and agricultural exploitation, carried out by the men and women of a single society, there is very little else to do but to respond with intelligence to radically varying conditions, from place to place, season to season, year to year. Perhaps with fewer goats and sheep there would be more grazing in the central area for cattle. Perhaps technical innovations in wells would make the groundwater more available for cattle and more steady in supply. Perhaps massive applications of insecticides by an outside society might decrease cattle epidemics. Perhaps trade in cattle could bring a reverse trade in agricultural goods.

But for any of these to come about, the possibilities must become psychological and economic realities to the Karimojong. There are no internal possibility-exploring institutions among the Karimojong. Each person explores his or her own possibilities. Most of the alternatives outlined above would require venture capital institutions, socially organized research and development efforts, and changes in the conception of how people ought to live and what makes people worthwhile. Institutions for changing people's minds on a large scale are not built into Karimojong social structure. Karimojong society is not a self-transforming system.

It is, instead, a rather finely tuned anarchic exploitation system, which maximizes the probability that someone will find every case of the resources that are valuable in the productive system. As in many such anarchic systems, one suspects that each resource is overexploited so that it cannot sustain itself. The vegetation in the central area has gone the way of oil reserves, European and American forests, clean water, or the vegetation cover of the American dust bowl. Each person in pursuing his or her opportunities does not limit himself or herself too much in consideration of someone else's need some other year. One has a family to feed and a herd to maintain.

The devices to limit exploitation tend to be ad hoc, structured among the people around a water source, for example. The carrying capacity of a water source can be accurately estimated by the Karimojong. Each man who uses it carries knowledge of its past use and bets about how likely it is to be refilled by new rains (based on lore from the constant gossip about problems of maintaining a herd). When the estimated capacity is stretched, newcomers are discouraged (with sticks—not with spears). They must go find a resource not yet used. If each Karimojong person is supported by about ten cattle, then 60,000 people must herd about 600,000 cattle. Starvation of cattle reached as many as 10,000 head in 1950, a dry year. Although that is less than 2%, it makes a big difference if your 100 head are among the 10,000. Slaughter and aging of cattle are steady processes that can be more than compensated for by births. But the unpredictable death of 10,000 cattle can make people want water and grass very badly.

Other natural resources (in particular, agricultural land) are in plentiful supply, even with the long fallow periods used for exhausted land. Although Karimojong agriculture was probably increased four times by the introduction of the ox-drawn plow, much of the work is done by a woman with a hoe or a child on a bird-scaring platform. Each woman cultivates a small plot with her children, sometimes with shared work among kinswomen who get along well together. Each wife separately, however, owns usufruct rights (rights to the produce) of "her" garden. Garden lands are only scarce near the settlements. Between settlements there is considerable cultivable land unused except for browsing animals.

Well sites in the sandy river beds vary in ease of exploitation (they are washed away after heavy rainstorms), in the depth below the surface at which one finds water, in the total amount of water available, and other crucial characteristics. Rights to such resources are created by exploiting them, rather than there being an abstract system in which every resource theoretically has an owner as in Western legal systems.

The reason why water supplies rather than land are not crucial resources for most of the people of the world is that people usually do not settle densely anywhere where water is scarce. Thus, although the distribution of water explains more about humanity's distribution on the earth's surface than does the distribution of soil, *within* societies after the agricultural revolution, land has been a more vital resource, at least in the sense of being more expensive. In the United States most people pay a trivial amount for water, yet hardly anyone lives in the great western desert. When they do (as in Los Angeles), they ship water by the cheapest transportation devices (canals and pipes) from better endowed areas. Water becomes the crucial resource when its distribution is just dense enough to support certain water-conserving ecologies (e.g., grasses that wither in the dry season that can be used as fodder), but not dense enough for intensive agricultural exploitation of the land. This is the condition of much of the earth's surface, but of few of the earth's people.

Movement Patterns of the Karimojong

The Karimojong are a tall, beautiful people, and a man in good condition can walk 60 miles in a day. Further, he fairly often does, to maintain contact between the settlement and the herd. His more usual pace, of course, is that of a cow grazing or walking. Karimojong movements can be classified into two groups: (1) commuting with a return either to a settlement or camp at night and (2) nomadism, or the seasonal moving part of the social structure and daily round of life of a part of the people across the country. Migration from one settlement area to another is not uncommon (it is nearly universal for women after marriage), but is much less frequent than in the United States.

The camp in the dry season is usually from ten to 40 miles away from the settlement, though farther extremes are found, especially in bad years. The grazing and watering range during the course of a day rarely covers more than ten miles. Each camp or settlement is then a center for daily movement of two detached parts of the social structure, because herding cattle 80 miles a day would not get them fat. If the camp is in an area of relative military security, a man with grown sons (or one of the sons at a time) might visit the settlement for a day or a night. Women sometimes visit the camps in the dry season for short periods to bring agricultural goods and to have sexual relations.

But between October and March, the male part of the society is largely detached from the female and child part, and constructs its own round of life in the camp. Camaraderie and love of cattle can partly compensate for the lack of amenities of the settlement, but there are obvious lacks, as in life in the barracks in modern society. Though the nights are cold, the men sleep naked in the open, near the cattle corrals. Each man has a cow skin on which he sleeps, and between every two men is a small fire for warmth. If it rains, each man folds half his sleeping skin over him for rough shelter. Only in a real downpour will they huddle together in one of the crude grass shelters that have been built, and as soon as the rain stops, they return to their places near the corrals to keep closer watch over the stock.

Apart from a few small gourds of drinking water, there may be no water available in the camp unless visiting women bring it. All utensils are therefore washed in cattle urine: as in the settlements, long before the first morning light the herd boys are waiting in the corrals to collect it. Then follows the milking, the milk being collected in wooden tubs near the corral gate, with a separate tub for each of the men who share breakfast together.

After the sun has risen and the herders have had their morning meal of milk, the camp gates are cleared of the thorn blockades and the cattle file out, followed by the goats and sheep. Men and older boys call their dogs, and taking up sticks and spears and small water gourds, they leave for a day tending the herds. The smaller boys carry the suckling lambs and goats to small enclosures of cut thorn or living sansevieria, planted in a circle in the shade of a tree, then they drive the calves to wander with them around the outside of the camp.

During the day the camp is deserted. If grazing and water are near at hand, a man may be found near the camp sitting under a shade tree. But when water is scarce, or the camp is near enemy country, the men move with the herds, watching over them and supervising the watering to make sure each animal gets enough.

The herds return at sundown, or if the water source is far away, not until well into the night. Then the various stock herds converge on the camp, and the stock are driven to their separate corrals. The herd boys select an animal for bleeding, shooting a blocked arrow in the jugular vein to draw off several pints of blood. They collect the blood in a bowl, whisking it with a stick to remove the fibrin. The blood is then divided among wooden tubs set out for milking. Calves are collected one at a time by the boys, and their dams are milked. After suckling, the calves are returned to their separate pen, and the men and boys gather around the fire for the evening meal of milk and blood.

Thus, the transfer of energy from the grass and water in the region of the camp to the humans is almost entirely mediated by the cattle. The subeconomy of the camp is, except for occasional gathering of wild vegetation and some beer occasionally brought by visiting women, entirely an animal products economy. Further, it is one in which preservation of animal products is almost absent. It is this morning's product which is eaten this morning, and this evening's product eaten this evening. The camp herd must produce enough animal products at the worst part of the dry season to support at least the male part of the society.

The agricultural settlement economy involves much more energy stor-age, both in the form of stored grain and in beer. The storage techniques do not allow food to be preserved for more than one harvest year, so the food accounts must balance each year. This incapacity to use excellent harvests of one year to compenstate for bad harvests the following year increases the variability of the food available. Although it is fairly rare for the harvests to be equally bad all over Karimojong territory, there is no systematic exchange from one area to another. Some use can be made of the kinship ties in case of a bad harvest; for example, a woman may visit her home village with her children and eat out of a better-provided larder in that village. But the basic balancing of food accounts goes on at each settlement, and to some degree at each sub-household of mother and children within each settlement.

This lack of an exchange system covering Karimojong agriculture is reflected in or caused by low mutual transportation access between set-tlements. Fundamentally the things that move in Karimoja are people and cattle, not goods. Resources are used where they are; the people and cattle move to where they are to exploit them. As resources shift with the seasons and with chance meteorological conditions, a corre-sponding quick shift of the physical distribution of the people and cattle takes place.

Social Solidarity and Enmity in Ecological Perspective

Among the Karimojong, there is not a tight relationship between re-sources exploited by a group and the solidarity of a group. As we will see, in eighteenth-century France there was a close relationship between the *finage* of a village and the complex of resources exploited by the group of people who lived in the village. Each *finage* was designed to have a mix of resources appropriate for constructing a complete round of life. But as the Karimojong say, "The sun mixes us." In the dry season the group of people exploiting a particular resource area may come from different settlements, different families, and different sections. Further-more, the group may be different from the group which exploited that resource during the previous year, if only because the resource may support very different numbers of cattle in different years.

This does not mean, however, that solidary groups have no relation to territory. Each settlement area or neighborhood forms a loosely knit community. Each family within that area traditionally uses certain of the garden plots and can reclaim fallow garden plots if someone else starts to cultivate them. Sections and subsections of the tribe, which form ritual congregations, are associated with collections of neighborhoods. The ritual grounds at which cattle are collected for sacrifices pertain to the subsections and are located within the subsection areas. The Karimojong, however, do not concentrate attention so much on the borders of the area, but rather on the centers of settlement. The area associated with a section is thus the ceremonial grounds and the "nearby" territory, which gradually fades into the "nearby" territory of another subsection. Subsection membership is inherited in families, rather than being tightly linked to residence.

But the overarching identification is between the Karimojong tribe and the lands from which they can effectively expel enemies. This area again has uncertain and shifting boundaries. Enemies rarely make it to the central settlement area, but interpenetrate with Karimojong along the edges. The farther toward Turkana territory a Karimojong goes, the more likely he (basically only men go into border areas) is to run when he meets Turkana. He penetrates deeply only in large raiding parties. There is nevertheless a fairly definite area which is "ours," surrounded by area into which a Karimojong goes only with permission or as an enemy.

As the Karimojong tribe has grown since the disastrous years around 1900 when they were reduced to hunting elephants, their tribal territory has extended, and the mutual accessibility between the northern part of the tribal territory and the southern part has declined. The ritual unity of the society depends on bringing cattle together. Although considerable information can travel by word of mouth over large areas when men walk 60 miles a day and women perhaps 20 or 30, the movement of herds is slower, and conditions favoring the congregation of herds can change before the herds get there.

For the same reasons, the sun more often mixes northerners together with other northerners at northern watering places, and southerners with other southerners at southern water sources. The southern settlement area is dominated by a single large section, the Pian, of about 20,000 people. (There are ten sections.) This group of people is internally divided into subsections and river-course groups. The northern part of the tribal area is a mixture of many sections, dominated by the Bokora section (about 20,000), and the Maseniko (about 10,000), who together make up about three-quarters of the northerners. Thus, the men the sun mixes in the south mostly belong to the same ritual congregation, and those in the north mostly to one of two congregations.

The combination of greater internal differentiation of the Pian section, and their failure to use their old ceremonial grounds in the north, brings together a social and ritual boundary with an approximate ecological boundary. The Pian people (*Ngipian*) are more nearly a sub-society than the other sections of the Karimojong. They exploit in common a more or less distinct set of resources, and have within their social boundaries most of the institutions required for carrying on the Karimojong way of life. But this special condition of the Pian section serves to emphasize the normal dissociation among the Karimojong between solidary groups and a complete set of exploitable resources.

ECOLOGY OF FRENCH SOCIETY

A Brief Introduction to Soil Fertility

In order to understand variations in the ecological situation of different regions in France, it is useful to have a general idea of what makes soils fertile. The fundamental components of fertility are metallic ions (especially calcium, potassium, and magnesium), phosphate ions, and related ions with nitrogen in them. These are the things that, along with water, a plant absorbs through its roots. These ions normally occur attached to large molecules of clay or humus (decayed organic matter). They can be decreased either by a decrease in the number of clay–humus molecules (e.g., in sandy soil) or by being replaced by hydrogen ions, which makes an acid soil. Thus, soils are classified by the prevalence of clay–humus molecules into "light" soils with fewer such molecules and "heavy" soils with many, and into acid soils in which the ions have been replaced by hydrogen and basic soils in which they have not. Many sandy desert soils are light basic; fertile clayey soils like those of the western Seine River basin are heavy basic; sandy soils in very wet areas tend to be light acid, soils of clay mixed with sand, as in many alluvial soils, light basic, and so on.

Further, if a soil becomes acid, the clay tends to break down into its components, which then leach out of the soil into the subsoil. Thus acid soils tend to stay infertile. The decomposition of organic matter liberating minerals seems to be often reduced in acid soils, resulting in the accumulation of peat, undecomposed organic matter. This unused organic matter can, of course, serve to liberate nutrients if it is moved into an area where the accumulated organic matter decays.

There are several things that affect the acidity of the soil. One is the chemical composition of the rock subsoil. Limestone or chalk, found in the ancient seabottoms of France, and volcanic basalt found in some areas of the central massif, decompose or "weather" into soils with a basic composition, so that clays do not decompose and leach out and metallic ions are available.

A second variable is the rate of rainfall. Heavy, frequent rains dissolve carbon dioxide from the air and the resultant carbonic acid substitutes hydrogen for the metallic ions when it hits the soil. The carbonate salts thus formed can leach away in the flow of water downward.

A third variable is the vegetation cover. For example, prairie grasslands keep water from penetrating the soil, stopping the leaching, and in this way build up deep layers of rich humus-laden soil. Forest cover on the other hand, prevents drying of the soil and allows more rapid leaching. Some plants (e.g., oak trees) are more demanding of the soil because they use many metallic ions. The humus that results from these plants varies in richness according to these demands. Oak leaves, for example, are mineral rich. Trees that require many metallic ions may grow deep taproots and bring minerals that have leached into the groundwater to the surface. When an oak forest is cleared, the land tends to be very fertile.

Broadly speaking, in France the amount of rainfall decreases from the north and west (e.g, it is very wet in Brittany) to the south and east. The leaching action of water is greatest in Brittany. On the Mediterranean coast the dessication of plant life during the droughts has prevented soil formation, or allowed erosion to wipe out soils on land with slopes. The optimum of enough rain to support rich vegetation, but lower leaching, characterizes most of non-Mediterranean France.

Generally, the ancient granite massifs, such as those in Brittany and the Massif Central, weather into sand with no contribution to maintaining basic ions in the soil. The limestone and chalk of the ancient sea bottoms provide basic ions and maintain a clayey composition of the soil. Further, the soils on the relatively flat plains have more chance to build up without erosion than do soils where the relief is sharper.

Thus, a combination of factors reach near to their optimum in the Seine basin, especially from Paris westward to the English Channel coast and to the beginning of the Armorican massif (Brittany). This land is relatively flat so soils can be plowed, the land does not erode rapidly, rivers are navigable, and roads are cheap; it has a basic clayey composition; it is well watered but not leached out as happens in tropical rain forests. This area is structurally and climatically very similar to England (excluding Wales and Scotland), and has many of the same possibilities for a rich diversified agriculture tied together by inland waterways. (This account is derived from Samuel R. Eyre, *Vegetation and Soils: A World Picture*.)

Geography of France

Geologically, France can be divided into three broad types of land formation, with subvarieties of each, which provide different ecological environments in different places:

1. Old bottoms of flat shallow seas, on which a deposit of sedimentary limestone has accumulated. These form
   a. The fertile plains of the Paris basin (the Seine and Loire basins) and the Aquitaine basin in the southeast near the Bay of Biscay, and
   b. The limestone foothills pleated by the rising of the Alps and the consequent rising of the Massif Central and the Vosges—Black Forest massif (the limestone foothills of the Jura, upper Provence, the Causses)
   These areas are essentially similar to most of England.
2. Ancient granite or crystalline rock massifs that were not submerged in the shallow seas, but have been much smoothed by erosion. They are geologically and ecologically rather similar to Wales in Great Britain, except not so wet. There are three large important massifs: the Armorican massif covering the whole of the Breton Peninsula on the west, and extending into the Vendée on the southeast and Normandy on the northwest, the Massif Central between the Rhone River on the east of the massif and the Aquitaine basin on the west, covering the south center of France, and the Ardennes–Vosges highlands in the northeast. (The Vosges Mountains form a massif with the Black Forest of Germany, broken by the Rhine Valley). The Massif des Maures near St. Tropez is a smaller mass of this kind.
3. Alpine Mountains, of which the Alps proper in the southeast, the Pyrenees, between France and Spain, the mountains of eastern Corsica are examples. They are somewhat analogous to the Rocky Mountains of Oregon and Washington.

From the point of view of population and communication, the limestone plains were the most important. Most of the population of France lived in either the Paris Seine–Loire basin or in the Aquitaine basin. The ecology of this sort of region consists of two radically distinct types of environments. The tableland tends to be flat and well drained, with a tendency to be too dry for many crops. Its natural cover seems to be mostly grass; at least trees and bushes do not establish themselves quickly when the land is left fallow, as they do in the river valleys. The tableland is covered with a heavy rich soil that grows cereals well.

For our purpose the "natural cover" of an area is that cover that quickly becomes established when the land is left out of cultivation, and which then changes slowly (if at all) toward the true ecological equilibrium. Since grazing or fire frequently prevent the true equilibrium from being established if the rate of change toward that equilibrium is slow, the rate of conquest by the true equilibrium plant cover is crucial. Probably the true equilibrium of these limestone plains is deciduous forest of mineral-demanding trees (e.g., the oak), which once established could change the hydrological regime enough to flourish and so shade out the grasses. But this equilibrium is much more rapidly reestablished in the river valleys. Unfortunately, the quantitative assessment of rates of ecological succession under various conditions is in its infancy.

The rivers and streams often cut through the limestone covering, exposing the clay, sand, and marl underneath. The underground drainage encouraged by the character of the tableland comes out in numerous springs on the sides of the valleys, so the sides of the valleys are well watered. Fruit trees, vineyards, and garden crops grow well in river valleys.

Both of the major plains are drained by large, slow-moving river systems which are navigable far inland. The slow grades of the plains made it possible to connect the different river systems, especially the Seine with the Loire, with canals in the eighteenth century. The rivers together with the canals unified the Paris basin for bulk transportation, making Paris the most important port in the country even though it was not accessible to oceangoing ships.

In the limestone foothills and mountains of the south, the general tendency for water to be drained from the surface combines with the marked dry season to create a barren environment, a white rocky desert, except where erosion has cut through the limestone cover. Only sheep and goats, and not many of them, can make a living on these barren slopes.

The ancient eroded crystalline highlands of Brittany, the Massif Central, and Ardennes tend to have irregular patches of pebbly or sandy soil that is flat enough to cultivate. The soil has a different (especially more acid) chemical composition, and so has different natural vegetation cover. This, together with a different water regime, encourages the growth of forests. Except where it is enriched with volcanic (basaltic) deposits in the Massif Central, the land seems generally less fertile than the old seabottom limestone plains, but more fertile than the folded limestone hills and mountains around the Alps and the Massif Central.

Since the ground in these ancient granite massifs is irregular, and higher than in the surrounding plains, the headwaters of the rivers that rise in these ancient crystalline rock masses tend not to be navigable. The irregular relief, the forested countryside, the widely spaced farms, all discourage the penetration of adequate roads. The relative infertility of the soil means that any given road would not give rise to as much commerce per farm reached as it would in the plain. For all these reasons, the interior of these highlands tends to be more isolated than the surrounding plain. The farmers tend to live separately on their pieces of land rather than together in villages and to enclose their fields with hedges and trees.

The Alps and Pyrenees have the same effect as the ancient highlands, but much intensified. The average slope of the relief is much steeper, the patches of alluvial soil deposits are farther between and rockier, the difficulties of communication are multiplied. The difference between the agriculture of the Alps and the ancient highlands is something like the difference between the Rockies and the Appalachians in the United States.

Animals and Plants in Energy Transfer

The basic energy transfer of French agriculture outside the Mediterranean area in the eighteenth century took place in two stages. First, the work animal, either a horse or an ox, collected energy from the pastureland or fallow and transferred it to plowing, cultivation, and hauling on the arable, and to providing fertilizer. The arable land then produced grain that was consumed by humans and perhaps by transport animals, or occasionally by animals being fattened for market. A subsidiary energy cycle transferred animal products (especially butter, cheese, and meat) directly from the pastureland to human consumption.

> A characteristic trait of the rural economy of the 18th century is the great quantity of uncultivated land and rough pasture. The extent is variable according to the regions. In Brittany they occupy about 40 percent of the surface (more or less according to the nature of the soil). In the mountainous regions (Rousillon, Alpine regions) they are still more considerable. On the other hand in Picardy, and above all in Flanders, Alsace, in the Ile-de-France [the Paris basin, bounded by the Seine, the Marne, the Oise and their affluents], the cultivated lands much surpass uncultivated land. Throughout the forests, in the lower valleys of rivers, insufficiently drained, much of the land escaped cultivation. Sée *Esquisse d'une histoire du régime agraire*).

On the plains, much of the pastureland could be used for arable, and during the eighteenth century some land was cleared to produce more grain. Consequently, one main way to increase total productivity of arable products, principally grain, was to decrease the amount of pastureland. There are two main ways to do this, both of which were used especially by noble landlords during the century. The first is simply to drive other people's animals off the pastureland, and then to reduce the pasture to enough to support one's own animals. Much of the conflict over the enclosure of common land (i.e., pasture) had to do with who it was going to be enclosed against, whose animals were to go hungry. Likewise, when cattle and work animals traditionally graze on the fallow, a decrease of fallow and introduction of more "modern" crop rotations often has the side effect of pushing some people's animals off the land.

The second way to decrease the amount of land devoted to pasture is to increase the productivity of pastureland by planting artificial meadow in place of the natural cover, or planting fodder crops and using stall feeding. Naturally the technique of letting other people's animals go hungry tends to exacerbate the class conflict, while planting artifical meadow or fodder crops on already enclosed land merely increases one's own productivity. But because the high productivity policy usually required enclosure, the two techniques were often employed simultaneously.

In the ancient granite highlands and the mountains, the basic parameters of this energy exchange were far different. The ratio of natural pasture to arable land was much higher, so that there was plenty of pasture for everyone. There was no pressure to turn low productivity pasture into higher productivity arable or artificial meadow because the pasture land was not suitable for cultivation anyway. Nature kept the eyes of greedy landlords off the common pastureland in the highlands by making it too steep, rocky, and forested. Perhaps this, as well as the lower commercialization of agriculture in the highlands, helps explain their general tendency to support reactionary movements during the revolutionary period, especially in Brittany. (Most of the lawsuits about common pasture seem to come from the plains, and lawsuits tend to indicate conflict fueled by self-interested indignation.)

Both because pasture is plentiful and because animal products have a higher value per pound, many of the mountainous areas nowadays export animal products, especially cheese, which does not decay, and animals that can be driven out. This commerce in animal products was undoubtedly much less important during the eighteenth century, both because transport costs were higher and also because a poorer population cannot afford animal products since they cost a great deal more per calorie. Where the highlands were cut by a navigable river, as in Alsace-Lorraine, the area became famous for animal products. It is difficult to estimate accurately the parameters of the energy exchange. It seems from English information from approximately the same geographical situation that on heavy, clayey soils, a team of five horses could plow about 50 acres (20 hectares), while on lighter soils, four horses could cultivate 80 acres (32 hectares). (These are estimates of Arthur Young. See George Fussel, "Animal Husbandry in Eighteenth Century England," p. 213 for work capacity, and p. 114 for the amount of grass needed to raise a cow, which I take to be equivalent to a horse.) Each horse apparently needed about 2.5 acres (1 hectare) of unimproved pasture. So the necessary ratio between natural pasture and arable would range from 1:4 to 1:8, if no one uses any animal products and no resources are devoted to feeding pregnant or nursing mares or young horses before they enter the labor force. A more realistic estimate would be one acre of pasture for each two to four acres of arable. It was generally alleged that this ratio was higher for oxen, because oxen work slower but eat as much. In the long run in the nineteenth century, horses were substituted for oxen, which probably indicates that horses more efficiently transformed food into work.

A landlord who shipped only grain would presumably aim toward a minimum ratio of one-ninth to one-fifth pasture. A peasant or farmer who wanted to vary his diet with animal products would want the right to keep a couple of cows and a few pigs. Since a peasant family worked about 30–70 acres, and for this would need from two to four horses (see R. Forster, "The Noble as Landlord in the Region of Toulouse at the End of the Old Regime," p. 235; for various farms in the Armorican massif [bocage], see Charles Tilly, The Vendée, Chapter 7), this desire for meat products could easily double the amount of pasture needed. Tilly says that often a 25-hectare farm in the bocage area of the Armorican massif had from six to ten oxen for plowing. These were also fattened and sold for meat when they got old. Note, however, that natural pasture is more plentiful in this area.

Apparently, by cultivating fodder crops and planting artificial hay, the productivity of an acre of land, in terms of animal flesh or animal energy, could be about doubled (Fussel, 1937, p. 114). On the other hand, this meant that the pastureland had to be plowed and cultivated as well. So fodder crops tended to be introduced in those old seabottom plains where there was no surplus of natural pasture. As in England, the "improving landlords" of the eighteenth century were found in the flat champaign country, while "backward" landlords who used natural pasture were found in the granite country of Wales, Cornwall, Brittany, and the nearby bocage, the Ardennes, Vosges, the Massif Central. The most "improving landlords," in the restricted sense of the eighteenth century, were those on arable plains nearby large rich markets for animal products; there cultivation of fodder for stall feeding of animals became profitable. Flanders and the immediate environs of Paris provide examples.

In Provence, where the Alps and their foothills come down to the Mediterranean, and to a lesser extent in Brittany, where an ancient crystalline rock highland is surrounded on three sides by water, the coastal and river valley population dominates the isolated mountainous groups. A Provençal person typically participates more in the Mediterranean as a social system than in any land-based geographical social system. One indication of this is the localization of the plague of 1720. The plague was sufficiently drastic to kill nearly half of the population of Marseille, yet it did not really spread outside Provence. It seems that, similarly, some half of the population of Brittany has always lived on a narrow belt of seacoast, where agriculture based on alluvial soils is combined with fishing, the Navy, and other seafaring occupations. The seacoast is partly protected from frosts, which makes certain tender tree crops possible.

The agriculture of the coast of Provence and of the lower Rhone Valley is affected by the yearly droughts of about half the year. The "natural" cover is *maquis*, whose dominant plants are low-growing, drought-resistant shrubs. (Here again the previously given definition of "natural" cover applies. This is the cover that first grows when land goes out of cultivation, which is succeeded only slowly, if at all, by other plant cover. It seems likely that in the long run a broad-leaved evergreen forest or deciduous forest whose leaves drop in the dry season is probably the long-run equilibrium. But the long run here is very long indeed.) During the rainy part of the year, one gets occasional light frost near the ground and every once in a while a real freeze. The *mistral* is a cold, dry wind created by the movement of an Arctic air mass formed over the Alps, which moves toward the low pressure areas formed over the western Mediterranean. This cold, dry, fast wind tends to break and to dry out agricultural plants. The drying winter wind and the dry summer require either irrigation or "dry farming" to get a good crop. Dry farming involves storing one year's rain in the soil for the following year, by keeping unplanted fields plowed all during their fallow year (this decreases run-off, keeps weeds from using the water, and decreases capillary evaporation).

This complex of climatic and soil conditions tends to produce marked variations from one place to another in favorability to agriculture, with protected coastal valleys supplied with irrigation water from a stream or river, protected from the *mistral* by a row of landward mountains, and protected from frost by the warm Mediterranean waters, being the most favorable. It now seems a waste to use such a favorable conjunction for grain rather than fresh fruits, vegetables, and wine, particularly since the productivity of these lands for grain is generally much lower than in the north. Furthermore, the only animals that can live easily on the "natural" cover of the south of France are goats, who do not pull a plow as well as horses or oxen. Now the Mediterranean areas of France either grow nothing but scrub, or else grow luxury fresh crops and wine.

But this concentration on wine and fruits is to a large extent the product of commerce with grain-growing northern Europe. The Mediterranean coast was commercialized early, because of the easy access to the sea. Nevertheless, the production of local requirements for bread was probably mostly carried out in the area in the eighteenth century. It seems likely that vine growing spread more rapidly in the first half of the century than in the second half, because the prices of wine relative to wheat declined in the last half (Pierre Vilar, "Geographie et Histoire Statistique, Histoire Sociale, et Techniques de Production: Quelques Points sur L'Histoire de la Viticulture Mediterraneenne," pp. 121–135. The specific data come from Barcelona, which is physically and economically similar to Mediterranean France).

Access to the Mediterranean was also important in turning Marseille into an international *entrepot* port, where goods were transferred from one ship to another and where much organization and finance of Mediterranean trade was organized. None of France's North Sea or Atlantic ports competed with the Dutch in this *entrepot* business. But in the western Mediterranean, Marseille, perhaps pushed by its physical isolation from the interior by a set of infertile limestone foothills, developed around its sheltered inner harbor a meeting place for sailing ships and a warehousing and trading elite that died of plague or became wealthy, depending on the circumstances.

Ecological Types of Social Systems

French social scientists have been especially interested in the types of social systems that grew up in different types of geographical environment since André Siegfried (1913) observed that the conservative political persuasion of an area in elections varied sharply with altitude. (André Siegfried, *Tableau politique de la France de l'ouest sous le Troisième Republique*.) Siegfried showed, and others have confirmed since, that this relationship between elevation and politics, between rock types and attitude toward religion, extends back to the French Revolution (Charles Tilly, *The Vendée*, and Paul Bois, *Paysans de l'ouest*. Bois attacks Siegfried's explanations, but not the basic finding. Tilly comments at one point, "As in so much that Siegfried wrote, the intuition is unerring, even when the facts remain vague" [*ibid*. p. 40].) Several variables seem to have varied

TABLE 2.1

Contrasting Social Systems in Ecological Areas

Ancient sea bottom and river valleys	Crystalline massif
Open fields worked jointly in three-field rotation	Enclosed fields *(bocage)* worked on two-field rotation system
Nucleated settlement of farmers in villages	Dispersed settlement in hamlets and farmsteads
Much interdependence of city and country	Little urban contact
Higher productivity on arable per man year	High productivity on pasture per man year; low arable fertility
Wine produced for market	Little wine produced
Large percentage of crop marketed	Low percentage of crop marketed
More bourgeois and peasant ownership of land	More noble ownership of land
More monasteries (regular clergy)	More secular clergy (parish clergy)
Higher literacy	Lower literacy
Higher royal penetration	More "feudal" government

together over most of non-Mediterranean France, with the main distinction being limestone and chalk versus granite (plains versus hills, headwaters versus navigable rivers, heavy soils versus sandy soils, forest cover versus grass cover, all cut the map in about the same place). The variables in Table 2.1 (taken from Charles Tilly, *The Vendée*) show the contrast between the plains or river valleys and the *bocage* in the southern half of the Department of Maine-et-Loire in western France. With the difference of a variable or two, the same contrast is found between the Aquitaine and Paris basins on the one hand and the Massif Central, and between the Paris basin and the Ardennes-Vosges highlands.

This contrast between the plains and highlands is the geographical basis of a kind of two-party system in the social history of northern France. In the eighteenth century the agricultural improvers liked the plains and got their bad examples from the granite *bocages*. After the Revolution, the faithful flocks of the western *bocages* got their examples of perfidy and sin from the urbanized plains. The Midi with its Mediterranean climate was irrelevant to the discussion of whether fodder crops were a sign of progress. The southerners were also, in a way, an uncomfortable third party in the fight over the Revolution and its values. Commercialized and modernized like the northern plains, the Midi supported the great Revolution. But one could almost say they were waiting for the communist movement so they could support the Revolution, but oppose the French government. French historians of the eighteenth century have ignored the Midi as much as they could until very recently.

On the plains the property-owning system had two levels, the *communauté* or village which "owned" the *finage,* and the individual family which owned a "share" in the *finage,* the *champs* or *labor.* If one owned a *champs,* one was a *laboureur,* and as a consequence had rights in the common land, which often consisted of forest or rough pasture (*forêt* or *landes*) and of meadow near a river (*prés*). If one was not a *laboureur,* he was often called a day laborer, *journalier.* The day laborers had lesser rights in the common land and were excluded from the government of the *communauté.*

The arable land of the *finage* was divided into three great fields, the *soles.* Each shareholder in the village had a proportionate share in each field, generally in the form of long strips. Sometimes there would be several strips in each field for each shareholder, so that each got a proportionate share of the good and bad land. One *sole* was generally sown with winter wheat in the fall after it had lain fallow, then sown with summer grain the following year, and then kept plowed clean the third year. It seems that the clean plowing or fallow was for the purpose of killing the weeds which otherwise came to dominate the grain crops. After the harvest, the cattle of all the village were allowed onto the fields in a number in proportion to the landholding (*vaine pâture*); if the harvest had been done with a sickle rather than a scythe, the amount of straw left was substantial. But one official of the district of Cluses was not so generous in his evaluation in the year III. He spoke of *vaine pâture* as "fields abandoned, I wouldn't say to pasture, but to the promenade of animals" (Festy, *Les conditions de production et de recolte des céréales.*)

When agriculture and cattle raising are combined in the same small area, one can either enclose the fields and let the cattle run free or enclose (or guard) the cattle and leave the fields open. The basic choice of the three-field plains was to leave the fields open and guard the cattle. (This description is extracted from Lizerand, *Le régime rural de l'ancienne France,* Chapters XII to XV, especially XV.)

There are two competing theories about why the *bocage* areas on the ancient granite highlands had a different human geography (*paysage*). The fields of isolated farms were enclosed with hedges or with low, wide walls of loose rock. The simplest theory is merely that there were more rocks in the fields and that hedges grew more easily, and that furthermore such arable as the country provided was not scarce, so the tenth of the fields taken by hedges and walls was not missed. The lower value of arable is also shown by the general practice of a two-course crop rotation, with half rather than a third of the arable land in fallow.

The second theory is more complicated and more sociological. The basic idea is that the walls and hedges constitute a property claim. "In sum, hedge and low wall are the equivalent of a notarized deed." ("*En somme, haie et murette sont l'équivalent de l'acte notarie*" [Delaspre, "La naissance d'un paysage rural au XVIIIᵉ siècle sur les hauts plateaux de l'est du Cantal et du nord de la Mageride," *Revue de geographie alpine*, vol. 4, 1952, p. 494]. The area referred to is not alpine, but in the Massif Central.) The argument is that when the village as such is a solid property-owning entity, then individual ownership is sufficiently effectively asserted by having a share in the village. But where cultivation is not in a form requiring (or permitting) corporate village activity and ownership, individual assertions of ownership become necessary. Hence, *bocage* (or individual enclosed fields) occurs outside areas of common three-field cultivation. (I have never seen this argument stated in its full form, though its elements all occur in the French literature. The nearest to a straight statement of this theory that I have seen occurs in George Homans, *The Thirteenth Century English Villager*.)

The Midi in the south of France was still influenced by the large, defensively oriented agro-town, much larger than the northern three-field village. The median size of agricultural villages along the line of main contact between Christianity and Moslem areas, from Spain across southern Italy and Sicily, the Balkans, and on into the Caucasus, is still today much larger than in the north of Europe. (See Folke Dovring, *Land and Labour in Europe: 1900–1950*, Chapter 1, especially the map between pp. 14–15.) The royal government was less successful in the south at preventing attacks from "pirates" than in the north, and since much of the most productive agriculture was near the sea, the defensive organization of the population was a much more important ecological force.

The fields were often individually enclosed, though generally with rocks rather than hedges because goats eat hedges; even goats have trouble eating rocks. The fields tended to be square in shape, and there is little to indicate any communal organization of cultivation.

Ecological Uncertainty: Famine and Plague

Whether people could stay alive in their physical and biological environment in the eighteenth century varied from year to year. A disastrous famine occurred throughout France in 1709–1710. As a result the price of wheat at Rozoy in Brie and Albi increased by four times the 1708 price, the price at Douai was about three times as high, and the price at Grenoble about two and one-half times as high (cf. Abbot Payson Usher, "The General Course of Wheat Prices in France: 1350–1788", pp. 159–169; and R. Latouche, "Le Prix du Blé a Grenoble du XVe au XVIIIe Siècle", pp. 337–351). When we realize that estimates of the proportion of a worker's wages that he ordinarily had to pay for enough bread to feed his family ranged around 60–80% (cf. Georges Lefebvre, "Urban Society in the Orleanais in the Late Eighteenth Century", pp. 46–75, at p. 62), we can see that on the averge, consumption by the poor was probably cut at least in half by such prices. A similar disastrous harvest had taken place in 1693. Other bad harvest years throughout northern France came in 1698–1699, in 1713–1714, and 1740–1741, and there was considerable death during the two years after the 1709–1710 disaster, and again in 1725.

After 1741 there was a long period with no really bad harvests until 1788. During this latter half of the century, the correlation between the price of wheat and the death rate almost disappeared.

The size of the effects of these famines is hard to estimate, partly because in time of famine people wander about looking for food and then die in places where they are not registered. The data we have, however, are from local areas. It seems, however, that the great famines of 1693–1694 and 1709–1710 may have tripled the death rate in the Parisian basin. If about 3% of the population normally died per year, this would mean about a tenth of the population would die in a famine year. (This estimate is based on scattered figures in Meuvret, "Demographic Crisis in France from the Sixteenth to the Eighteenth Century," 1965, pp. 517–518.) Of course, the poor were more likely to die than the better off.

> [At Saint-Godard in Rouen] we find the number of burials broken down into burials "on charity" which can then be compared with the number of fee-paying burials. We find that a normal year saw on an average, out of 121 deaths, 92 burials which were paid for as against 29 charity burials. The harvest year 1693–94 includes 208 burials paid for: that is to say, double the usual number; 116 were performed on charity; four times the usual number [Meuvret, 1965, p. 519].

But furthermore, the effects of these famines were highly variable from one place to another. For instance, in the village of Le Houlme (Rouen) deaths increased in 1693–1694 to 50 from 15 in normal years, but in Les Mesnil-Vigot (Manche) there was no increase in these years. There is evidence that places near the English Channel had much lower variation in grain prices. This could, of course, be due to accessibility to seaborne trade or to supplementary fish supplies, or to the moderation of bad winters near the seacoast improving harvests.

A similar effect was produced by epidemics, both among people and among animals. On about May 25 of 1720, the ship *Grand Saint Antoine* arrived in Marseille carrying the bubonic plague. The ship and crew were isolated in the lazarette for two weeks, but some of the textiles it was carrying were smuggled out. During the quarantine period, several sailors and longshoremen died, but the diagnosis of plague was not made with certainty. The plague spread into the city of Marseille, and to Toulon, Apt, and Arles. A commission of physicians sent by the King's physician, Chirae, investigated the outbreak but did not diagnose plague. They nevertheless took some precautionary measures based on the theory that the disease was contagious. The well-to-do tended to flee the cities, to go to their country houses where the incidence of the disease was lower.

We now know that the plague is mainly spread by insect parasites which feed on the blood of both human beings and rats. The two theories of the eighteenth century were that a "miasma" in the air caused plague (this explained such facts as its concentration in port cities, its prevalence in the Mediterranean, its seasonal character, its association with the smell of rotting garbage); and a "contagion" theory that contact with the sick and the dead caused it (this explained the epidemic character of the plague, its concentration in commercial cities and its importation by ships on which men died of it). The preventive measures suggested by the idea of contagion were isolation of the affected people and deep burying of the bodies of the dead, and also the quarantine of ships coming from plague-infected ports. These, especially the last, may have some actual value in restricting the spread of infected rats and fleas. (These facts about the plague are taken from L. F. Hirst, *The Conquest of the Plague*, pp. 58–62.) The result of this plague was that something like a third of the populations of the affected cities died, and an unknown number of rural people in Provence died.

In 1763, an epidemic among cattle spread over the eastern part of the Paris basin, with some outbreak in the west. Government policy was organized mainly by Fleury, the *procureur general* of the *Parlement* of Paris. It was mainly based on the idea of contagion, and consisted in isolating the affected animals, burying their corpses, and restricting commerce of cattle in affected areas. Various empirical remedies were suggested for curing the cattle. An example is

> Roots of milk weed, (d'annee), of masterwort, of angelica, at a dose of a half ounce each; boil in two liters (a little over two quarts) of vinegar with red rose petals, until a third is boiled away. Add, after having strained it, a half ounce of theriaque [treacle—a panacea or sovereign remedy of medieval medicine made of a combination of over sixty drugs]. Give in two doses to the animal, one in the morning, one in the evening. [Bandois, "L'Epizootie de 1763", p. 354].

The epidemic died out during the year, whether because of the preventive and curative measures, we cannot tell.

The point of these examples is that there was great regional and temporal variability in the relations of people to their physical and biological environment. The ideas they had to use to form actions to deal with such disasters were not sufficient to bring them under control. Furthermore, the society as a whole did not effectively provide insurance, so that famine could ravage one part of the country, while other parts were little affected.

The Ecology of Paris

The population of Paris in 1789 was probably between 600,000 and 650,000. Of these, perhaps 120,000 were nobles, clergymen, officials, and middle and upper bourgeoisie. The other half million or so were *menu peuple:* artisans and craftsmen, apprentices, shopkeepers, peddlers, domestics, putting-out workers who did manufacturing in their homes on materials provided by merchants, and a large floating population of temporary rural in-migrants. If we estimate that an adult eats two pounds of bread a day, while a child on the average eats one pound, and estimate that half the population might be children, then such a population would need a daily supply of about a million pounds, or 500 tons, of bread. Over the course of a year, then, each urban family of four would require about one ton of bread, or a little more than a ton of grain (about three *setiers* in the measure of the time).

The productivity of a farm family varied considerably over the country, and there were also nonfarm families serving rural areas. At a very rough estimate, it probably took the surplus of two farm families near Paris to support the necessary rural nonfarm population (blacksmiths, priests, etc.) and one urban family in an ordinary year. Thus, to support the Parisian population at a minimum level of subsistence, the full surplus of about 1½–2 million rural people had to be shipped into Paris. Of course, the upper classes did not live at a minimum subsistence level. In an area of 25 miles around Paris, all the surplus grain was required to be sold in the Paris markets. In addition, grain merchants bought grain outside that perimeter. The grain was distributed to several thousand mills to be ground into flour, then distributed to bakers. There were stalls of some 300 bakers in the *Halle aux Blés,* the central bread market of Paris. This concentration of bakers led to the concentration of housewives, and in times of short bread supply and high bread prices, this facilitated bread riots.

Typical residences in medieval Paris were five-story houses. The ground floor often contained shops. The first floor (i.e., what in the United States is called the second floor) tended to be occupied by upper- and middle-class families, the higher floors by working-class families, and the top floor by servants, students, transients, and apprentices. During the eighteenth century, there appears to have been an increased tendency for different social classes to be segregated in different parts of town, with the west and southwest becoming fashionable districts.

The concentration of government and the luxury market in Paris tended to concentrate manufacturing, cultural, and finanial institutions in the city. This concentration helped, and was helped by, the concentration of international and national trade in Paris.

Paris was the largest, and by far the most important, urban agglomeration. But it seems that from 1726 to 1789, "The population in cities of 50,000 or more rose about 30%, and that in cities of 20,000 or more, almost 60%. If correct, these figures would mean that about 4% of the French population was in cities of 50,000 or more (of which about half were in Paris, A.L.S.), and about 7.5% in cities of 20,000 or more" (Tilly, *The Vendée*, op.cit, p. 23; he is citing Roger Mols, *Introduction à la démographie historique des villes d' Europe du XIVe au XVIIIe siècle*, pp. 514–515).

Government was probably the chief city-forming industry, with trade, especially in agricultural products, second in importance. International trade, especially in sugar, coffee, and tea, grew by some 900% during the century. (Tilly, 1964, p. 21, citing Reinhard, *Histoire de la population mondiale* pp. 93–94). The prices of colonial goods were very much higher (in comparison to wheat) than in the modern world, so this was trade in "luxury" goods, not goods for mass consumption. Bordeaux especially had as a principal economic base trade in sugar from the West Indies.

Tableau de la France

We can simplify these details into an overall division of eighteenth-century France into three important regions, with a cross-cutting distinction between rural areas and cities within two of these regions (see Table 2.2).

The main sustenance of the royal government in Paris, and the population of Paris itself, was drawn from the first region of rich commercialized grain agriculture, especially the northern plain stretching from the North Sea and the Bay of Biscay on the west to the Rhine and German states on the east. This area was the core of French status as a world power in the eighteenth century.

The mountain regions were more backward, tending much more often

TABLE 2.2

Outline of the Major Regions of France and Their Characteristics

Type of region	Areas included	Distinguishing features
Rich plains	North of France except Brittany, Vosges-Ardennes, plus Acquitaine basin near Bordeaux	Fertile grain agriculture with *charrue;* 1 acre of pasture required to feed work animals for 4 acres of arable; corporate villages with three-field open-field agriculture; introduction of crop rotation, fodder crops, stall feeding of animals, by "improving landlords"; scarce pasture, "enclosures of the common;" much peasant and bourgeois ownership of land; highly commercialized agriculture; good river and canal transportation and dense road network; bureaucratic government royal officials; monasteries as well as parish clergy; dominance by nearby cities.
Well watered granite mountain	Brittany, Vosges-Ardennes, Massif Central, Alps, Pyrenees, (Jura somewhat similar)	Low fertility grain culture with *araire;* 1 acre of pasture required for work animals for 8 acres of arable; dispersed villages with individual enclosed fields; alternate year cultivation of fields; little crop rotation or growth of fodder; plentiful pasture, little "enclosure of the common;" much noble ownership of land; low commercialization; nonnavigable rivers and poor roads; less bureaucracy, more noble control of government; parish clergy only; few cities and little urban dominance.

Type of region	Areas included	Distinguishing features
Mediterranean, hot, dry summers, wet winters	The Midi	Dry farming of grain (alternate year cultivation, with intervening year plowed surface) with *araire*, with some irrigation, especially grapes, near rivers; little pasture available near fields; large villages with individual enclosed fields and no cultivation in common; few fodder crops; poor pastures, herds must go to mountains during dry season; much peasant and bourgeois ownership of land; highly commercialized; often near sea transportation, but poor road network; recent penetration of royal bureaucracy into a local, already somewhat bureaucratic, government; monasteries as well as parish clergy; dominance by cities.
Cities	Sea and river ports in the rich plains and Midi	Based mainly on wholesale trade in agricultural goods and on government; wholesalers and officials and abbots or bishops constitute the upper class; guild-organized artisians, mostly serving the local population, form a middle group; porters, stevedores, day laborers, make up the poor; royal officials divide authority with city oligarchy; monasteries and cathedrals are usually located in cities.

to be run as *pays d'etat* in which the royal government negotiated with a local assembly of nobles and notables. The population generally spoke dialects rather than French, and were less open to the new ideas of agriculture. They were settled on more or less isolated homesteads, each farmer having a separate relation to the local lord rather than a relation through his village.

The Midi was essentially part of Mediterranean culture rather than northern European culture. The agriculture of the northern plain of France was quite similar to eastern and southern England, whereas that of the Midi was similar to Spain and Italy and Morroco. Winter wheat, olive trees, and extensive vineyards were cultivated in the Midi. French cultural hegemony was only relatively recently instituted even in the lowlands, whereas in the mountains the local dialects of Provençal and Langue d'oc were still often spoken.

The cities had roughly the same structure and economic base in the north and the south, but the poor mountain cultures had difficulty supporting cities. Instead of being manufacturing cities such as grew up after the Industrial Revolution, most French cities were "local metropolises," engaged in trade, finance, and government, with an artisan population to make goods that were mainly consumed locally and a population of laborers, especially involved in physically moving the goods that the upper classes traded.

ECOLOGY OF AMERICAN SOCIETY

The dominant characteristic of American ecology is the degree to which all human activities are carried out in artificial environments. Most important American activities are carried out inside buildings; these buildings have controlled temperature, lighting, humidity, and biological environments. Each such building has a reliable supply system that provides fuel, water, food, raw and semi-finished materials for the work done there, and capital equipment for doing the work.

Transportation in American society takes place in air-conditioned machines, and these are in specially constructed transportation environments furnished with pavements, rails, radar beams, lights, and signals. In cities, about a third of the land area is devoted to these specialized transportation environments, and in the countryside great gashes are cut in the hills and mountains to provide appropriate grades and drainage for them.

The biological supplies for the society come from farms that also have an artificially altered environment: the chemical environment is changed by fertilizers and pesticides; species composition is determined by species agricultural productivity; the hydrologic regime is changed by irrigation, drainage, contour plowing, and bulldozing; the soil's physical structure is changed by plowing vegetation or mulches under; the animals live in barns and chicken factories.

This all means that the dominant determinant of ecological organization has changed from the features of the natural environment to the socially organized conditions of access of one activity to another. Another way of saying this is that American society is an urban society, for the distinctive feature of a city (or now, of a metropolitan area) is the high mutual accessibility of the people and activities in it. A city is traditionally a place of dense settlement, but dense settlement has given advantage for some activities only because of high mutual access. The exurbs of rural Connecticut are functionally urban even when they are not dense, because the people there choose that place to live because of its accessibility to the activities of New York City.

Even cities themselves tend to be located to a large extent by their access to other cities. Those manufacturing industries that use manufactured products in their own work have a strong tendency to be located in the industrial belt that stretches from New York–Philadelphia–Baltimore on the east to Chicago–Milwaukee on the west, including Buffalo, Pittsburgh, Cleveland, Detroit and many smaller industrial cities with high mutual accessibility. Great cities no longer primarily buy in and sell to a resource hinterland. Instead, they buy and sell to each other.

The Economic Base of American Cities

The economy of each American city can be divided into a part of about 25% that produces goods or services for a national or regional market, and a part of about 75% that produces goods and services for the local population. The housing construction and real estate industry, the retail trade industry, local manufacturers of goods like newspapers or bakery products, police, primary and secondary schools, urban transport workers or parking lot attendants, all look pretty much alike in all large American cities. The difference between cities is in the export industries: automobiles and other machines from Detroit; financial and shipping services, apparel, and some sophisticated manufactuers from New York; airplanes and weapons from Los Angeles and Seattle; grain from Minneapolis (cf. Otis D. Duncan *et al.*, *Metropolis and Region*.) For instance, the occupational class structure of the local 75% is almost the same in different cities. Differences between cities in social class structure are almost entirely accounted for by the 25% export sector. (Omer Galle,

"Occupational Composition and the Metropolitan Hierarchy", pp. 260–269).

The export quarter of the economy tends to be organized in larger firms. These firms could move part of their activities elsewhere, since they do not depend on the local market. It is the location decisions of these nationally and regionally oriented firms that determine whether a city grows or declines. This in turn determines whether local real estate and retail trade enterprises boom or bust. This asymmetrical dependency of local economy on national firms, but low dependency of the export sector on the local economy, tends to create a concentration of power in the hands of national firms. Tax concessions, subsidized industrial park developments, subsidized docks or other transportation facilities, special credit arrangements at the local banks, and other economic privileges are generally granted such national exporting firms. It is very rare for a community to encourage its economic growth by subsidizing new department stores, supermarkets, workers' housing, or by giving tax exemptions to real estate dealers.

The city-building or base industries have changed substantially during American history. The first large cities during colonial and early post-colonial times were foreign trade centers. They developed to gather the agricultural products of the countryside for shipment to Europe, and to handle the return cargoes of tropical products from the West Indies and manufactures from Europe. In 1790 the largest cities were New York, Philadelphia, Boston, Charleston, South Carolina, and Baltimore. As the interior started to open up by 1840, New Orleans surpassed Boston and Charleston in size, while Cincinnati and Albany passed Charleston. Two further cities on the Mississippi and Great Lakes system passed New Orleans in size: Chicago growing to third in size by 1880 and St. Louis to fifth. In 1880, then, the list of largest cities was: New York, Philadelphia, Chicago, Boston, St. Louis, Baltimore, Cincinnati, San Francisco, Pittsburgh, and New Orleans. New York was then over a million, and Philadelphia near a million, in population. (See Beverly Duncan and Stanley Lieberson, *Metropolis and Region in Transition*, pp. 29–58.)

Up to about 1880, the dominant manufacturing industries were those that produced biological products: textiles, clothing, boots and shoes, lumber products, flour and grain mills. These industries tend to be located on the lines of agricultural trade and to confirm the dominance of trading centers.

The character of manufacturing started to change quickly around 1880 in three respects. First, a larger proportion of manufacturers were working up metals rather than biological products. Second, the growing railroad network and the growing number of machines produced tended to increase the proportion of all the materials used by a particular manufacturer that were bought from other manufacturers rather than from farmers or loggers. Third, heavy capital investments in large factories became more important. Steam power was not easily transmitted to small shops scattered around town as electricity was later; there are great economies of scale in the furnaces and rolling mills for steel production. Metal working, intercity railroad trade, and factory production, therefore, became the core industrial institutions.

Most of the new manufacturing activity was added to the traditional trading centers. In 1900, "Nearly 11% of the nation's manufacturing workers lived in New York, in contrast to 5% living in Chicago, (and 4.7% in Philadelphia)" (Beverly Duncan and Stanley Lieberson, p. 81). But Pittsburgh, Cleveland, and Detroit, all showed marked development of those types of manufacturing that buy from other manufacturers and sell to still others.

This mid-Atlantic to Midwestern metal fabrication belt continued to grow, so that in 1939 the large cities with an exceptionally high ratio of manufacturing to wholesale commercial activity were all in that belt: Detroit, Buffalo, Cleveland, Milwaukee, Philadelphia, Baltimore, and Pittsburgh (Duncan and Lieberson, 1970, p. 131). Perhaps Chicago should be included here, though it is also a great wholesaling center.

In addition, between 1900 and 1939 three noncommercial, nonindustrial centers grew to large size: Washington, Miami, and Los Angeles. The particular reasons are different in the three cases, but all three seem to reflect the relative growth of services other than commerce as city-creating industries. (Whether film manufacturers should be classified as service industries or as manufacturing is a more or less arbitrary decision. The census calls them services.)

As the proportion of all products sold in an area that must be further processed by other firms before final consumption increases, the proportion of all trade of the base industries that goes to other metropolitan areas increases. The great national firms that make up the 25% base industries of a metropolitan area mainly ship to, and receive from, other base industries of other metropolitan centers. Rather than being oriented to an agricultural hinterland, today's metropolises ship to each other. About 40% of the population of the United States in 1980 lived in the metropolitan regions and SMSAs (Standard Metropolitan Statistical Areas) shown in Table 2.3. About another third lived in other urban areas. Only a quarter lived in rural areas (towns of under 2500 and open country not in urban districts).

Thus, because of the advantages of performing the "export" activities in great metropolitan complexes about 10% of the total United States

TABLE 2.3

1980 Census Count of Metropolitan Regions
of the United States
(to the Nearest 1,000)

SCSA and SMSA	1980 Population (x 1,000)
New York SCSA	16,120
New York SMSA	9,120
Nassau–Suffolk	2,606
Newark NJ	1,965
Los Angeles SCSA	11,496
Los Angeles–Long Beach	7,478
Riverside, etc.	1,557
Anaheim, etc.	1,932
Chicago SCSA	7,868
Chicago	7,102
Gary, etc.	643
Philadelphia SCSA	5,549
Philadelphia	4,717
Bay Area SCSA	5,182
San Francisco–Oakland	3,243
San Jose	1,295
Detroit SCSA	4,618
Detroit	4,353

work force is concentrated in metropolitan areas of over a million population. But this 10% draws to it another 30% of the total United States work force to service its local needs, so that each metropolitan work force is about one-fourth "export" or "base" industry, three-fourths service and local industry.

The export sector of each city's economy largely ships to other metropolitan areas inside the United States. These metropolitan base industries fall into four main types: (1) commercial centers with little manufacturing (e.g., Dallas, New Orleans, Seattle, and Kansas City); (2) manufacturing centers of the heavy industry type with relatively little wholesaling (e.g., Detroit, Philadelphia, Houston, Buffalo, Milwaukee, Baltimore, Cleveland, and Pittsburgh); (3) commercial centers that successfully added diversified manufacturing (e.g., Chicago, New York, St. Louis, and Cincinnati); (4) specialized service centers (e.g., Washington and Miami). Not all cities fall neatly into these types, of course, and there are marginal shadings between them. Some cities change over time; for example, Miami looks more like other metropolitan areas now than it did when dominated by the tourist industry. Smaller cities seem to be more specialized than the great metropolitan areas.

SCSA and SMSA	1980 Population (x 1,000)
Washington D.C.	3,060
Dallas–Ft. Worth	2,975
Houston	2,905
Boston	2,763
St. Louis	2,355
Pittsburgh	2,264
Baltimore	2,174
Minneapolis–St. Paul	2,114
Atlanta	2,030
Cleveland	1,899
San Diego	1,862
Miami	1,626
Denver	1,620
Seattle	1,607
Tampa	1,569
Phoenix	1,508
Cincinnati	1,401
Milwaukee	1,397
Kansas City	1,327
Buffalo	1,243
Portland, Ore	1,242
New Orleans	1,187
Indianapolis	1,167
Columbus, Ohio	1,093
San Juan, P.R. (Preliminary Count)	1,084
San Antonio	1,072
Total	97,377
Total U.S. population (preliminary count)	226,505

The Physical Structure of American Cities

American buildings are permanent, in the sense that with maintenance they will continue to provide services until they are knocked down. The value of new construction in 1975 was 5.6% of the total value of all structures in the society (*Statistical Abstract 1979*, pp. 773 and 472). This means that in 1975, about 95% of the physical structures were a deposit of past history and only 5% were marginal adaptation to current needs.

The capital value of a given building depends on the expected flow of income or services from that building in the future. If a community is growing normally, that means that the capital value of most buildings is greater than the value of the site without the building (i.e., with a new building on it). In fact, it is usually only rapid growth of a city that increases the capital value of the site as compared with the old building. (See the analysis of housing characteristics related to the time when an area was built up in Beverly Duncan et al., "Patterns of City Growth," pp. 418–429 and Beverly Duncan, "Variables in Urban Morphology" pp. 17–30.) When most of the commercial and industrial life of the city took place in the center of town, near the port, the railroad terminals, and the center of the streetcar system, rapid growth of a city rapidly increased the value of central sites. This resulted in constant rebuilding of the center of the city, and especially the replacement of old dense housing ("slums") by commercial and industrial buildings. Thus, there used to be a ring of old residential buildings around the center of town which everyone thought would soon be torn down.

But the speed and flexibility of the automobile have changed the speed of travel from an estimated 4 mph on the city streets of New York in the 1870s to the 60 mph of a Los Angeles freeway. (The speed in New York is still about the same on downtown streets, but the subways and sub-urban roads have much higher speeds.) Furthermore, a much larger proportion of freight is now carried by flexible truck transport. Both access to customers and access to freight transportation can now be had in the suburbs. People who work in the center of town can get there daily from the suburbs.

Both of these forces have led to a decline in the rate of expansion of the central business district. For a while this left speculative real estate holders with dilapidated tenements that they had hoped to wreck for high-rise buildings. Urban renewal was essentially a project to sell these speculative properties to the government, so that the government, rather than the real estate holders, would take the loss. Many of the sites cleared by urban renewal had a good deal of difficulty finding a buyer, because new commercial and residential ventures were looking to the suburbs. This downtown decay, speculative slums, and unsuccessful urban renewal happened mostly, of course, in slowly growing cities in the Eastern and Midwestern industrial belt.

Generally, each new layer of housing added to the rim of the city is newer, and is also built to modern standards of luxury. Both the middle and working classes are richer now than they were when the older residences were built. Further, the amenities that come with low land costs are more available in the new automobile-access suburbs than in the old streetcar-oriented downtowns. Finally, the rich move to the suburbs to avoid the poor. All these forces tend to concentrate the poor in older, more central sections of town, and to concentrate the rich, educated families toward the periphery. Broadly speaking, then, social characteristics of residents vary systematically with distance from the center of the city, and with the age of housing. The poor live near downtown, and the rich live on the very rim of urbanization.

This tendency towards a ring-like structure is reinforced by racial segregation. The *overall* location of black people toward the center of cities is probably due to their generally greater poverty. But individual wealthier black families live much closer to the center of the city than white familes of the same wealth. Racial segregation of suburbs tends to push middle-class black people into old working-class housing, working-class schools, working-class street life, and center-city crime rates.

But the tendency to social segregation results not only in ringlike structures. It also means that newer construction for a given social group will probably be done on that part of the ring nearest their sector of the old city. And it means that a disproportionate share of the people who move into vacated housing on the edges of a group will be members of the group. Both of these tendencies tend to produce a structure of sectors. For example, in some older Eastern cities one can identify a "Jewish quadrant," like a slice of pie, with poorer Jews living toward the point of the pie slice and richer Jews living toward the rim.

Recent Migration and City Growth

In recent years the net population migration has been out of the machinery-building industrial belt to the Southern and Western metropolitan areas. The SMSAs that depend most on heavy machine-building industry tend to have had the largest net outmigration in recent years (e.g., Cleveland, Detroit, Pittsburgh, Buffalo, and Toledo). Those that mix wholesale commerce, light industry, and heavy industry have had somewhat less net outmigration (St. Louis, Chicago, Philadelphia, and Boston). SMSAs in the New York region show relatively large net outmigration if they are more central (the New York, Newark, and Jersey City SMSAs) and stagnation if they are suburbs (the Nassau-Suffolk SMSA, e.g.). The Washington SMSA is a government service center for the East and Midwest as well as the national government, and grew rapidly in the 1960s, but had net outmigration in the 1970s. Denver, the government service center in the West, boomed during both periods.

In the South and West, traditional machine-building centers like Birmingham, Alabama, had a large net outmigration in the 1960s, then stagnated in the 1970s. The pattern for the Southern California region paralleled that of the New York region, but at a higher rate of growth.

The central Los Angeles–Long Beach SMSA had some net outmigration in the 1970s following slow growth in the 1960s. But the peripheral SMSAs of the region (Anaheim, Oxnard, Santa Barbara, and Riverside) boomed throughout the last two decades.

In the rest of the South and West, two types of city growth were prominent. There was explosive growth of SMSAs that were popular retirement centers, such as Ft. Lauderdale, West Palm Beach, Tampa–St. Petersburg, and Orlando in Florida; Austin in Texas; Phoenix and Tucson in Arizona; and San Diego in California. Second, there was substantial expansion in traditional southern and western commercial centers such as Las Vegas, Atlanta, Denver, Miami, and Dallas–Ft. Worth, and in centers of new and sophisticated industries such as Houston, San Jose, and Portland, Oregon. The distinctive feature of the retirement centers is a low ratio of labor force to population—the labor force is just about a quarter smaller than we find in northern cities of the same size, as if there were no "export" sector in their economies. In some sense, of course, such cities "export" housing services to be bought with retirement money earned elsewhere.

These net migration patterns are the results of a much larger gross migration. From 1975 to 1978 about one out of every three people changed houses (34.2%). About half of these moved within the same SMSA (16.1%), leaving about a tenth of the population who moved across SMSA boundaries (between SMSAs or from and to small town and rural area—9.6%) and about a twelfth of the population who moved between small town and rural houses (*Statistical Abstract 1979*, p. 40). These numbers are very much larger than the total net migration in all the cities of the society during those three years. They cumulate so that nearly half of the population now lives in a different state than the state of their birth (44.1%) (*Statistical Abstract 1979*, p. 39). Consequently the stability, slow growth, or slow decline of the population of a given area is the balance of a large outflow and a large inflow into the area. The composition of a given area, for instance, the racial composition, changes when white (or black) people stop moving *into* an area. Since in the normal course of events nearly a fifth of the population of a given neighborhood will move out during that year, only if the fifth that moves back in has the same composition will the neighborhood remain stable.

Thus, a city at a given time is a cross section of migration flows. Its composition will be determined by the history of the net balance of inflows and outflows. Cities that have a large growth at a given period will tend to cumulate that kind of people who dominate the migration streams of the society, and these may be different from the general population.

TABLE 2.4

Percentage of Foreign-Born and Second Generation in the United States Population

Date	% Foreign born	% Native white of foreign or mixed parents	% First and second generation of non-Western European stock[a]
1900	13.6	20.6	4.4
1910	14.7	20.5	
1920	13.2	21.4	12.0
1930	11.5	21.0	
1940	8.8	17.6	
1950	6.7	15.6	
1960	5.4	13.2	9.4
1970	4.7	11.8	9.3

[a]These are all foreign born and native whites of foreign or mixed parents whose ancestry is *other than* northwestern Europe, Germany, Austria, or Canada. The largest groups of non-Western European stock are Italians, Poles, Russians (largely Jewish) and Mexicans. The largest groups of northwestern European stock are the Germans and Austrians taken together, then Canadians, English (including Scottish and Northern Irish), Irish and Swedes.

The Recent History of American Immigration

At the turn of the century about one out of every eight residents of the United States had been born abroad; another one out of five had at least one foreign born parent (see Table 2.4). A total of one out of three people were immigrants or children of immigrants. But most of these "foreign stock" were from northwestern Europe, or Germany, Austria, or Canada. Only about one out of twenty-five American residents were recent migrants from southern or eastern Europe, Latin America, Asia, Africa, and Oceania. Though the Germans and the Irish were at that time considered somewhat more "alien" than they are now, the dominant "foreign stock" origins were fairly similar to the "native stock" ultimate origins.

Between 1900 and 1920 the national origins of the streams of immigrants shifted. In 1920 approximately the same proportion of the population were foreign born or had a foreign-born parent as in 1900. But now a third of the "foreign stock," or about one-eighth of the American population, were from southern and eastern Europe, especially Italy, Russia, and Poland. The immigrants tended to settle in the cities that were growing at the time, the new industrial cities of the Northeast and

Midwest. Therefore, they were a much larger proportion of the population of cities like Chicago, Pittsburgh, or New York. They were a political challenge to continued control of those cities by "native" or "Irish" political elites. (Most of the "Irish" politicians were, of course, born in the United States of Irish ancestry.)

Much of the political history of the first part of the century consists of the response of the native populations (i.e., those who had immigrated earlier) to this change in the composition of the immigrant population. The prohibition movement in rural America received much of its impetus from the fact that the drinking and gambling population were ethnically alien and lived peculiar sorts of lives in the centers of dirty cities. From 1920 to 1924 this anti-alien sentiment resulted in an attempt to control the ethnic composition of the flow of immigrants by legislation, the "quota system." (For a detailed analysis of the political history so drastically compressed in this paragraph, see John Higham, *Strangers in the Land*.)

The long-run effect of the quota system on the individual potential immigrant is to require higher qualifications for immigrants from countries of eastern and southern Europe than for immigrants from northern Europe, Canada, and (to some extent) Latin America. The effect of the system on the flow of immigration is mainly to reduce the overall quantity of the flow, by making it hard to immigrate from those places where more people want to leave. There is probably some change in the ethnic composition of the flow due to the quota system, but it is difficult to estimate this effect. We have very little way of knowing who would have immigrated had they been free to do so. The flow of immigrants maintained its southern and eastern European character despite the quota system. In 1970 over half of the foreign born and of the people with foreign or mixed parentage were of southern and eastern European or Mexican extraction. In fact, the ratio of eastern and southern European stock (immigrants and their children) to the total population changed relatively little from 1920 to 1970, going down from about an eighth to about a tenth.

The higher qualifications required for immigrants under the quota system have changed the impact of immigration on American society. In 1910 immigrants were a little over a third of the urban working class, about a fourth of the small businessmen and managers, but less than a sixth of professional, clerical, and sales workers. That is, the immigrant communities occupied a distinctive place in the class system, toward the bottom of the urban sector. By 1960 the immigrant population was distributed more or less evenly throughout the class system, except that there were very few foreign-born farmers.

The immigration act of 1965 abolished quotas, and several groups of refugees have changed the ethnic composition of the flows. It is perhaps too early to assess the effect of these arrangements on the ethnic structure of the United States.

In rough outline, then, immigration during the first two decades of the century created distinctive lower-class urban ethnic groups of southern and eastern European extraction. The limitation of immigration after 1920, first by an emergency quota act and then by the immigration bill of 1924, has not changed the ethnic significance of immigration. It is still southern and eastern European ethnic groups that are created by immigration. But it has drastically reduced the size of these ethnic groups by reducing the flow into them.

The flow out of ethnic communities in the United States has consistently been at a high level throughout the century. The principal device for reducing the size of the ethnic groups created by immigration is the school system, which in the United States has taught the children of immigrants English, and has introduced them into the occupational system at a level slightly above that of "native stock." (Peter Blau and O. D. Duncan, *The American Occupational Structure*, pp. 231–238.) The children of immigrants do not occupy a distinctive place in the class system, except that they are almost all urban. A large proportion of all the foreign born have become naturalized throughout the century, so that their political incorportion was carried out without extensive fights over suffrage. The combination of strong forces of assimilation and decreased supply of new recruits to the unassimilated ethnic groups has tended to reduce the structural importance of ethnic groups. (See Table 2.5).

Throughout the century, American immigration policy has also had an effect on the ethnic composition of the country by limiting immigration from the nonwhite parts of the world. During most of the century either no, or an insignificant number of, immigrants from Africa, Asia, and the nonwhite parts of the Pacific Islands have been admitted to the United States. This has changed somewhat in very recent years. By various devices British citizens of the Caribbean Islands, who are mostly black, have also been pretty much excluded. Thus, the normal expectation that immigration from poor countries to richer countries would change the color composition of the richer countries (which has happened, e.g., in the Caribbean during the century) has not worked out. The immense majority of the nonwhite population of the United States are native born (though a number of the leaders of the Negro movement, such as Marcus Garvey and Stokeley Carmichael, have been of Caribbean extraction).

In recent years the main source of net migrants has been the South.

TABLE 2.5

Percentage of White Male Working Force Who Were Foreign Born,
by Major Occupational Group for the United States, 1910–1960

Major occupational group	1910	1920	1950	1960
All occupations[a]	24.7	22.4	9.9	6.9
Professional, technical, and kindred workers	15.6	14.3	7.5	6.1
Managers, officials and proprietors, except farm	26.4	25.6	13.0	7.5
Sales workers	18.0	16.1	7.0	5.8
Clerical and kindred workers	10.9	9.9	5.5	4.5
Craftsmen, foremen, and kindred workers	29.6	26.4	11.3	7.7
Operatives and kindred workers	38.0	31.8	10.1	6.7
Laborers, except farm and mine	45.0	37.4	13.1	7.9
Service workers, including private household	36.8	36.3	18.7	13.0
Farmers and farm managers	12.8	11.0	4.5	3.0
Farm laborers and foremen	8.4	8.3	7.4	9.5

Source: 1910 to 1950, E. P. Hutchinson, *Immigrants and Their Children, 1850–1950* (New York: Wiley, 1956), Table 38, p. 202 (indices given by Hutchinson were converted back into percentages; the latter are, therefore, subject to rounding errors).* 1960 U.S. Bureau of the Census, "Occupational Characteristics," Subject Report PC(2), 7A, *1960 Census of Population* (Washington: Government Printing Office, 1963), Tables 3 and 8.
[a]Gainful workers 10 years of age and over for 1910 and 1920; experienced civilian labor force 14 years of age and over for 1950 and 1960; includes occupation not reported.
*Taken from Peter Blau and O. D. Duncan, *The American Occupational Structure* (New York: Wiley, 1967), p. 229.

For example, between 1950 and 1960 there was a net migration out of the South of some 1,405,000 people. West Virginia, North Carolina, Georgia, Kentucky, Tennessee, Alabama, Mississippi, Arkansas, and Oklahoma all had net outmigration of both white and black people. The Washington area (Maryland, D.C., and Virginia) had a net inmigration (mostly white), and Louisiana and Texas gained whites but lost black people. On net balance, the South gained a few whites by net migration (53,000) and lost a great many black people (1,457,000). Thus, the growing metropolitan areas tend to have had their populations shifted in a Southern direction, and to have rapidly growing black populations. This pattern has changed in recent years with the growth of the sun belt metropolises, as discussed above.

American Migration Institutions

The migration institutions of a society are those that determine the social environment of the three main stages during the migration process: (1) the selection and socialization in a local community of those people or groups who will later migrate; (2) the structure of group attachments and activities during the movement; and (3) the process of attachment to the institutions of the receiving area.

American society is distinguished from primitive and feudal societies by the fact that many of the young in any given local community are being prepared for positions that do not exist in that community. The institutions of the community must therefore be formed under the influence of institutions of the receiving social structures.

Undoubtedly the school is the primary channel by which the metropolis reaches down to form rural and small-town children for metropolitan participation. The "universalistic" standards of schools often do not prepare children for local positions. In old small town school systems all sorts of concrete considerations about who controls what position, when it will be open, and what social circles the position is embedded in, permeate the system. In modern small town schools, however, counselors read Labor Department books about *The Occupational Outlook*, rather than looking at positions developing locally downtown. Colleges themselves are often made up of migrants, and form the first stage of the migratory process of the future middle class. Even when colleges have a local clientele, they form them for society-wide professional groups or society-wide corporations. Thus, the school is a principal migration institution, preparing those who will migrate for nonlocal stratification positions.

The telephone, the mail, and the freeway all provide mechanisms by which some of the group structure of the sending community may be carried, in attenuated form, into the receiving community. Usually the group that migrates is an adolescent or young adult alone, or a nuclear family of husband, wife, and minor children. Vacations, as a part of the structure of roles in the receiving community, are crucial institutions for the sending community—especially as families reunite in vacation time, and lapsed courtships come alive as Christmas and summertime bring students home from college. The group structure of the migration stream itself tends to be preserved by the increased flow of communications from sending areas and by reverse travel during vacations.

In the receiving community the first attachments of an immigrant are usually to work institutions and to the real estate market. Legal incorporation into the receiving polity is governed by residence rules; the receiving community's lower schools often cause the first involvement in neighborhood affairs; churches make valiant efforts to induce attachments from the passing stream of families. American community institutions are much more welcoming to migrants than institutions of traditional societies. There are few political, legal, or participation disabilities associated with being a migrant.

Thus, all American community institutions are shaped by the fact that many present members of the community will in the future be members of other communities, and many members have in the past been members of other communities. The qualification process for immigrants from abroad serves much the same function, much more formally and obnoxiously, of selecting those socialized for metropolitan life, forming the group character of the migration process, and ensuring the successful attachment of the immigrant to the American metropolis.

ECOLOGY AND THE ROLE OF NATURE
IN ECONOMIC SOCIOLOGY

Social scientists often observe that some feature of the social structure varies with natural conditions: improving landlords and conflicts over enclosing the common are found on clayey plains but not on granite hills and mountains; patrilineal extended families managing large herds of grazing animals are found where there are seasonal rains in areas too dry or too mountainous for reliable agriculture; traditional steel machine building is more tied to the East–Midwest industrial belt than is the building of silicon-chip machines; commercialization of manufactures and agriculture is a feature of river valleys and seacoasts, at least until the railrood age.

Such correlations between natural conditions and social structures are often spoken of as direct geographical or climatic determination, as when the Karimojong formulate their summer search for grass and water as, "The sun mixes us." From the point of view of the sociology of economical life, the central point is that *every mode of production is a transaction with nature*. It is therefore simultaneously determined by what a society is prepared to extract with its technology from nature and by what is there in nature. For example, before the development of heavy wheeled plows drawn by several animals, it was very hard to cultivate the heavy soils of northern France; the ground was therefore covered with forests. But the heavy *charrue* of northern France cannot put clay molecules into the sandy soil of Brittany, nor level the rocky pastures there into cultivable plain. (With the invention of dynamite, which made a millionaire of a man from a rocky country, at least one could build a road or a railroad to the farm in granite hills; but in the eighteenth century there was no dynamite, and mountain folk walked, driving their animals to market.)

Economic structures have to solve the problems posed to them by nature. Since nature poses different problems in different places, the economic structures vary. The large families of the Karimojong are understandable if one knows how many fragments there are of a viable herd, and what the requirements of defense of the herd are when looking for grass and water near the tribal boundaries. The large family solves a productive problem that would not be solved as easily with nuclear families.

Of course, the social organization of the economy also shapes the solutions to problems posed by nature. While a nineteenth-century American ranch in the Southwest had many of the natural problems of a Karimojong herd owner, a free labor market enabled one to hire cowpunchers. The all-male group that followed the herd could therefore be formed by labor contracts rather than by family authority. Different social forms can have an underlying productive similarity and will therefore be correlated with the same natural conditions. The all-male cowboy barracks and the all-male Karimojong cattle camp of kinsmen both occur under conditions of marginal seasonal rainfall.

This means that an analyst interested in the social effects of a given mode of production, such as revolutionary movements of village-organized agriculture, ought first to look at the variations in nature that determine the boundaries of that mode. The three-field village central to Skocpol's explanations of rebellion during the French Revolution had natural limits, and beyond those limits there was the individual farm family confronting a noble landlord who was also the *seigneur,* rather than a corporate village in a dispute over seigneurial dues payments and over plowing up common pastures or clearing common forests. It strengthens Skocpol's argument that the *bocage* areas of Brittany and the Massif Central hardly supported the Revolution, and that the Revolution was quite a different phenomenon in the rural Midi. But it gives a false impression of eighteenth-century France to describe it as if the core basis of the French state, the three-field system of fertile northern plain, was the only mode of production in French territory.

Natural boundaries are often overcome by technical development. Ecological theory deals with this fact by building transportation access into the center of the theory. From the Karimojong who can walk their cattle to grass and water in the highlands, to the aqueducts and air freight that make it possible for Los Angeles to be an industrial center, the activities possible in a place depend on what can be brought there and what can be taken away, as well as on the resources of the place. Commercialization in the eighteenth-century depended in a fundamental way on the slow-moving rivers of the plains or on access to the sea. Tucson, Arizona, is a commercial and industrial center about the same size as eighteenth-century Paris. It has no navigable rivers, and would have been impossible to supply in the eighteenth century. To carry on a government of the size of eighteenth-century France, one had to choose a seat of government with easy water transportation from a large fertile plain.

Transportation is thus not mainly part of the "services" we consume, as the modern fashion of dividing urban industries into "secondary" (manufacturing and construction) and "tertiary" (services, including transportation) would have it. It is instead a part of the material productive system. In a twentieth-century city roughly a quarter to a third of the value of all the goods and services used is produced outside the city and two-thirds to three-quarters in the city. The hardware and machines that are produced in the industrial belt and imported to other cities, for example, are retailed, maintained, and used by local labor. The flour produced on Midwestern grain farms and milled in Midwestern market centers is only a small part of the value of the bread we buy, and the rest is local labor. Most of the labor that goes into a newspaper is local labor, because logging is highly mechanized and papermaking is a continuous process, capital-intensive industry. But this means that local construction, automobile repair, printing, or baking craftsmen could not do their work unless the city had easy access to the industrial belt.

The network of transportation and communication in societies ranges from the Karimojong, for whom resources further than walking distance are inaccessible, to the United States, in which up to a third of the labor one depends on is done in cities beyond a Karimojong's range; this accessibility of resources is intimately tied to the level of development of a society. In modern societies most of the social structure does not vary with natural conditions, because all sorts of deficits for all sorts of activities can be filled by fast efficient transportation systems. All environments in which it is worthwhile for people to live can be made similar in almost all respects important to the social order. In the twentieth century, instead of Arizona cowpuncher barracks having some similarities to Karimojong cow camps, Phoenix is indistinguishable from Los Angeles, even to the point of building aqueducts from the same river. The natural characteristics of a place, its "resources," therefore have to be analyzed in modern societies in conjunction with what can be brought there to modify the local environment. And this means that features of the social structure are no longer strongly correlated with features of the natural environment.

The third ecological principle is that some activities at a place make it possible to carry out other activities nearby, because they provide vital inputs. It is an "external economy" for the milch herd at a Karimojong settlement that it is possible to graze bulls, oxen, and cows not in milk, in the hills, even in the dry seasons. Otherwise one could not support a milch herd on the overgrazed area near the settlement. Similarly the way hardware and machine manufacturers in the Mid-Atlantic–Midwestern industrial belt buy and sell to each other makes each dependent on the whole industrial complex. But this means that a mode of production at a given place is actually a network of interdependent activities.

There is therefore no one industry that accounts for the cities of the Mid-Atlantic and the industrial Midwest being heavily populated by descendants of southern and east European immigrants, and having a Democratic Party heavily influenced by industrial unions. It is the whole industrial complex of this area that grew and attracted immigrants from about 1880 to about 1924, and which provided fertile ground for industrial unions from about 1936 to 1943. Similarly one cannot understand why pasture was so crucial to class relations on the plains of northern France without realizing that it took the "output" of an acre of unimproved pasture just to support the work animals to plow four acres of the heavy soil. One had to grow the energy for plowing near enough to the grain fields so the oxen or horses could walk back and forth. Access to the pasture was thus technically necessary to the mode of production.

But on the plains (unlike on the granite hills and mountains) the pasture could be turned into arable; it had been "enclosed" in England and put under the ownership of the lords.

Thus, while the mutual external economies between pasture and arable constituted the peasant mode of production both on the plain and in the mountainous regions, the possibility of enclosure and feeding work animals fodder crops presented an opportunity for the lords, for which the peasant use of unimproved pastures was a diseconomy. This competition of pasture and arable did not take place in mountainous regions. In the Midi there essentially were not pastures for work animals, so small underfed animals pulled small plows that merely scratched the ground—sometimes the plows were pulled by humans. It was therefore the complex of feeding work animals and growing grain using the animals' energy whose mutual relations produced different modes of production in different parts of France.

Although the general point of this chapter is captured in the slogan that every mode of production is a transaction with nature, that empty statement must be fleshed out with the analysis of the ecological concepts of resources, access, and external economies. To explain why the mode of production that Skocpol analyzes was located on the northern plain, we need to know how fertile land is distributed in France (the natural distribution of resources), which fertile areas have river or sea transportation to cities (the distribution of access), and which activities were external economies for each other (such as pasture and arable).

Similarly the ethnic cities with strong industrial unions of the Mid-Altantic and Midwestern industrial belt are to be explained partly by where coal and iron ore were to be found (resources), by where the rail network first became dense (providing mutual access), and by the fact that machine and hardware manufacturers buy from each other (producing external economies for each other).

These concepts then are used to describe the social shape of the transaction with nature that constitutes a mode of production.

3

Technology and Manipulation of the Environment

THE SOCIAL IMPACT OF TECHNOLOGY

Virtually any set of activities carried on by social groups has an aspect of *knowledge, skill, and material means* which determines (or is thought to determine) how much results of what kind are obtained from the activity. We call this aspect of a system of activities its *technology*. That is, the technology of a set of activities consists of those aspects of the pattern of activities that influence, or are thought to influence, the *effectiveness or efficiency* of the activities for achieving the ends for which they are carried out.

"Things" play a very important part in technology, for things often make activities more efficient. Machines, implements, buildings, chemical compounds, fertilizers—all influence the effectiveness or efficiency of activities. The crucial aspects of things, from the point of view of their impact on society, are their uses. Technology can be thought of as a *set of uses of things*, rather than a set of things.

For example, the Karimojong use rocks to castrate animals, by pounding the animal's sexual organs with them. Clearly it does not make much sense to say that rocks are "part of the technology of herd control" among the Karimojong. Instead the *use* of rocks to modify the genetic environment, and so to increase the efficiency of the herd, is the crucial aspect of technology. As a contrary example, when the flintlock musket and the bayonet were introduced in eighteenth-century France, this made an infantry more efficient if it were reorganized by a different deployment (thinner ranks facing the enemy, so that more of the infantry could fire the more rapid-firing weapon) and different division of labor (reduction of infantrymen's roles from two—pikemen to charge enemy, and fusiliers to fire at them—to a single role of a gunman with a bayonet). For a considerable part of the eighteenth century, these innovations in social organization were not made. There was no real use of the added fire-power, and of the added flexibility of the flintlock with a bayonet affixed. Hence, although the physical implements of warfare that were to dominate infantry tactics in the nineteenth century were there, the uses of these implements in a rational fashion had to await the reorganization of the infantry.

The fact that the set of uses of things is what technology really consists of, rather than the things themselves, becomes very obvious if we consider what happens to a modern society after a war. A great many *things* in Japan and Germany were destroyed during the Second World War. Yet, shortly after the war, certainly within five years, both countries were among the most technically advanced countries in the world again. African countries, which ended the war with *neither* the things *nor* the traditions and skills to use the things, were not technically advanced five years after the war. Things are easily replaced. The patterns of use of things are cultural accretions of great complexity.

Components of Technology

It is convenient to divide the problem of the effectiveness of activities into four components: (1) knowledge of how to accomplish something; (2) the set of ends for which the activity is carried out, by which its effectiveness is judged, (3) the organization of the pattern of activity itself, and (4) the environment in which the activity has to be effective.

Knowledge

We can distinguish two main kinds of knowledge. First, there is knowledge of general causal laws, of scientific theories applicable to many situations. Second, there is knowledge of concrete environments, how these environments vary, how they can be manipulated, and so forth. A skilled veterinarian might have a very hard time keeping a herd alive in some of the semi-desert conditions where primitive herders manage. He or she would have to learn the concrete details of when water and grass were available in each of hundreds of locations. The point is that by very detailed knowledge of the particular environment and how to manipulate it, primitive nomads can do things that a person with much better general understanding cannot. Of course, the nomads would have greater difficulty than the veterinarian adapting to new conditions if they moved to South American Patagonia, or New Zealand, or some other environment which they do not know in such detail.

It seems likely that, as a rough generalization, this kind of detailed knowledge of particular concrete environments does not grow with advancing technology. A Karimojong knows his way around his territory to the places where there is good grass about as well as an American university professor knows his way around the library to the places where there is knowledge. But general causal knowledge applying to a wide variety of situations, and in particular applying to situations that do not yet exist, is a feature distinctive of modern societies.

To be sure, part of this abstract knowledge is applied to the development of measuring procedures—thermometers, analyses of soil chemistry, aerial photography, etc.—which gives us better knowledge of concrete environments. But just as among the Karimojong, or in the eighteenth century, we generally do not care, and so do not know, whether it is 86 or 90° F, but only know that it is hot. Most of the time we do not use the available instrumentation.

General causal knowledge is very much dependent on schools, on written communication, and on specialization of people so that they know how to analyze a class of situations in their specialty according to general standards. Schools primarily teach general principles, rather than about specific situations; written materials in almost all cultures are more generalized, more divorced from particular situations, than oral materials of the same cultures; specialists in modern societies are most often specialists in a certain kind of causal connection common to a large number of situations, rather than specialists in particular environments. Schooling, literacy, and intellectual specialization are distinctive features of the technological systems of modern societies. This is the main dimension which differentiates the technology of a modern society from a feudal society, and that of a feudal society from that of a primitive tribe.

Ends

Effectiveness or efficiency of an activity can only be evaluated in relation to the ends of the activity. For instance, the French government during the eighteenth century spent much of its time at war, pursuing the territorial ambitions of France and the dynastic ambitions of the kings. This meant that the central government evaluated many policies toward technical improvements (e.g., the policies on roads and bridges) according to military ends. People who do not approve of those ends, and who evaluate the policies in the light of, say, economic development and the welfare of the lower classes, might find the policies directed toward maintaining royal military control of rebellious distant provinces obnoxious. Different societies have different ends institutionalized in various sections of the social structure. Dynastic ambition has virtually no influence as an end in either Karimojong or in American society, so technology cannot be evaluated against that end in those societies.

In addition to more or less "free" variation among societies in the ends they choose to follow, there are ends induced by the environment. For instance, much of Karimojong technology is devoted to protection against drought—ensuring that there will be enough food during the dry season. Ensuring that one has food every day is an end in all so-cieties. But societies living in environments in which the rainfall is plen-tiful, or societies with a developed storage technology, do not need to keep the specter of drought constantly before them in order to ensure that they eat every day. A common human end of eating all year-round then becomes a pressing end of living through the dry season among the Karimojong.

In modern societies, many of the ends people follow in their work life are ends of someone else, which they have been paid to follow. That is, the ends by which technology is to be evaluated are not the ends of those who use the technology, but ends induced in them by social arrangements which make *other people's* motivations into purposes of people's activities. Modern societies have carried the differentiation of the ends toward which technology is directed from the ends of the people who do the activities farther than primitive or feudal societies. From the point of view of the individual, this differentiation of his own ends from the ends to which his work is directed is generally called "alienation" in the Marxian sense. From the point of view of the pro-ductive system as a whole, it is called the division of labor. The con-nection between the division of labor and alienation was first analyzed extensively by Karl Marx. Marx used the word *alienation* to mean the divorce of the ends of work from the personal ends of the individual.

Technical Aspects of the Organization of Activities

There are three major features of systems of activities that seem to vary directly with technical factors. First, different systems of activities have different degrees of *dependence on the environment*. Second, they *use wealth or capital* to different degrees. Third, they have different degrees of *variety of simultaneous activities*, or division of labor.

By dependence on the environment of an activity, we mean either that the results of the activity vary a great deal depending on varying characteristics of the environment (as for instance, cows give less milk in the dry season), or that in order to achieve the same end, activities have to change a great deal with changes in the environment (for instance, the Karimojong have to vary activity very quickly in response to changes in the distribution of water or grass). In the United States, when there is a change in rain in one area or another, there is little activity in the society which changes. There are mechanisms for adaptation, for storage, for transportation, for redistribution, for decreasing the consumption of affected crops by increasing their prices, etc. But only a few of these mechanisms change as we move from summer to winter, drought to hurricane, or flood to still water.

In the eighteenth century there is a certain sense in which the armies had to run around and hunt up a field that was flat enough for them to fight on according to the technology that they used. They had great difficulty fighting in forests, jungles, and mountains. The American Revolutionary Army learned to discipline troops in the forests so that they did not all go home as soon as they got out of sight of their officers. This enabled them to use the cover of the forest, and of the night, to avoid defeat by the flat-field strategy used by the British and other eighteenth-century armies. The results of general British military superiority in America varied a good deal, then, with natural conditons. Under flat, open-field, daytime conditions, they could almost invariably win against the Americans. Under the conditions they ordinarily found, they could not usually win, and even occasionally got defeated. Thus, eighteenth-century armies' fates were more "dependent on the environment" than is a modern army's fate.

The differences in dependence on the natural environment in the three societies show up most clearly, perhaps, in the supply of food. The supply of food varies very intimately with natural conditions among the Karimojong. When it gets dry, the Karimojong hardly eat. In eighteenth-century France, there were still very substantial famines, but considerable control had been introduced by the end of the century by some modernization of cultivation, improvement of roads and water transportation, and the like. In the United States one can hardly tell what kind of weather they are having out where they grow food by going into a grocery store.

A major difference among technical systems, then, is how much the activity, or its results, varies according to natural conditions. In more primitive societies, much more of the activity varies with natural conditions. Primitive societies adapt to the environment rather than controlling it. In modern societies very little activity changes as natural variables change, because part of the technology is directed as creating special, controlled environments that facilitate steadiness and certainty in various activities. Modern societies control the environment rather than adapting to it.

A second major way in which activities vary is the degree to which they use wealth or capital. That is, some activities are carried out more effectively if they are carried out with some implements, or in some special environment that has been specially created to facilitate that activity. By wealth or capital we mean something that satisfies three criteria: (1) it can be appropriated, that is, I can exclude you from using it, (2) that it makes some activity more effective or efficient than it would otherwise be, that is, that it produces things of value, and (3) that it is scarce, or that it takes effort or resources to produce it, hence that it is itself a value.

The main form of wealth in Karimojong society is clearly the cattle. The main form of wealth in eighteenth-century France was probably agricultural land. In the United States, the main forms of wealth are implements (machinery, tools, and equipment) and changes in the environment (roads, buildings, docks, etc.), though of course land is also of value.

It is most convenient in discussing the relation of wealth to technology to start at a lower technical level than the Karimojong, that is, the gatherers. The distinctive thing about gatherers, people whose technology involves gathering food as it grows wild, is that wealth is virtually absent. The things that produce wild fruits are not easy to appropriate (to keep other people from using) because people have to cover such a wide area in order to get enough to eat. Gatherers cannot defend such a wide area very well. They do not produce many implements that might be appropriated to help them gather food.

In general, as the technical level of societies increases, activities use more wealth. The total wealth, in the sense of accumulated implements, land, and other appropriable objects in the United States, runs to about three times the yearly national income. That is, the value of all capital (including land) in the United States is roughly equal to the value produced during the course of three years' functioning of the economy. It is possible that herding and agricultural societies have a higher ratio of capital to current production, but any such estimates would involve imputing values to agricultural land or to cattle, that is, capital not produced by human action, in nonmarket economies. The technical difficulty of such estimates is very great. It is, however, quite clear that constructed capital equipment and human modifications of the environment play a much larger role in an advanced economy than in primitive or feudal economies.

A third aspect of the technical system that varies among societies is the degree of division of labor, or the degree to which a variety of activities are carried on simultaneously in the society. During the dry season among the Karimojong, nearly all the men are engaged in herding the animals to good sources of grass and water, and nearly all women are engaged in caring for children and settlement herds. At the other extreme, thousands of industries in the United States are being carried on simultaneously, and within each of those industries many different activities are being carried on by people with different occupations.

The division of labor depends on the technical level of societies for several reasons. One is that unless vital activities, such as the production of food, are carried on with a high degree of certainty and reliability, people will try to ensure themselves of vital necessities by doing the activities themselves. When the results of an activity vary a good deal with natural conditions, as they do in primitive technology, this discourages the division of labor. In fact, we find that in modern society those aspects of an organization's environment that are highly variable and uncertain tend to be incorporated into the organization itself (cf. James D. Thompson, *Organizations in Action*). Organizations may be prepared to be wrecked by environmental uncertainty; but if they do they will insist that whether the uncertain environment is dealt with properly be under their own control, rather than in the hands of a supplier. Thus, uncertainty produces a tendency for everyone to do the same things. (An excellent example is the discussion of why each Soviet machine factory has its own foundry in David Granick's *Soviet Metal Fabricating*. The reason is that even though specialized foundries serving several factories are more efficient, a factory cannot run without castings. Since buyers have little control over suppliers in the USSR, each factory secures castings by making them themselves.)

A second reason is that, with high productivity of all activities, those activities directed at necessities occupy a smaller role. People's wants are more various than their needs. In advanced technologies, much more activity is directed at satisfying people's wants, and hence is more various.

A final reason that advanced technologies have more division of labor is that a high degree of division of labor is *part* of an advanced technology. If a social unit, such as a factory, a store, or a police department, can be designed for a specific purpose, it will achieve that purpose better. The norms appropriate for policing are not very good for producing cars, people trained to police are not trained to produce cars; the guns used in American police work are not very effective tools for assembling cars. (There is some debate about whether guns are effective policing tools either. But at least they come closer to being useful for a policeman than for an assembly line worker.) Thus, dividing the work of the society among social units that are especially set up to do a particular kind of activity generally increases the efficiency of each of the activities. Within the social units (factories, police departments, etc.) so set up, it is quite often useful to divide labor in a stable way among the people who work there. Not only are social units distinct from each other in their activities, but within the social units people do different things. The division of labor is itself an aspect of improved technology.

Changes in Technology over Time

In advanced societies there are very large shifts over relatively short periods of time in the overall composition of activities. Although activities in the United States do not vary much with the seasons, they have varied a great deal between 1900 and 1960. Economic development (i.e., increasing productivity or efficiency of activities) tends to change the composition of activities as well as the efficiency of each. Some activities (agriculture, for instance) produce goods for which the demand goes up *less* rapidly than the increase in productivity. Some other activities (education, for instance) produce goods for which the demand increases *more* rapidly than the increase in efficiency. As all activities become more efficient, the extra "income" produced by this greater efficiency will be spent in a different manner than the income that people already had. In particular, it will be spent more for education than for agricultural goods. Hence as technology improves, educational activities will become more prominent in the total composition of activities in the society, and agriculture will become less important. (This observation is sometimes known as "Engel's law," that the consumption of necessities increases less than the consumption of luxuries during times of prosperity, and decreases less in times of dearth. Modern economists consider the dimension from "necessity" to "luxury" to be a continuous variable, which they call the "income elasticity" of the good.)

Change in the composition of activities also takes place directly because of the advance of knowledge. If they had known how to make penicillin in the eighteenth century and to use it to cure infections, they undoubtedly would have. We grow penicillin in part simply because we know how. The composition of activities of a society changes, then, as knowledge of how to carry out new activities is developed, or is borrowed from another culture. Invention and the development of science, which had already become massive by the eighteenth century in France, have become a torrent in modern times. People are now paid salaries to innovate or to improve the knowledge that is the basis of technology or to introduce new inventions into the pattern of social activities. This torrent of innovation is constantly changing the composition of social activities in modern societies.

A third source of change in the composition of activities of a society is a change in the ends to which technology is directed. This is most marked in modern times with the shift from war to peace, or peace to war. Up to half of the national income of a modern country is devoted to warfare during time of serious war (e.g., in the United States the Second World War). That is, half of the economic activities of the United States were different during time of war than during time of peace. Before modern times no societies could devote such a large part of their activities to warfare, because they would not have enought left over to live on (except for a few societies that lived off warfare itself—off booty). But such shifts of activities of a social organization as it changes ends are quite common and marked, and make a static analysis of the technology of a society a rather precarious operation.

HERDING TECHNOLOGY IN KARIMOJA

Among the Karimojong, technology has marked consequences because there is so little of it. Something in the region of three hundred items would give an effective Sears-Roebuck catalog of Karimojong material culture. But we have to speak of a primitive technology, rather than a minimal technology, for there are still very substantial technical knowledge and skill in the activities of a Karimojong. In technological equipment, the Karimojong are very primitive; their skills in the use of that equipment are very considerable.

If we say that technology is the series of skilled labors and tools that act upon a natural environment (or upon a set of natural resources) to create an economy, the Karimojong economy is marked by the continual use of human beings. Their numbers, energy, experience, and skills, are the determining factors in the effectiveness or efficiency of Karimojong activities. These are the factors enabling them to extract a livelihood from a somewhat marginal and unpredictable environment. Karimojong technology is an attempt to combine limited material culture with maximally developed skill to construct a mode of livelihood that is based principally on herding, but with agriculture as an important auxiliary activity. Occasionally, in response to a crisis they gather wild foods. It would be statistically untrue, but nevertheless sociologically and economically completely sound, to say there is no hunting in this society.

Housing Technology and Herding Requirements

This split technology, pastoral herding technology and agricultural technology, is reflected in two styles of housing technology or living technology. There are two styles of human dwelling, two styles of settlement, and so on. First, there are homesteads, which are permanent settlements near agricultural fields; and second, there are stock camps, which are temporary settlements. The Karimojong use these two kinds of settlements in an attempt to do a split exploitation of resources by herding and agriculture. All sorts of consequences follow from this, and the distinction will recur in our discussion of the property institutions as well.

It will be convenient for us to simplify the geography of the district in which the Karimojong live for purposes of exposition. The region where they live is something like a triangle on its point, and is divided into two distinct ecological regions. There is a central strip that is occupied by the homesteads, or permanent settlements; the rest is occupied by stock camps. The only distinction between the types of settlements is that one is even more crude than the other. (See especially Chapter 2, Section 10 of Dyson-Hudson, *Karimojong Politics* and the relevant plates showing settlements.) The agricultural homesteads are, on the whole, relatively warm and waterproof, but they are made of very simple materials—thatched roofs, wattle and daub walls, and smoothed earth floors. But they have a permanent quality because they are responding to the agricultural technology. The settlement house is related predominantly to agriculture with herding as a subsidiary activity (e.g., the homestead has a corral); the stock camp housing is oriented predominantly to herding—and particularly to herding of a highly wandering and nomadic kind, where permanence of settlement would be a curse rather than a blessing.

We have treated the sources of this differentiation, or bifurcation, of technology, in more detail in Chapter 2. To recapitulate, there has to be this split because there are not enough water and vegetation resources in the central area to allow cattle to be kept there all year around. So the herds have to move. On the other hand, the fields that can be used are near the main water courses, and are all in the center of the tribal area. That means that field exploitation is centralized, territorially speaking. Once crops are raised in a particular place, there are requirements for storage of the crops themselves, of the implements, and a residence for a labor force which is going to be working in approximately the same place day after day. This leads to a much more permanent form of settlement.

The basic layout of the housing at the settlement is of a farmyard with a fence all around. Outside of that fence, a number of stilted storehouses are used for storing implements and unthreshed grain. On the inside there is an area divided up for humans, but with also smaller constructions for the grain, a place for cattle, and in the middle a place for the goats.

The temporary camps are just a series of thorn enclosures made of thorn bushes hacked down and arranged in a loose ring. Their only purpose is to protect the stock at night from wild animals and to make it somewhat more difficult for human enemies to get in. Hopefully the thorn enclosures will slow down enemies enough so that the men on guard will have time to go for their spears before all the cattle are gone.

Herd Management

When we say that the Karimojong have a herding technology and economy, what do we mean concretely? The milk and the blood of cattle are drunk, the meat of cattle is eaten, cattle fat is used as a food and as cosmetic, cattle urine is used as cleanser. (The only hot water tap in Karimoja is a beast. Small children gather around the corral early in the morning when it is very cold and misty. They all stand there by the cattle corral until they see some cow lift her tail and then run to see who can get there first to get under the warm tap.)

Cattle hides also make sleeping skins and shoulder capes and skirts, and collars for more cattle (for more hides, for more skirts, etc.). Hides also make sandals, armlets, and anklets. Cattle horns and cattle hooves provide snuff holders and boxes for keeping feathers in. Since the Karimojong do not wear very much, what they wear is precious, and they mostly wear cattle products. Hides are used to make food containers. Bags are made from bull's scrota. Cattle intestines are used for prophesying, and cattle chyme (partially digested grass) is used for anointing. Cattle droppings are used for fertilizer. Cattle are the only recognized form of wealth in the society. This monocapital situation gives herding enormous social consequences, because Karimojong are involved in using wealth for establishing social status and social connection in many of the complicated ways found in modern society.

The herding technology for maintaining the animals that provide so much of the good things of life for the Karimojong develops from three main principles. The first we will call the "interest" use of livestock resources. The second is a specification of the general point we have made about Karimojong technology—that the matter of experience and skills outweighs the equipment for herd management. The third general principle is the pressure to move livestock and its consequences for the pattern of herding activity.

The Karimojong firmly believe that, on the whole, people should live off their income and not off their capital. Concretely this means that they try to live off of cattle produce without actually killing the animals—they live off milk and any of the various dairy products: butter, soured milk, and so on. They also use the blood of the animals, but as far as possible they do not use the meat, their "capital."

For example, a simple hollow arrow is used to extract blood from a live ox (see Dyson-Hudson, *Karimojong Politics*, pp. 83–87). The arrow is shot a little way into the jugular vein, to take off quite a lot of blood. They can take four or five pints of blood from an ordinary animal, and they insist that given a big animal they could take a good deal more—up to eight or nine pints. Then they let the animal go again and leave it for six or seven months before they tap it again. This way, then, they are continually taking interest from the animal without depleting the capital.

Obtaining this interest in a regular fashion from a herd of cattle involves a great deal of skill, but very little capital equipment (except for the cattle themselves—the most important form of capital in the society). For instance, the device for harvesting blood is really very simple, but applying it in the right place and taking the right amount of blood to get maximum use out of the animal without endangering its life is a matter that has to be learned. Likewise, the devices for milking are very simple—essentially a wooden jug so shaped so that it can be gripped between the knees while the cow is milked. Again, the material culture is very simple, but holding the jug steady between your knees while you milk and leaving just the right amount of milk for the calf to be healthy but not pampered takes a great deal of skill and practice. There are similar difficulties in turning the milk into clarified butter. Since they have no devices for storing dairy products, they either have to turn the milk into edible sour milk (which they do by mixing it with cattle urine), or turning it into clarified butter (butter with the milk solids removed). Their device for churning is simply a big gourd hung with a couple of long leather strips. The process of churning is simply to swing this gourd back and forth for sufficient time to make butter. Thus, harvesting and processing of herd products involve little equipment but much skill.

The management of the herd itself likewise uses very little equipment. For example, the Karimojong carefully design their herds so that there are no surplus bulls nor any low-quality animals. They try to keep a high standard of breeding; this involves careful selection of breeding stock and castration of the remaining bulls. They do this with great skill, and there are very few "whole animals" in their herds. They castrate an animal simply by holding it down and pounding its testicles with a couple of hard rocks or a mallet.

The husbandry side of herd management—the provision of fodder—likewise involves a good deal of knowledge, discernment, and skill, but very little equipment. For example, controlled burning of grasses is used at certain times in order to stimulate the growth of new grass. The whole procedure is very carefully timed so that there is minimum destruction of usable resources. The only "tool" involved is a torch.

Likewise, it is apparent that nothing is required for watering the animals except a hole in the ground into which water comes, and some sort of trough so that the animals can get it. From an equipment point of view this is very simple. But knowing where to dig for water, knowing when each animal has had enough water, and making sure that all the animals get access to the hole all depend on human knowledge, care, and skill.

Overall, then, the Karimojong's technology of herding demonstrates their exceptional skill in the use of natural resources, which is supplemented with a bit of rather simple material culture and a lot of human effort.

The third main principle of herd management, around which the technology is organized, is environmental pressure to move livestock. Livestock cannot be raised in this semiarid area without moving the herds (given the limits of the technology that they have). There is not enough water or grass, and the rainfall is too irregular so that the inadequate amount of grass is in a different place this year than it was last year, and so on.

This is counter-balanced by a need to make a conjunction of the livestock and the humans for whom they produce. On the whole, at any time, the greater part of the herds are out toward the edges of the triangle. On the whole, at any time, the greater part of the humans are in the middle. They have to keep the cattle out and moving because it is the only way they can survive. The scheduling of the movement of the components of the herd, so that there are enough cattle producing their "interest" in the central area, but enough cattle accumulating their interest in the outside grazing area, is a very complicated matter involving a great deal of skill and judgement. The technology of actually moving the herd consists, at a minimum, of a small naked boy with a stick in one hand and a water gourd in the other.

The first major constraint that this pattern of movement has to respond to is that, of course, cows do not produce milk all the time. Only cows with suckling calves produce milk, which is the main form of "interest" on the herd. This is even more the case with Karimojong herds of animals not very carefully bred for regular milk production (some modern dairy cattle are much more regular producers). If a herd is to provide a continuous milk supply, it needs a relatively large herd of cows, and the management of the herd involves scheduling their pregnancies so that some of them are in milk all the time. This means that the herd has to have a larger number of fertile animals, and a low number of sterile or insufficiently productive animals. Because the herd has to have enough cows to offset the interval between periods of yield or milk, it needs enough bulls to make sure that the service of the cows is what it ought to be, and the bulls have to have high fertility. If there is any limitation on any of these factors, then the herd produces a spasmodic milk supply. When the humans live off the milk, a spasmodic milk supply is a catastrophe.

The second major constraint on the pattern of movement is that the individual yield of an animal depends on the animal's general condition. Its general condition depends on its regular access to grass and water. In the rainy season, grass and water are usually sufficient, and the animal yields are good. But in the dry season, water and grass are on the whole not sufficient, and the cattle lose condition quite rapidly. The first thing that happens then is that the milk supply falls off. During the rainy season, the Karimojong harvest four or five pints of milk from a cow a day and still leave it with enough milk to rear a healthy calf to add to the capital stock. In the dry season, very often a cow yields only a quarter of a pint a day, unless the herd manager is willing to risk killing the calf. The same goes for the harvest of blood—it is possible in the rainy season to take a great deal of blood from an animal and still leave it in good condition. In the dry season the possible harvest is much smaller. In other words, the size and design of a herd that would carry a family through a wet season will not necessarily keep people alive during a dry season.

These two factors constraining herd movement combine with the problem of bringing the producing herd together with the humans, who depend on that herd and who may live 40–60 miles away, to produce very complex problems of management. The material technology for solving this management problem for greatest efficiency in accomplishing the purpose for which the Karimojong keep herds is the man or the small boy with a stick. Obviously, technical knowledge involved is again the important factor: the small boy with a stick must head the right number of cattle, of the right mixture of cows, calves, and bulls, in the right direction at the right time.

EIGHTEENTH-CENTURY FRANCE: A GRAIN
TECHNOLOGY WITH IMPERIAL AMBITIONS

The two great enterprises of eighteenth-century France were growing and distributing grain and fighting wars. Grain economies dominated the temperate zones of both the northern and southern hemispheres in the period immediately before their industrial revolutions, in Europe, North America, Argentina, Uruguay, Australia, and New Zealand. Understanding grain technology is therefore essential in outlining the economic environment in which industrialization has taken place.

The great advantage of grain over most agricultural products is its storability and transportability. This historically enabled agricultural products to be the food base of peoples in the temperate zone, for grain could be stored through the winter. It facilitated the growth of cities in temperate zones, because grain could be transported to cities from relatively long distances. The spread of civilized societies into temperate zones has gone hand-in-hand with the introduction of grain culture. The technology of a grain economy is conveniently broken into two parts: agriculture, or the actual growing of crops; and transport, or the movement of food from the fields to the cities, to famine areas, and to areas specializing in other crops.

Agricultural Technology

The basic technology of temperate-climate grain growing consists in an intervention in the natural ecology of a field so that the grain grasses (rye was the main crop in eighteenth-century France) get a head start on the natural cover at the beginning of the season. The natural vegetation (there are two main dominant temperate-zone covers—forest and grass, with grass becoming dominant when a forest has been cleared) is destroyed by plowing cleared fields, which also provides a proper consistency of the soil for the germination of the grain seeds. Once the grain has a head start, it tends to choke out other plants by providing a complete cover for the ground and thereby shading sunlight from "weeds." Unlike "bare-ground" crops (e.g., maize, cotton, tobacco, most truck-farm crops), grain crops do not need constant cultivation to kill competing plants. They are, in fact, similar in structure and physiology to the grasses, which are the naturally dominant cover on cleared ground in temperate climates.

This basic intervention in the ecology of fields was carried out with different technology in the plains of northern France than in the Center and South. In the North, in a broad band from Normandy to the German border, the dominant type of plow (*charrue*) had a set of two wheels in a fore-train (in front of the share, the iron part that cut the earth) which regulated the depth of the cut. The share itself had an attached mold-board to turn the earth over after the furrow was cut. (See the plate in G. Duby, *Rural Economy and Country Life in the Medieval West*, plate II after p. 390. This picture is from a somewhat earlier time, but apparently the structure of the plow stayed fairly stable for a long time.)

During the Middle Ages, the yoke had been developed which dis-tributed the force of the pull over the shoulders of the draft animal, rather than on its neck or horns. This was accompanied or followed by a change *from* a team of four to six oxen for draft (requiring a total of two men and a boy) to a team of two horses manageable by a single man. However, the details are not clear because it takes more draft power to plow the heavy clay soils than the lighter sandy soils, and the available drawings do not specify the weight of the soil. The smaller team had a shorter turning radius than the great teams of oxen. This facilitated the enclosure of fields into family farms, as did the lower capital requirements of fewer draft animals and the lower labor require-ments for managing the team.

There is some evidence that during the seventeenth and eighteenth centuries, the plains of the north were evolving from a system of co-operative tillage to a more family-organized tillage, with corresponding changes in the property system. This evolution corresponded with the technical changes to a small team drawing the plow as described above, and perhaps was caused by it. This technology of plowing was common across the northern European plains, in the Danube basin, and in south-ern Russia.

In central and southern France, the dominant type of plow (*araire*) merely broke up the soil, without turning it over. (Its effect was more similar to the "cultivator" of American farming than to what we call a "plow." Another way of describing its effect is that the *araire* corre-sponded more to a horsedrawn hoe than to a horse-operated spade— see the drawings in Georges Duby, Armand Wallon, and E. Le Roy Ladurie, *Histoire de la France Rurale* Vol. 2 pp. 22–23). It lacked a mold-board and wheeled foretrain. Perhaps this is due to the thinner rockier soils of the South, perhaps to the shortage of pasture for draft animals, or perhaps to cultural influences from Italy and Spain where similar plows were used. In some areas in France, the plow that turns the soil was not introduced until the middle of the nineteenth century. Perhaps the dominance of the *araire*, which requires less draft power, was due to the more parceled and enclosed, family-run, property arrangements of southern and central France. It is fairly clear that dispersed settlement on individual farms, family-organized rather than village-organized tillage, and the plow without a moldboard went together in southern and central France and in the Breton Peninsula.

A second major technological variable in grain growing derives from the fact that grain exhausts certain compounds from the soil that are needed for a good crop. The yield from a given field declines steadily unless these elements are replaced. There were four basic devices used in varying degrees in eighteenth-century France for restoring these elements: (1) leaving the field in longer or shorter periods of fallow (sometimes allowing the natural plant cover to take over the field and grazing animals on it) until the chemical composition of the soil is restored; (2) rotation of crops so that successive crops extract different elements and sometimes actually restore depleted elements; (3) systematic fertilization with animal manure or human excrement; and (4) systematic fertilization with inorganic materials, especially marl, limestone, or turf from uncultivated lands.

Variations in fertilization practices caused very great differences in yields. The most advanced grain agriculture was in Flanders, and during the late eighteenth century was spreading along the plain southward and eastward toward Paris. Slicher Van Bath (1964, pp. 330-333) estimates the rate of advance of this system across the plains at about 30–45 miles in 30 years, or about 10–15 miles per decade. The ratio of yield to seed in this agriculture was, for rye, somewhere near 10:1 or 12:1, occasionally up to 20:1; agriculture depending only on fallowing gave yields of about 4:1 or 5:1. Flemish agriculture involved stall feeding of animals, spreading manure, collecting human excrement from cities; rotating crops with fodder crops, especially nitrogen-fixing crops, so that stall feeding could be alternated with grain crops; and fertilizing with inorganic compounds. The spread of such complicted, but effective, agriculture was encouraged during the last half of the century by high grain prices (perhaps due to increasing use of horses for transportation and for military maneuvers) and by the organization of agricultural societies that propagandized for improvements.

The greatest amount of human labor was used for harvesting and threshing grain, although this was not crucial in determining yields. The scythe, a knife with a long handle swung with the whole body, was replacing the sickle, a short knife swung with the arm, in harvesting. The scythe was especially being used more in areas where animals were stall-fed. This was because the straw from the grain plant was used for bedding, and hence the plant needed to be cut next to the ground. In areas where cattle grazed on the fields after the harvest, the straw was left for them to eat; hence, the farmers only wanted to cut off the head of the grain rather than the whole plant. For this, the more maneuverable sickle was more efficient.

Threshing was done either by beating the grain with human force, or by driving animals to walk over it. Then usually the chaff (the "leafy" inedible part of the head of grain) was separated from the grain by throwing it into the air and allowing the wind to carry off the light chaff.

Very roughly speaking, the yield from a harvest of grain under the dominant fallow system was sufficient so that it could be divided approximately into thirds: one-third for seed for the following year (allowing for some loss in storage); one-third for a very poor subsistence for the laborer that produced it and his family; and one-third for rent. In many cases, in eighteenth-century France, the "rent" was eaten up by the peasant himself, who owned the land. But much of the rent went to support local nonagricultural people (local lords, priests, artisans, and transport workers) and to feed transport animals. The surplus available for urban and military consumption was thus well below half of the net yield. The movement of that surplus, both for urban and military consumption and for famine areas, depended on the network of transportation.

Transportation Technology

In a basically agricultural economy with animal traction there are two crucial questions to ask about transportation technology: (1) How much of the food is eaten by the animals and teamsters, or by the sailors, for each ton-mile of transportation, and what proportion of it spoils? (2) How many tons of surplus food does each mile of road, canal, or river, give access to? Compared to most other types of agriculture, grain growing results in high productivity of transportation investments in both these respects. Relatively little of the grain spoils in transit, so any economies in traction efficiency pay off. And compared to jungle, desert, or mountainous ecologies, grain-growing plains give access to a large amount of food for each mile of transportation developed. One of the great advantages of grain-growing areas in preparing for industrialization is that they result in a dense network of roads, canals, or railroads. This in turn means that the agricultural population is generally more involved in commerce, more in contact with the city, and generally more open to modern influences. These forces were at work strongly in the grain-growing plain of northern France in the eighteenth century, making the rural inhabitants of that area considerably more "modern" than the peasants of the South and West (see especially Charles Tilly, *The Vendée*).

There were two basic variables that determined how much grain was eaten per ton-mile of transportation: (1) whether the route was by water or by land, and (2) if by land, whether the roads and bridges were well constructed and in good repair.

Water transportation was very much cheaper than land transportation for all goods in which its slowness did not cause wastage. The great advantage of Paris for urban development was that the Seine was navigable, and gave access to most of the rich northern plain. Besides supplying Paris, the Seine basin also exported grain during the eighteenth century. Several canals were built during the century, mainly to connect different river systems to each other. Transportation by sea (between river valleys) was also used, especially for goods of relatively high value for the weight (e.g., wines from the Bordeaux region). Practically all foreign trade of France moved by water.

The hours of animal and human time needed to move a ton of goods over land depended mainly on the condition of the roads. Better roads allowed the same animal to pull heavier loads, and permitted greater speeds. This reduced the amount consumed for each ton-mile. At the beginning of the century, there was general complaint about the quality, maintenance, and extensiveness of the road system. The roads of each area were under the authority of the *Intendant* or the local government.

In 1714 an office of roads and bridges (Ponts et Chaussées), was established which became a new type of social structure for managing technical change during the century. The central office developed a systematic apprenticeship program to train civil engineers, which grew by 1747 into a full-fledged professional school. The same office had responsibility both for the design of royal projects and for technical advice to local authorities on all road and bridge enterprises. The school in its turn encouraged the development of technical culture and the writing of textbooks on civil engineering. A constant stream of technical innovations flowed from this professionalized central authority and were rapidly spread throughout the realm by trained engineers working for the authority in various parts of the country. By general consent, France had the best road system in the world by the end of the eighteenth century.

The conformation of this road system was shaped by the economic forces outlined above for transportation systems in grain economies. The network of royal roads was considerably denser in the northern plain, from Normandy across to the German border. Each mile of road was cheaper in the plain. Each mile gave access to a larger surplus of food, because of the relatively high percentage of the land farmed. The grain was transportable and storable. This relatively rich network of good roads in turn involved northern farmers in more commercialized production, and made them more responsive to price shifts. With the high grain prices of the last half of the century, technical innovations in agriculture spread much more rapidly in this plain than in the South-west and South. Urban concentrations became greater in this northern area, especially in Paris.

The combination of increased agricultural productivity and better transportation considerably decreased the risk of famine. The periodic famines of the Middle Ages and the Black Death had kept the population growing slowly. During the eighteenth century, the population of France grew substantially. This same combination of increased productivity and improved transportation also increased the capacity of northern France to raise and supply an army. The military preponderance of the royal government compared to local "feudal" military formations by the eigh-teenth century is partly due to the increased mobility of grain supplies. Certainly the size of army raised by Napoleon at the end of the century would not have been possible without these agricultural and transpor-tation developments during the eighteenth century.

French Military Technology

There were four major innovations in French military technology at the beginning of or during the eighteenth century that substantially changed the nature of land warfare. These were (1) the development of the cadenced march (marching in a common rhythm, generally with drums), introduced about the middle of the century; (2) the introduction starting at the beginning of the century of the flintlock musket (*fusil*) in place of the matchlock musket as the main infantry firearm; (3) the introduction of the bayonet to be attached to the firearm, and (4) a radical decrease in the weight of artillery pieces and improvement and stan-dardization of the carriages for field artillery. The army was changed to take advantage of these innovations gradually during the century. The final adaptation of the structure of the army and of tactics to this new technology was made by Napoleon. Since a large part of the national income, and especially a large part of the activity of the royal govern-ment, was devoted to imperial aims, these technological changes were fundamental for French society.

Before the middle of the century, without the cadenced march, ranks of troops had to be kept a relatively long distance apart, or else when they started to maneuver they would get all mixed up. This long distance between ranks in turn meant that the distance between files (files are the lines in the direction of march; ranks are the lines perpendicular to the direction of march) and the distance apart that they ought to be when facing an enemy, was much less than the distance between ranks. Therefore, when the troops had to form into a battle line on one or another flank, they had to go through complicated movements to adjust their spacing. Further, each batallion had its own set of movements for getting from a marching column into a battle line, because a general armywide regulation of infantry movements was not introduced until mid-century.

All of this meant that it took most of a day to get an army from its marching columns into position ready to fight. The battles of the late seventeenth and early eighteenth century often started about three o'clock in the afternoon, and they could only take place if the defending army waited for the attacking army to get into position. Thus, both armies had to decide that they wanted to give battle, and neither could force battle on the other. Wars tended to reduce themselves to matters of maneuver, rather than matters of battle. With the introduction of the cadenced step and drill in deployment, armies could shift from marching order to fighting order in very much shorter periods of time, and the offensive general could therefore force battle on the defensive general. Further, both generals could move around after the battle started, to take advantage of shifting circumstances, to press an advantage, to retreat, etc. The simple device of the cadenced step, with its clear superiority in organizing and deploying large masses of men, shifted the nature of warfare from one of maneuvering for advantageous position to one of destroying the enemy's forces.

The flintlock musket had a much faster rate of fire (roughly one shot per minute) than the matchlock musket, and this rate of fire was further increased by the introduction of the iron ramrod and the cartridge around the middle of the century. In order to make use of this more rapid rate of fire to concentrate fire on the enemy, the infantry needed to be thinned out so that only a few soldiers were loading in back of each soldier on the front lines who was firing so that all the infantrymen's weapons could aim at the enemy. In the Middle Ages, when a main infantryman's weapon was the pike, the massing of infantrymen gave force and compactness to their function as a group that charged the enemy and fought up close. But around the turn of the century the line was thinned down from six to four ranks deep, and then later to three, to take advantage of the faster rate of fire.

A further impact of the flintlock was that small bodies of men detached from the main body of the army could pin down and distract parts of an advancing army. The detachment of skirmishing units from the main body of the army, to operate more or less independently on the flanks or in dispersed strong points in order to disrupt the organization of the opposing army, was introduced on a relatively large scale during the eighteenth century.

The bayonet had the effect of making a given infantryman *both* capable of firing from a distance *and* also capable of charging the enemy and fighting up close (not until the development of automatic weapons could firearms be used while in physical reach of the enemy; if the enemy is close by, he will not give you a minute to reload). This reduced the number of types of infantrymen to one, with a single multipurpose weapon for both firing and charging, instead of the two (or more) types for each different function, which had been characteristic of the seventeenth century.

From about the middle to the end of the eighteenth century, the weight of a four-pounder field artillery piece decreased from about 1300 pounds to 600 pounds. This was mainly the effect of reducing the charge and making the balls fit the cannon barrel more tightly, which gave about the same range for a much smaller amount of explosive force; cannons were built with thinner walls when less explosive charges could be used. At the same time the carriages for field artillery were improved and standardized, with as many interchangeable parts as possible. These developments combined to make field artillery much more maneuverable, and enabled artillery to be used in support of mobile troops as well as in defense of fixed strong points.

The combined effect of these innovations was to make the army much more mobile, both in the sense that one could move the whole army with artillery pieces to a place of battle, and also in the sense that the army could reform and maneuver on the field of battle itself and attack when an opportunity was presented without the "consent" of the opposing general. The firepower of an attacking army could equal that of a defending army, and the firepower could be rapidly converted into a charging group of men. These developments in land warfare provided the basis of the rapid conquests by revolutionary and Napoleonic armies at the end of the eighteenth and beginning of the nineteenth century on the European continent. They made the Napoleonic wars much more bloody and much faster moving.

At the same time, developments were taking place on the seas that drastically changed France's colonial position. France held Canada and had three bases in the Caribbean at the beginning of the century. During the century France intervened sporadically in the Mediterranean, especially in Corsica, finally permanently securing Corsica at the end of the century. She had two major bases and a minor base in India and held an island in the Indian Ocean.

But during this century, England's navy grew very fast, eventually completely surpassing the French and Spanish navies and becoming capable of denying France access to any of her colonies, as the English government saw fit. During the century England drove France from Canada and, to a considerable degree, from India. This meant that by the beginning of the nineteenth century and the Industrial Revolution, England had the capacity to defend her monopoly of access to her own colonies and to force entrance into colonies of other powers if the market looked good. The market looked good especially in India and South America. The Indian and South American markets were the mainstay of the rapid growth of English textile production, which was in turn the backbone of her industrial revolution.

The overall result of these combined developments was to make France by the end of the century by far the most powerful land force on the continent but very clearly militarily inferior to England on the seas. The imperial growth of France in the Napoleonic era in the first part of the nineteenth century was essentially limited to Europe, where she confronted powerful and industrializing enemies, rather than distant colonies where she might have confronted more primitive peoples, and might have reaped trade monopolies which might have encouraged her industry.

An Overview of Technical Change
in the Old Regime

It is tempting when examining a society just before the industrial revolution to read backwards from the innovations of the following century. Manufacturing played a relatively small role in the eighteenth century. The main enterprises of French society were the production and transportation of agricultural goods and warfare. In these areas, especially in transportation and land warfare, we find substantial changes in the efficiency of activities due to technical changes.

But perhaps more important than any of these concrete innovations was the growth of a new set of social structures that encouraged a constant search for profitable innovations. Probably the most important of these was the increase in the publication and distribution of what might be called technical monographs. The debates among military thinkers on how to adapt tactics and strategy to the new technology were carried on partly by competing printed monographs. There was a plethora of books on agriculture—reports on foreign practice, arguments for one or another agricultural "system," almanacs with agricultural advice, economic analyses by physiocrats, etc. The technical practice of the office of roads and bridges was promptly translated into textbook form. That is, even questions of the internal administration and technique of a single government department were argued in print. And through print, men learn technology more easily from strangers and foreigners. The rapidity of dissemination of innovations and knowledge was greatly increased by the introduction of the technical monograph.

A second major structural innovation was the technical profession, devoted to the improvement of a particular art, disseminating innovations through a school, and using governmental powers to increase the impact of trained men. The profession of civil engineering started as a quite ordinary government department, but ended up as a new device to secure constant technical innovation in its area of competence throughout the country.

A third structural innovation was the voluntary association of interested men to encourage the search for, and dissemination of, innovations. In the eighteenth century these were especially prominent in French agriculture.

Though these structures for innovations may seem vestigial to people accustomed to great universities and laboratories that pay high salaries to people for nothing but innovation, such vestigial structures made France a self-transforming technological system. This self-transforming character was much more prominent in the North and in the cities, and especially prominent in the northern city of Paris. From a technological point of view, France was no longer changing randomly as people found solutions to technical problems in their own work roles. By the end of the Old Regime, France had built transformative processes into the center of the social and technological structure. These processes would lead France to be the second great power, after England, to engage in substantial industrialization. The transformations rooted in these institutions of systematic change would give France the role of one of the two greatest world powers for a century.

THE UNITED STATES: MODERN TECHNOLOGY
WITH SCHOOL-TAUGHT PRACTITIONERS

Twentieth-century American technology shows in full flower the transformative patterns that were beginning to develop in the eighteenth century. The most significant thing that can be said about American technology is that by the time you have said anything about it, it will be outmoded. Small parts of a technology form curricula for the Ph.D. at the Massachusetts Institute of Technology (MIT); ten years later a person who has not kept up is almost hopelessly outdated. Describing

TABLE 3.1

Percentage Composition of the Labor Force, by Industrial Sector

Date	Agriculture, forestry, and fisheries	Manufacturing, mining, and construction	Trade, transportation, and services except government and education	Educational services and government[d]	Total
1900[a]	38.6	29.9	28.2	3.3	100
1940[b]	19.1	30.4	43.0	7.5	100
1960[c]	7.0	35.4	46.9	10.6	100
1979[e]	3.6	30.2	53.3	12.9	100

[a]Gainful workers; taken from U.S. Bureau of the Census, *Historical Statistics of the United States*, 1789-1945 (1949), p. 64, Table D 47–61. Not quite comparable to later years.

[b]Employed civilian labor force, excluding "emergency" workers (i.e., workers on public relief work). Computed from 1940 *Census of Population* "U.S. Summary, Labor Force" p. 233–234, Table 81, excluding those without reported industries.

[c]Employed civilian labor force. Taken from 1960 *Census of Population* U.S. Summary 1-557-562, Table 209.

[d]Not elsewhere classified.

[e]U.S. Bureau of the Census (1980) Current Population Reports, Series P(20), No. 350, Population Profile 1979, Washington: USGPO. Table 23.

such a technological system is necessarily a radical act of abstraction, in which most of what people learn at MIT is excluded.

In the first part of this section I outline the general features of American technology and how it has changed since about 1900. In the second part I consider the main varieties of technology in fabrication (manufacturing and construction), agriculture, wholesale and retail distribution of goods, and services to clients.

The General Transformation
of American Technology since 1900

From a sociological point of view perhaps the most important effect of the transformation of technology is the change in the composition of activities in the society (see especially Daniel Bell's *The Coming of Post Industrial Society*). In Table 3.1, we present estimates of the proportion of the labor force in different industrial sectors of the economy, for 1900,

1940, 1960, and 1979 (the data are not exactly comparable because of changes in census definitions).

In 1900 about two out of five of all the employed in the United States worked in agriculture. By 1979 this was down to about one out of 28. From being the dominant activity of the society (i.e., more important in terms of people than manufacturing or services) agriculture has become less important than education and public administration alone. The proportion of the labor force working on fabrication of commodities or buildings, or the extraction of minerals, has remained more or less stable near one out of three persons. Trade, transportation, and various sorts of services (entertainment, medical and legal services, repair services, personal services, etc.) have increased substantially, from occupying a little less than one-third of the labor force to occupying about half. The most explosive growth has been in the public sector, in education and public administration, which occupied about one out of every 30 employed Americans in 1900, but about one of every eight in 1979.

Corresponding to these gross shifts in the industrial sector of activities in the economy are shifts in the activities of particular people, changes in the *occupational* composition of the economy ("industries" are classifications of the activities of organizations; "occupations" are classifications of the activities of individuals). Table 3.2 shows the 1970 occupational composition of the industrial sectors used in Table 3.1. For example, agriculture was less than 3% professional workers in 1970, while education and public administration were over 40% professional. Thus, as agriculture declines and education and public administration grows, we will expect the percentage of all workers who are professionals to grow. In addition to this change, there has been professionalization within each of the sectors. For example, in 1940 only 3% of all workers in mining, manufacturing, and construction were professional workers. By 1970, 9% were professional workers. Similarly the minute proportion of professionals in agriculture in 1979 (2.9%) was an even more minute 0.2% in 1940. The major source of the shift in the occupational structure of the labor force is the net shift away from an agricultural economy to a service economy and especially to an economy in which government and education are increasingly important services. But an additional factor is the professionalization of all sectors of the economy.

The overall shift toward a distribution and service economy, and a corresponding shift away from an agricultural and fabrication economy, has been accompanied especially by a radical increase in the proportion of professional workers. In 1910 there were about 1.6 million professional workers in a total labor force of about 37 million, or a little over 4%. By 1940 professionals constituted about 7½% of the labor force. By 1960, professionals were about 11½% of the labor force, over 7 million in a

TABLE 3.2

**Percentage of the Employed in Industry Groups Who Were
in the Occupational Groupings Specified, 1970 Population Census**

	Industry grouping			
Occupational grouping	Agriculture, forestry and fishing	Mining, construction, and manufacturing	Services except public administration and education	Public administration and education
Professional technical and kindred	2.9	9.0	12.3	42.2
Managers and farm owners	49.5	6.0	10.7	7.3
Sales and clerical	2.3	13.5	34.1	25.9
Craftsmen and foremen	1.6	26.5	9.1	3.9
Operatives, laborers, and farm laborers	43.8	45.0	34.0	20.7
Totals	100.1	100.0	100.2	100.0
Numbers, in 1,000's	2,868	25,135	38,380	10,386

Source: Computed from U.S. Bureau of the Census (1972). Census of Population 1970, Occupation by Industry, Final Report, PC(2)-7C. Washington: USGPO.

labor force of about 65 million. By 1979 there were about 15½% professional workers in the total labor force, or over one out of seven workers. That is, professional and technical workers have gone in a half century from about one in every 23 workers to one in every seven workers. The younger age groups now in the labor force are much more highly educated than older workers, and a higher proportion of them are professionals. There is some dispute about whether we can expect this professionalization of the labor force to continue (see my "On Softheadedness on the Future," *Ethics,* October 1982).

The gross facts describing the American economy in 1960, which distinguish it sharply from traditional economies, are that: (1) approximately one out of every seven people uses some kind of specialized abstract knowledge, usually certified by the educational system; (2) one-half of all the people are engaged in services or in distribution of goods produced by the other half. These gross features distinguish the United States, at least in degree, from any previously existing society; western European societies are similar in structure to American. We are interested in the social consequences of this extreme advance—the extreme of application of specialized knowledge to the transformation of the productive apparatus.

Some Gross Consequences of Advanced Technology

The most important consequence of this advanced technology is a fantastic productivity of activities. That is, by systematically applying specialized knowledge in a routine fashion to improve productive processes of all kinds, the productivity of all activities has greatly increased. This is very clear in manufacturing activities and agriculture. Productivity per person in the manufacturing industries is much higher in the United States than virtually anywhere else. Perhaps New Zealand agriculture is more productive per person than United States agriculture taken as a whole, because much of agriculture in the southern states is so inefficient.

Greater productivity in service activities in the United States is much harder to demonstrate. In the educational industry we can infer from the fact that people come to the United Sates from elsewhere to study that the United States has some advantage over other countries. Trying to shop for a week's groceries in an underdeveloped country will soon convince one that distribution activites are much more efficient in modern countries. Roads, postal service, parks, and other governmental activities are clearly better in the advanced countries than in poorer countries. These differences in the productivity of service activities among countries are obvious to people who have had experience with both a modern and underdeveloped economy, but they are quite hard to measure precisely.

A second major social consequence of such a knowledge-intensive economy is that storage and transportation problems are solved. That is, people do not starve because of a bad harvest in the United States. In fact, many times it is hard to notice that there has been a locally bad harvest without reading about it in the local newspaper, because the slight upward push on the prices of fresh foods is small compared to seasonal fluctuations, and it requires some statistical skill to ferret out the price increase.

A third major consequence of such an economy has been implicit throughout our treatment above: that increasing effort is spent on innovation rather than on running the system. The productive system, more or less, runs itself; it does not really take much human effort to get things done. Instead, to an increasing degree, the effort that goes into the economy is spent on changing things rather than on running them. For instance, much of the effort goes into the preparation of the professionals who will be applying specialized knowledge. This preparation is concentrated in research universities where the most advanced specialized knowledge is taught. But another way of looking at this phenomenon is that people who do what they are taught to do in universities will be innovators if their older colleagues have been still doing what they were taught to do in universities when *they* went to school, because what new graduates learned in school will be new knowledge. The point is that the research traditions of universities are constantly transforming the content of the abstract knowledge that specialized applied professions use, which in turn transforms the technology.

It is increasingly the case that the really rapidly growing industries are not so much those that introduced one major innovation, which gave them large profits, as used to be the case in the beginning of American industrialization during the last half of the nineteenth century. For instance, when Sears and Montgomery Ward introduced mail-order catalog distribution into the countryside they became very big from that one innovation. Instead, the rapidly growing companies are increasingly those that *constantly* innovate. The chief advantage of Du Pont, for instance, is not that it makes specific chemicals better than anyone else (we do not know whether it does or not), but rather that the company figures out how to make new chemicals faster than other companies. The same general principle is true of universities: those which innovate most get richest and grow the most. This principle also applies to hospitals, branches of the military, and so forth.

Thus, increasingly, in both the governmental and the private parts of the economy, success depends less on what one is doing, than on how fast one is innovating. (The analysis of the economic consequences of innovations in the market part of the economy was a major part of the life work of Joseph A. Schumpeter. See for instance his *Capitalism, Socialism, and Democracy*.)

Varieties of Technology in Manufacturing and Construction

The social organization of production can be identified by examining the routine of the worker: Does the worker typically do the same activities every day? By looking at the varieties of American industry with this question in mind, we can distinguish three main types of fabricating technology.

First, there are production systems that produce one item of a kind, usually one at a time. For instance, in the construction industry a firm will ordinarily be building only one skyscraper at a time, and in any given city there will ordinarily be only one skyscraper with that design. In the movie industry a crew makes one movie at a time, with a different script and generally a different set of actors than other movies. The same is true of building rockets, of building big airplanes, of book publishing, of ship building, of tailoring to measure or dressmaking of "originals," of research organized into projects and so forth. We will call these industries "one-at-a-time" technologies. Their central feature is that of adapting the activities of the organization each day to a slightly different task, with major changes of tasks coming periodically when a major project is finished.

A second major type of technology is large-batch or mass production, where a large number of identical products are in the process of fabrication at the same time, going through a sequence of nearly identical operations simultaneously. In such a system, if it takes, say, five days to assemble a car, and it is 15 minutes between cars coming off the end of the production line, then there must be 160 cars in the plant being worked on at the same time. People doing these tasks are very likely, when they come in tomorrow, to go to the same place as they did yesterday and do the same set of activities as they did yesterday. We generally call this type of technology "mass production." From the point of view of the worker its essential feature is boring routine, the same thing day in and day out.

Finally, most fluids (gasoline, beer, natural gas, many chemicals, electricity) are produced in a continuous process. Usually the activites done to the product are done automatically by machines, and the function of the production workers is to watch gauges and take corrective action. Most of the manual workers are maintainence workers whose activities vary from day to day, depending on what has gone wrong. New devices to control mechanical processes (computers, etc.) may make it increasingly possible to produce hardware in the same general way we now produce fluids (the movement to do so is generally called "automation").

In Table 3.3 are outlined some main features of social organization of the activities of production that tend to be associated with the variation in technology of one-at-a-time production, mass production, and continuous process. (The original work in this area was done by Joan Woodward and her colleagues. See *Industrial Organization: Theory and Practice.* See also Arthur L. Stinchcombe, "Bureaucratic and Craft Administration of Production.")

The one-at-a-time industries, generally speaking, have something approaching a craft system, and quite often there is a good deal of sub-

TABLE 3.3

**Outline of Some Characteristics of Different Technologies
in American Manufacturing and Construction**

Typical features of organizations using the technologies	Type of technology		
	One-at-a-time	Mass production	Continuous process
Examples of the type	Construction; movies; shipbuilding; machine tools; rocket construction; oil well drilling; book publishing; tailoring	Automobiles: refrigerators; ready-made apparel; hardware and small tools; meat packing; most liquor; steel production	Oil refining; most chemicals; beer and soft drink bottling; electricity production
Archetype of manual worker	Craftworkers who can read blueprints	Operatives and machine tenders	Maintenance and "blue-collar clerks" (few manual workers)
Length of hierarchy	Short (3–4 levels)	Long (6+ levels)	Long (6+ levels)
Role of line and staff	Vestigial staff; professionals (e.g., architects) supervise work	Strong line and strong staff; some conflict	Vestigial line; most supervisors and professionals engaged in innovation rather than supervision of production
Proportion of work force "middle class"	Around 15–20% (many small proprietors and subcontractors)	Around 15–20% (many officials and clerks)	Around 35–65% (many professionals and clerks)
Amount of paperwork (% clerical workers & accountants in production administration)	Little (few)	Much (many)	Very much; (very many)
Labor intensity	High (e.g. 35–75% of sale price in labor cost).	Intermediate (e.g., about 25% of sales price in labor cost)	Low (e.g., 5–15% of sales price in labor cost)

contracting. The central requirement on the system as a whole is that it be capable of adjusting its activities quickly and responsively, according to the plans for the particular project that they are making. In the movie industry, this plan is, of course, the script, and the skill involved is to turn it into a pattern of activity in front of the cameras. But for most commodities, the plan comes in the form of a drawing, and either the manual worker or the foreman has to be able to read those plans and adjust activities to them. In addition, the activities of the whole organization have to change as the project advances—as, for instance, a skyscraper moves from the excavation stage, to the frame-construction stage, to the attachment-of-the-shell stage, to the internal finishing stage. This necessity for adapting the whole organization to what is essentially a different task each day tends to result in subcontracting as a typical administrative sytem. The subcontractors that come in after excavation and before the shell attachment are specialists in foundation and frame construction and iron workers.

The reason such firms generally have short hierarchies is that the activity of the lowest levels has to adapt very rapidly to decisions at the highest levels as the higher levels take on new jobs. And the highest levels, when they take on new jobs, cannot be too far from the operative level, or they will not be able to understand the problems involved in the new job very well. A staff structure of professionals concerned with the long-range problems would not make much sense when the firm will probably be doing a different thing next year than the problem the staff analyzed this year. The staff structure in these firms is generally quite small and oriented to the short run.

Usually these industries have a high labor intensity—most of what the firm sells is its capacity to organize labor to get a special job done. The ratio of middle-class people to manual workers is generally low, and many of the middle-class people tend to be proprietors of subcontracting firms, often recruited from among craftsmen themselves.

Mass production systems can be thought of as people-driving systems. That is, the management has to run the activities of people in a systematic fashion. The activities that make up the continuous production line are interdependent, so that one person has to do his or her job before others can do theirs. Workers have to do their jobs rapidly and reliably or the entire line will slow down; supervisors have to solve problems immediately or else everybody will stop working. In general, then, management has to drive supervisors to solve problems fast in order to run such a system successfully. This results in a strong line authority structure supervising semiskilled workers who, generally speaking, do the same thing today that they did yesterday.

A long line hierarchy—often with up to eight or ten levels—is fairly typical. But also the continuous, large-scale character of the production process means that there are meaningful long-range problems. A steel plant is still probably going to be producing steel in ten years, therefore having a staff department planning over a ten year span makes good sense. Consequently, the authoritative line structure, oriented to short-run "emergency" problems, is confronted by a staff structure with young college graduates trying to tell them how to run the plant over the long run. There is often quite a lot of tension between staff and line people in this type of production system, because of the radically different orientation toward authority problems in these two structures.

The structure of the labor force in mass production typically involves (1) a good deal more "bureaucracy"—information processing by clerks—than in the craft industries; (2) many officials in the line structure; and (3) some professionals working in staff advisory capacities. Labor is still a substantial enough cost of production to be a major worry, though, capital and materials costs are a much larger part of the gross cost than in most one-at-a-time industries.

In the continuous process industries such as beer, oil, or chemicals, we have essentially a self-regulated production system. It is here that the extreme form of a system that runs itself is approximated; effort goes into innovation and changing the system. Insofar as these industries have a manual working force, it is usually highly skilled, but a very large share of the labor force in these industries is middle class.

The hierarchies in continuous process industries tend to be very long, and they do not have the same significance they do in mass production industries. The hierarchy is set up, essentially, to *solve problems* rather than to *run people*. Relative to mass production or one-at-a-time production, there is almost no line structure; everyone is either staff, planning what new to do in the long run, or maintenance, planning what to do about imperfections in the old plan. There are not very many people engaged in managing workers because, in the first place, there are not very many workers to manage, and second, because being a worker is a responsible position in which it would be easy to damage millions of dollars worth of equipment or goods in process by making a substantial mistake.

The emphasis of the effort on innovation and long-run planning influences the structure of the middle-class labor force. There are a great many natural scientists and accountants in such firms. Analyzing the effects of some major innovation in the self-regulated productive system (a new product, new process, or expansion of the old process) involves both a complicated projection of the physical, chemical, and control processes that will operate in the new system, and also a complicated projection of the future economic productivity of such an investment. A chemical plant or oil refinery will probably have to be profitable for 20 years without much change. Mass production systems and one-at-a-time systems can be easily redesigned after ten years, because their basic components are people. People are pretty flexible components of technical systems, as compared with massive complexes of pipes, valves, cracking towers, and so forth. In continuous process industries, this dependence on self-regulated, complex systems rather than labor to produce the goods also means that the component of labor cost in sale price is likely to be quite small. Capital costs are the most important. (Of course, usually around 75% of the cost of a piece of capital equipment is labor cost, because capital-producing industries are very labor intensive. For instance, in an oil refinery about half of the total *labor ever used* in the plant goes into building it, the other half into running it. As Marx long ago observed, capital is basically "embodied labor." Thus, the statement that "labor cost is a small part of sales price" is deceptive.) Hence, relatively speaking, one has more specialists in capital costs (accountants) than specialists in labor costs (labor negotiators and line management).

Varieties of Agricultural Technology

We can roughly classify types of American agricultural technology by the degree of person–machine intensity per acre; that is, the amount of human or mechanical effort put into the land to create a special environment for plant or animal growth.

The lowest level of person–machine intensity are forests and ranges for grazing livestock. These are relatively little modified from their natural state, except perhaps for changing the genetic composition of the plant or animal populations on the forestland, providing water wells on ranges for animals, and providing various sorts of winter protection for animals. Mountainous, desert, and swamp country is often exploited this way in the United States.

At the next level of person–machine intensity are the grains, especially wheat, and cultivated pasture. Typically the environment of the plant is modified by plowing, fertilization, application of insecticides, drainage management (*e.g.*, contour plowing), and crop rotation, in addition to the interventions listed above for forests and ranges. Chemical control of competing plant growth is also used (although under a system of crop rotation, the chemicals have to be compatible with several varieties of plants or otherwise applied with discretion).

Somewhat higher in person–machine intensity than grain cultivation is the cultivation of various bare-ground crops which do not enter the fresh produce market, such as yellow corn or maize, cotton, tobacco, soybeans, sunflowers, sugar beets or cane, potatoes, etc. At about the same level of intensity is the stall-feeding of cattle and pigs—in fact, it is often done on the same farms where corn is grown. In addition to the interventions made for grain farming, bare-ground crops require more extensive weed control, either by mechanical cultivators or by chemicals. The stalls for pigs, beef cattle, and dairy cattle provide for temperature control in winter, convenience to stored feed, and capacity to control the composition of feed. Dietary and chemical control of pests and diseases is common. In addition to the work of intervention in the ecology of the farm to grow the product efficiently, many of the products of this kind of agriculture require further treatment on or near the farm, such as fermentation of corn or grass for silage and the separation of sugar from the beets or sugar cane.

At the next higher level of intensity is truck farming, or irrigated vegetable and fruit farming. In addition to all the interventions of the previous types of farming, a higher degree of intervention is required in truck farming because of the importance of scheduling for the market and the requirement of uniformity of quality and of appearance. Truck farmers typically provide special warmth for starting plants earlier than one can start them in the fields (in greenhouses or something similar); provide special watering; and provide special additives related to the physiology of particular plants. Truck farmers pay close attention to a variety of genetic stocks, whereas farmers of grain, cattle, and bare-ground crops usually choose one variety of their major crops and adjust everything else to that. Very often truck farmers change the contours of the land by bulldozing, if they do not like its shape.

At the highest level of person–machine intensity are florists and chicken breeders, who artificially control virtually all aspects of the environment of the plant or animal.

Obviously 20 or 30 acres of greenhouses or of multi-storied chicken coops may be a much "bigger" farm than several square miles of Nevada range, both in terms of economic value produced and in terms of the labor required. In almost all censuses and land tenure studies, acreage is taken as a measure of size. This makes it very difficult to compare farming technologies in different countries, or to compare farms over time within the United States. It seems, for instance, that oriental rice paddies are roughly as labor and machine intensive as greenhouses in the United States. Comparisons of farming technology between Japan and the United States would have to compare the dominant form of

Japanese farming with the most intensive form of the American technology.

Generally, the acreage of American farms *adapts to the technology* so that the family farm remains the basic unit of organization. That is, ranches and forests are much larger than grain farms, which are in turn larger than corn–hog–dairy farms, which are larger than truck farms, which are larger than greenhouses. The farm tends toward the size that needs (given the intensity of intervention) about two full-time (about 120 hours per week) workers. This size is several square miles for ranches with range livestock (in the mountain states, average acreage per farm was 2262 acres in 1974 [*Statistical Abstract, 1979,* p. 688]), a couple of acres for greenhouses or chicken factories. Corporate farms or large-scale proprietorships seem to be somewhat more common toward the more intensive end of the scale, especially in vegetable farming, cotton, chickens, and flowers.

But the dominant tendency in American agriculture is to adapt the technology to the family farm (destroying many family farms as technology gets more efficient, of course) rather than reorganizing agriculture corporately to adapt to rapid shifts in agricultural technology. The average farm in 1930 was 151 acres; by 1978 it was 444 acres, so it took three 1930 farms to make one 1978 farm. Yet 90% of the people living on farms in 1977 were members of the farm operator's family (*Statistical Abstract, 1979,* pp. 682–683).

Technology of Wholesale and Retail Trade

The most convenient starting point for analyzing the technology of modern wholesale and retail trade is the inventory of the retailer. If that inventory comes from many different manufacturers (as, for instance, in hardware stores, apparel stores, department stores, and grocery stores), then the distributive apparatus has had to *mix many flows of goods* to make up one flow through the store. This entails dealing with many original suppliers, keeping track of large complex inventories, scheduling the reordering of many separate lines, making thousands of separate price decisions, and so forth. If, on the contrary, the inventory all comes from the same supplier (as, for instance, new automobile dealers, paint dealers, gasoline and fuel oil dealers, and frozen bulk meat dealers), the flow has the same mix at the retail end as at the factory end. Such a single flow with low mixing entails dealing with only one supplier; it simplifies inventory control; it simplifies coordination of production scheduling with sales scheduling and reduces inventories; and it allows a unified price policy.

Variation along this dimension of *complexity of mixing* creates, then, variations in the *complexity of the information and decision system*. The more mixing that has to be done, the more hours of clerical work there will be per ton of goods. It is obvious from the discussion of the evolution of the labor force above that clerical workers form a large part of the "service sector." Complexity of information and decision systems is concentrated in the trade and transportation industries, and creates a large burden of paperwork. It takes very few of these clerical workers to see many tons of oil or gasoline through to the consumer. It takes a great many to process an equal tonnage of nuts, bolts, and spare parts.

As in the manufacturing sector, there are organizational differences that correspond to these technical differences (unlike the situation in agriculture in which the technology is adapted to a given organizational form, the family farm). But in commerce, what varies is the *set* of organizations dealing with a particular commodity flow, rather than a particular organization. The main work connected with mixing flows of many different commodities is making very numerous decisions rationally. This in turn involves numerous problems of processing information on who owns the flow at a particular place and time, what that organization paid for it, to whom it is promised at what other place and time, how much that receiver will in its turn pay for it, and when. The organization of commerce in commodities with high amounts of mixing before the retailer receives the goods reflects the attempt to minimize this information cost.

For instance, if a heterogeneous inventory from many manufacturers is to be maintained in a warehouse ready for shipment, it is convenient if it all belongs to the same firm. Hence, the wholesaler will *buy* the flows of commodities from the manufacturer. Hence, merchant wholesalers or chain retailers, both of whom buy from many manufacturers to create an inventory that they themselves own, dominate the branches of commerce with high mixing. Flows with lower mixing do not have such complicated problems of keeping track of who owns particular parts of the flow, therefore merchant wholesalers or chain stores provide relatively smaller economies, so manufacturers branches or brokers or franchise dealers handle more of the trade.

As an extreme case, consider the different problems of selling new cars, and selling repair parts for those same cars. The parts in both flows are produced by the same parts manufacturers. But when they are sold to the new car manufacturer, they are unified into a single product, which is easy to keep track of and which goes directly to the retailer from the plant. But to provide an inventory of repair parts, a merchant wholesaler buys parts from the parts manufacturers, maintains them in

TABLE 3.4

Organizational Characteristics of Commercial Flows
with High Mixing and Low Mixing

High mixing	Low mixing
(Hardware, groceries, dime stores, department stores, apparel stores)	(New cars, gasoline, paint, coal, bulk food)

1. Merchant wholesalers
     OR
   chain retailers
	1. Manufacturers branches
	     OR
	   franchise holders and brokers

2. Many "buyers and department heads" (commodity specialists) among retail executives	2. Few "buyers and department heads" among retail executives
3. Trade concentrated in metropolitan centers (information centers—e.g., New York)	3. Trade concentrated for cheapest freight rates (efficient docks, e.g., Norfolk, Baltimore)
4. Communication by catalogs	4. Communication by price quotation, futures markets, etc.
5. Many salesmen per million dollars of sales	5. Fewer salesmen per million of sales

his ownership until the retailer (a repair garage, usually) needs them. In short, to sell parts as a car, the system uses a structure of manufacturer's branches and franchise holders; when selling the same parts separately as needed by consumers, the system uses merchant wholesalers.

The other differences outlined in Table 3.4 have the same source. Information needs in many separate commodity lines create the need for commodity line specialists (in the census classification, "buyers and department heads"), while goods that flow directly from manufacturer to consumer do not need such specialists. Metropolises like New York are places where a rich environment of market information and facilities for mixing many flows of goods are found. Hence, flows with high mixing are likely to go through New York, often through wholesalers, before going abroad, whereas coal, oil, or grain are more likely to go through the more physically efficient ports of Norfolk or Baltimore. Homogeneous flows of goods need only a single price quotation to communicate sufficient information to the consumers or retailers for their decisions. A heterogeneous inventory needs a catalog attaching a price to each flow of commodities. The information that the retailer (and the consumer) need when buying from a complex inventory is generally greater than the information needed to decide on a purchase of coal or fuel oil. Hence, both for wholesaling and retailing more sales personnel are generally needed for more complex flows.

Varieties of Service Technology

The main variable differentiating different types of services is not, in a sense, technological. The main influence on the social structure of service activities is whether the person rendering service knows what the consumer "needs" (as in medicine, law, or education), or whether the consumer himself decides what he or she "needs" under the pressure of competition from other service enterprises (e.g., restaurants, dry cleaners and laundries, and whorehouses). In the former case, the person who renders service gives orders to the clients and is classified as a professional. In the latter case, the person who renders service takes orders from the clients and is classified as a menial.

Presumably, the technological base of this distinction is mainly the true technical complexity of the problem of the client. When great technical wisdom is needed to judge what is possible and useful to the client and to obtain it, the normal result is a "professional" service. When little technical wisdom is needed, and clients can supervise the achievement of the ends themselves, an unskilled menial worker is more appropriate.

TECHNOLOGY AND SOCIAL STRUCTURE

Up to this point, we have been discussing the inherent characteristics of activities that are causally related to their efficiency or effectiveness. But, of course, the reason we want to do this is in a text on the sociology of the economy (which is quite different from the purpose in a text on engineering or agronomy) is that efficiency and effectiveness of activities influence their roles in social life. If we look at any variable related to the technical effectiveness of a system of activities, what effect can we expect such a variable to have on social life—how can knowing about it help explain the structure of activities?

Technology in the Determination
of Social Structure

In general, people are purposive—they do whatever they do in order to achieve certain ends that seem valuable, satisfying, or necessary to them. Insofar as people want the things that their activities are supposed to produce, they will be oriented toward, or motivated by, efficiency or effectiveness of those activities. They will, in general, be happier to get more of what they want; they can do this by making their activities more effective and efficient. If it is true, for instance, in American distribution of goods that make up complex inventories, that merchant wholesalers and chain stores are more efficient in minimizing information costs, then we will expect people who want to get complex inventories distributed will choose to organize merchant wholesale firms and chain stores. Merchant wholesalers or chain stores are less prominent in the commerce for bulk goods.

An analysis of the technology of a system of activities gives us insight into the *derived motivations* that people will take up if they want to achieve the ends of the system. Off hand it does not seem likely that people who distribute spare parts for cars should have a stronger "instinct of ownership" than people who distribute new cars. Once we understand that the different technology of distribution makes ownership of goods in transit much more efficient in the spare parts business, but makes virtually no difference in the new car business, then we feel that we understand this more powerful "instinct of ownership" of spare parts wholesalers quite well.

That is, technology for a sociologist or anthropologist is a description of the causal connection between the ends people have and what they have to do to achieve those ends. The motivation to do those things that have to be done to achieve those ends is a derived motivation. But to understand how it is derived, we need to understand the technology.

We now need to ask what parts of social life are likely to be dominated by these derived motivations—that is, in what parts of social life will the effects of technology be most pronounced? While it is undoubtedly true that no motivations that people take seriously are completely without an effect in all areas of life, yet there are parts more affected than others. Julian Steward (1955) introduced the term *cultural core* to distinguish those parts of social practice most affected by technology in *Theory of Culture Change*. (Apparently the reason that Steward chose the somewhat invidious word *core* for this part of culture is that he is interested mainly in evolutionary theories, and evolutionary theories apply best to this part of culture.)

The aspects of society that seem to be most thoroughly infused with derived motivations, that is, connected to the values of the society through technical causation, are (1) the organization of production groups, (2) the wealth of society, the devices for owning a managing wealth, and the division of income among different goods and services, and (3) the degree of interdependence on a large scale of the society.

Organization of Production Groups

The aspects of the organization of production groups that seem to vary closely with variation in technology are (1) the structure of authority—who evaluates whose work, who gives orders to whom, and what sanctions they have to back up their evaluations and orders; (2) the size of the group—the number of workers and the proportion of their time that they spend in the group; (3) the education and skill of various members of the group—the content of abstract knowledge learned outside the group, the amount of experience and manual skill needed to do various jobs well, and the amount of discretion based on this knowledge and skill which is built into various work roles in the organization; (4) activity cycles—the degree to which work in the group is sporadic or constant, varies with seasons or not, changes during the course of a day or not, depends on the richness of the results or not, etc.; (5) the relation of the work group itself to the wealth it uses in doing the work—whether the wealth is owned corporately by some organization that employs the workers, or whether each owns his own tools, for instance. Concrete examples of these points can be shown by contrasting the construction industry with the chemical industry: (1) accountants have a greater role in evaluating outcomes in the chemical industry; (2) employment of workers is stable in large chemical plants whereas subcontractors hire craftsmen for temporary employment; (3) physical scientists play a large role in the chemical industry and experienced manual workers play a dominant role in construction; (4) chemicals are produced constantly whereas work in construction is seasonal; and (5) construction firms are owned as small firms whereas large chemical companies are owned by large corporations.

All of these are dimensions of the social structure of the activities carried out to achieve some ends. These are aspects of the structure that are most likely to vary with technical requirements for achieving those ends.

The Wealth of Society

We have already discussed how the general wealth of a society depends on the efficiency with which activities in general are carried out in that society, and how this in turn produces variations in the composition of the activities of society. The more efficient agriculture becomes, the fewer farmers are needed. The more efficient education becomes, the more education people consume.

It seems likely also that the general level of wealth influences the degree of stratification of societies. Wealthier societies generally have greater differentiation of levels of consumption among social classes than very poor societies. It may be true that feudal societies have the greatest amount of inequality, and the further advances in wealth with industrialization tend to be paid disproportionately to the middle and lower classes. But, in general, when the production of a society is just above subsistence, so that any great inequalities would push some of the people below the subsistence line, these great inequalities are not instituted (cf. Rae Lesser Blumberg, *Stratification*, and Gerhard E. Lenski, *Power and Privilege*).

Different technologies also create different degrees of interdependence of activities using different pieces of valuable goods. For instance, in a modern assembly line, the tools used by a given worker have to be used in conjunction with a conveyor belt, and have to be used *after* the tools used by the worker before him, and *before* the tools used by the worker afterwards. It would be quite inconvenient for these tools to be owned by different people, who might decide not to use them for that particular purpose some week. Hence corporateness of ownership of wealth, with workers being employed by owners of wealth rather than owning their own, tends to be produced by technical interdependence of different pieces of wealth.

Degree of Interdependence

This interdependence in detail in particular work organizations is intertwined with interdependence on a large scale of all the activities in the society. The large sector of the population engaged in transportation and trade are busy knitting together the diverse activities of a multitude of people in diverse places. The converse of the fact that a local drought may influence food prices imperceptably is the fact that a drought halfway across the country or on the other side of the world may also affect prices. One's welfare depends on the activities of people never seen nor heard of, who live in distant places. The devices one has to control that other person's activities—money, law, or world cultural standards—are much more impersonal than the controls needed in more primitive technologies where the interdependence is on a smaller scale.

Social Structure and the Adoption of Technology

The key differences among technological innovations, from a social point of view, is whether or not they require reorganization of the social relations involved in the system of activities in which the old technology was embedded. Quite often there are rather direct relations between the adoption of different types of technologies and the requirements for social changes. In those cases, technological questions become infused with derived motivations from the social order which they are reorganizing. For instance, there is a building on the University of California, Berkeley campus dedicated, in large letters, "TO THE PRESERVATION OF THE NATIVE VALUES OF RURAL LIFE." These values are derived motivations that are threatened by the combined facts of rapid increases in agricultural productivity and much slower increases in the amount people eat. In fact, classes in agriculture are no longer taught in the building. As old structures of activity are undermined by technical advance, any inherent value they had is threatened.

Another example that recurs with technical development in all areas was reflected in a conflict between noble and bourgeois officers in the eighteenth-century French army. The new sciences of ballistics involved learning general principles of mathematics, trajectories, experimental methods of determining the appropriate charge, the smelting of steel, and so forth. Many of the noble officers had neither the talent nor the inclination to learn mathematical skills, nor to experiment with different types of cannon balls. Consequently many of the people (all men, as it happens) competent to be artillery officers were of bourgeois origin, educated in cities in schools rather than in the country on horseback. Giving an important role to field artillery in battles meant giving an important role to men whose only qualifications for leadership was their training in certain abstract and arcane fields, who did not even know how to *vivre noblement*. Although many of the technical developments making field artillery practical on a large scale for an offensive army were introduced in the Old Regime, their rational use and high degree of centrality in tactics waited until after the Revolution, when Napoleon (a highly trained but noble artillery officer) became Consul and Emperor.

Likewise, the social structure of the Karimojong and their cultural values are so arranged that cattle are the only things considered really valuable. In such a situation the introduction of a market distributive technology, by which Karimojong could get money for cattle and buy other things with the money, involves a good deal of reorganization of the whole pattern and style of life. The innovation is only adopted sporadically, when there seems to be no other way to get enough to eat in a particularly bad drought.

Finally, some technical innovations offend the symbolic system of a culture. The Karimojong shower system at the back end of a cow provides all-day protection, but is not likely to replace *Arrid* because it offends American aesthetic sensitivities.

GENERAL COMPONENTS OF TECHNOLOGY

Technology is the transformation of nature into products or services useful to people. In order to transform a natural object such as a block of ore into an automobile ready for a buyer to drive away, energy has to be applied: energy to refine the metal, to shape the parts, to move the automobile to the buyer. But also information has to be added: information about metal refining, forging and machining, the market for automobiles, and the credit standing of the buyer. Energy and information make nature usable by humans.

Energy comes in forms that are more or less expensive for humans. The Karimojong use the cattle's energy to move the herd to grass and water and back to the camp or settlement to be milked or bled, because using cattle energy is less burdensome than humans carrying animals. The French in the eighteenth century used oxen and horses for plowing for the same reasons and used sails to move heavy goods in preference to animal power because the wind was cheaper than animal power. In the United States gasoline or diesel fuel are cheaper than animal power, and (where usable) electricity is less burdensome than petroleum-based power. Much of technological advance consists of making more energy available to transform nature into goods and services.

The overwhelming source of information to control the application of energy throughout human history has been people. It is because the herder knows where to go that the Karimojong have milk to drink. The plowman in the eighteenth century directed animal energy into precisely defined furrows, making it possible for the grain to dominate the natural plant cover. Such plowing is "unskilled" work compared to that of some other humans, but not compared to anything other animals do; it adds a lot of information to draft animals' energy to direct that energy into furrows. Advanced Flemish agriculture in the eighteenth century involved human knowledge of crop rotations, fertilizers, soils, tools, and seasons. The *fusil* threw the bullet with the energy of gunpowder, but with the aim of a human. It is because human beings are the source of the information applied that one requires human "labor" to make goods.

In the United States, information is still supplied mainly by the labor of humans, but it is also stored in libraries and computer tapes to be easily available to those humans. And many processes that supply energy to transform nature are controlled directly by information built into the machine (as, e.g., the fuel and air moisture is controlled by the fixed adjustment of the burner in a furnace) or obtained from automatic recording equipment (e.g., from the thermostat that turns the burner on and off).

While modern technologies can be differentiated from more primitive ones by their use of more energy (obtained in ways that do not burden humans as much) and more information (in the extreme, information detached from humans and built into the machine), particular concrete technologies have their energy supplied and information applied in ways suited to their problems.

The "constraints" that technologies place on human interaction are therefore the constraints on applying energy and controlling it with information. It is because it takes the information of a human to guide cattle that Karimojong men live separately from women and children in the dry season. It is because keeping track of the ownership of millions of car parts would be a lot of effort that repair parts are dealt with by parts wholesalers rather than by the franchised dealers who sell whole automobiles. It is because the information supplied by a worker on an assembly line is reduced to a minimum that factory operatives are easy to replace, whereas the old-fashioned skill of the automobile-constructing craftsman lives on only in the repair shop, where each worker has to supply information enough to make the automobile run again. That is, the "constraints" of technology are the requirements of energy and the requirements of human supply of information.

In fact, most of the constraints are removable, but at a cost. Without the herdsman, cattle have a much higher death rate in semiarid climates, but they still live and can support a few hunters. Without a plowman humans can still grow a few grains with a hoe. One can still make cars by craftsmanship rather than by assembly lines—they do at Rolls-Royce but lose money at it.

In general, one can say that a technology is "constraining" to the degree that an alternative technology takes more (or more valuable) inputs per unit of output. The *araire* was used in southern France because the deep-plowing *charrue* required more animal power, animal power was more expensive (because southern summer pasture had to use arable land), and the output from southern light soils was not much greater if they were deeply plowed. Thus, the southern peasant with a *charrue* would work harder for less output for humans if he devoted much of his land to pasture for work animals. This technical "constraint" had been there since the early Middle Ages, and was part of the reason for the difference in social organization in the northern clay plain and in the South.

Similarly, the many small owners of wholesale firms in the automobile parts trade is a product of "constraint" in the same way: an integrated firm making parts and distributing them through franchised dealers would be a bureaucratic nightmare, and would require much more effort for the same number of parts distributed.

The "forces of production" of Marxist theory are patterns of combinations of energy and information in the production of a particular good with a particular kind of resources. They show a tendency to improve over time, using less human labor, cheaper forms of energy, and more information built into machines or into the genes of plants and animals (Gerald Cohen urges this as a main Marxist hypothesis in *Karl Marx's Theory of History: A Defense*). But they still take a form in particular industries suited to the concrete productive problems of those industries.

For example, we find both many unionized craftsmen and many small entrepreneurs in one-at-a-time industries like construction, movie making, book publishing, machine tool building, shipbuilding, and the like. The entrepreneurs are often subcontractors. This combination of small firms and a highly paid unionized male work force does not fit well with the recent vogue of quasi-Marxist thought on "segmented labor markets." For instance, Charles Tolbert *et al.* (in "The Structure of Economic Segmentation" in *American Journal of Sociology* in 1980) classify construction with stable market, oligopolistic, capital intensive, large firm, "core" sectors like chemicals and petroleum. But the technical constraints of construction do not allow the growth of large oligopolistic firms, the construction market is extremely unstable, and it is impossible to concentrate the skill of the craftsman in the machine as is done in the chemical and petroleum industries. Lack of attention to the technological variations between industries, to the way the forces of production are concretely organized, has led these authors to a foolish classification of construction. The predictions that they hope to draw, for example, about promotion of workers in bureaucratic internal labor markets, stability of employment, vigorous class conflict, lack of worker opportunities to become capitalists, and so on, do not apply to construction craftsmen. Such craftsmen are highly paid male workers, which is their only real similarity to chemical and petroleum workers.

The general point of the technical detail in this chapter is to illustrate that one knows very little about how a technology will be organized by knowing whether it is primitive, feudal, or modern. To understand the impact of technology on social life, Marxist thinkers must enter into the details of what has to be done to supply information and energy to particular classes of productive enterprises.

The same may be said of destructive enterprises, as the impact of the flintlock musket, the bayonet, and mobile field artillery on the social organization of eighteenth-century armies illustrates. A mode of destruction is also application of information and energy in concrete settings, and imposes constraints on those who want to win wars in those settings. Those technical constraints determine the relations people enter into during the course of trying to win wars.

Relations of ownership and of authority in economic and military enterprises, then, depend in part on the exact shape of the technical system, how information is supplied and what energy is used. The variety of technologies discussed in this chapter give rise to the large variety of relations of production, or relations between ownership rights and labor, that are the subject of the following chapter.

4

Economic Organization

In every society, natural and artificial scarce resources (land and capital) have to be brought together with human effort (labor) to produce benefits the society wants (goods and services). People want these benefits, these goods and services, and that is why they put forth the effort and use the resources.

Who gets these benefits? is always a question in which people's appetites combine with their sense of justice, and thus provides the fuel for some of the most passionate social conflicts. Rights to control resources (property rights), rights to parts of the benefits as a reward for human effort (the right to a job, for instance, or the right to a fair day's pay), and other economic rights tend to be strongly institutionalized, because disagreements about who is going to eat during a famine are the stuff of social explosions.

It is convenient to consider the institutionalizations of economic action as having three separate aspects that fit together to constitute a productive system. First, there is a system of *property rights in resources*, in land, buildings, cattle, machinery, and so forth. These property rights enable the property "owners" (which are usually social groups—not individuals) to set up a *system of administration* of the resources so that they can produce benefits. This system of administration, and its relation to the legal order through the property system, is the first fundamental economic aspect of a productive system.

A second fundamental aspect of a productive system is its equivalent of a labor market, a supply of human effort of an appropriate kind, with enough motivation, with a sufficient degree of discipline, and so forth. If the legal unit that constitutes the decision apparatus for controlling the resources (say a family or a corporation) is going to get the required work done, it must also control the right kind and amount of human effort. Getting people to do one's bidding is a different sort of problem than controlling resources; the combination of *authority* over humans and *property rights* over resources is the normative core of economic organizations.

The benefits are the motivation for such organizations, so the division of the benefits constitutes the reward system for guiding resource use and inspiring human effort. The fundamental energy of an economic group is organized around the dynamics of its reward system, that is to say, its division of benefits. If the normative order in economic organization is constituted by property rights and authority, the energy that makes the normative machine go is in the division of benefits.

Every economy above the Robinson Crusoe level must necessarily deal with problems of allocating resources to decision apparatuses, of organizing human effort in conjunction with those decision apparatuses, and of dividing the benefits of the resulting goods and services. We will call these problems the problems of economic organization of the society. They could also be called the problems of stratification of the society, since they deal with the determination of relative levels of goods and services received by members of society.

THE PROPERTY SYSTEM

By a "property right" we mean a socially defensible right to make a decision on how to use a resource. If I "own" a piece of land in the United States, I can decide what use it is to be put to, including any legal uses of my own and also (by sale or renting) any legal uses of my tenants. Most resources have a continuing existence, so such rights in a resource are very often divided up temporally—I control the object during one time period; you control it during another. Such temporal divisions may be for definite periods (*e.g.*, a lease of a farm for a year) or for certain contingencies (*e.g.*, a mortgage giving rights in the contingency that a debt is not paid).

Usually the social entity that has the *ultimate* right in the courts to decide on the use of a resource, the "owner," uses this right to set up some apparatus that makes the day-to-day decisions. Such an apparatus may be set up by legal contracts, as in a leasing arrangment; it may be set up by hiring agents, as when a corporate board of directors hires a company president; it may be a "naturally existing" body such as a family.

The decision unit that has power to decide on the use of a resource for some time period may be an individual (though this is unusual), a family, a corporation, a government, or any type of body with "legal existence." All these types of bodies can "hold property." If a government holds property, it may be held for specific governmental uses (e.g., a space rocket) or for general public (or "common") use (e.g., a public park or road or drinking fountain). Thus, we can distinguish individual or family property, corporate property, governmental specific purpose property, and common property available for various uses to some group of people.

Moveable and controllable goods (chattels) are almost never "common" property, and present different administrative problems than do fixed resources (real property) and so are almost always treated differently in the legal system. When people are thought of as "owned," they also form a distinct legal category.

These various kinds of rights related to resources are outlined in Table 4.1. This list is by no means exhaustive, and is only meant to illustrate that a property system is a web of socially instituted control over decisions on the use of various resources. It is *not* very common for *all* the rights to decide on the use of a fixed resource, say land and buildings, to rest in the same hands. That is, most natural resources in most societies do not have a single "dictator" who holds the rights in all contingencies. Most land and buildings have been leased, or mortgaged, or had feudal encumbrances on them, or otherwise had unclear titles, throughout most of human history. Chattels are much more likely to be owned by a single "dictatorial" decision apparatus (though leasing, mortgaging, and pawning chattels are also common social institutions).

We can think of a particular object, say a piece of land, as a focus of many property rights: rights to affect various decisions about the land between now and doomsday. This bundle of property rights will be divided in a way so that an economic use can be made of the resource, and the division may be quite different in different societies, and for different purposes within the society.

Another angle for looking at the same set of legal phenomena is to consider the resources used in a particular enterprise, say a farm or a

TABLE 4.1

Some Types of Property Rights

Dimension of distinction of property rights	Examples of categories of rights, distinguished by dimensions on the left
Temporal	Permanent ("in fee"); temporary ("leasehold"), contingent (e.g., mortage, life interest, insurance contract)
Object of the right	Fixed ("real property"); movable and controllable ("chattels"); people ("slaves")
Type of social unit with legal control	Individual; familial; extended familial; corporate; governmental
Type of access to property	Restricted ("private"); common (e.g., public accommodations: stores, streets, parks)

factory or an army. The various rights in various objects used by the enterprise will be a *fund* of resources. Many of those resources can be used in other enterprises at other times, so many of them will be held on temporary tenure. This fund of resources used by the enterprise will be constantly changing, as some resources are used up and others come into the control of the enterprise.

A third way to look at the same set of phenomena is that the property right aspects of any given going concern is that aspect that could be defended in the courts by a legal action if necessary, or by an action in the society's equivalent of courts. Because it could be defended by appeal to outside agencies, property is an aspect that does not have to be negotiated or bargained away by its "owner" if he does not want to.

Property rights can be looked at, then, as a bundle of rights in a given object, as a fund of resources of a given enterprise, or as a set of potential actions in the courts that could be taken if necessary. These would be, respectively, an engineer's view, an accountant's view, and a lawyer's view of property rights.

In Karimojong society, there are two broad classes of property. Natural resources, such as water, grass cover, wood, and agricultural land, are thought of as property of the whole tribe or of a territorial section of the tribe. All who are Karimojong (or members of the section) have a right to use these resources, if they get there first. Movable property, of which cattle are the most important form, and capital improvements are owned by families. The head of the family is thought of as owning the herd and owning the other members of the family. Thus the main types of property rights are "common" rights, similar to our rights to use parks or streets, and extended family property rights in cattle, people, and capital improvements. There are few important Karimojong property rights similar to government property used for special public purposes. There is little corporate property of nonfamilial groups. There is little individual property separate from that of the head of a household.

In eighteenth-century France, the dominant resource was agricultural land. Perhaps the most important feature of the property system related to the land is that particular property rights in particular pieces of land were derived from the particular history of tenures on that piece of land. That is, instead of a constant renegotiation of rights and duties in the peasant agricultural enterprise, historical appeals to the classical rights of the landlord and the classical rights and duties of the tenant established multiple property rights in any given piece of land. But these property rights had derived from a different type of landlord–peasant relation, in which the landlord typically lived in the countryside and participated actively in the administration of the estate and in local government. The "servitudes" that had historically been, in a way, payments for landlord services had become pure property rights, often paid to the nobleman in Paris.

The particular network of rights and obligations of the tenant and lord of a particular piece of land was immensely variable, since it depended on a long series of special historical arrangments. There might have been special deals between the tenant's widowed mother and the lord, for instance. These historical rights in turn were embedded in some places in a fairly complex pattern of cooperation in tillage, whereas in other places the isolation of farmsteads rendered cooperation impossible.

Very roughly speaking, the main forms of land tenure were *metayage* and *fermage*, both overlaid with greater or lesser special servitudes. In *metayage*, the crop is divided, usually equally, between the landlord and the peasant. There was, however, a great deal of variation in who bore various costs. The most important costs were seed (about a fifth of the crop), royal taxes, and religious taxes, the *dîme* or tithe. Usually *metayage* involved more active intervention of the landlord in actual operations which was indicated, for example, by shorter terms of lease. *Fermage* was quite similar to a modern lease, being an agreement by the *fermier* to pay a fixed rent for use of the land for a term of years.

The essentials of this agricultural tenancy pattern were common features of the property system in other areas of French life. The decisions about the use of a particular resource were typically encumbered by a variety of simultaneous rights. For instance, the goldsmithing shop "owned" by a goldsmith was subject to special controls by the guild of goldsmiths. The venal officer owned his office, but owed duties to the king. The rights of a craft or merchant guild of a particular town were typically granted by a charter that might be, for historical reasons, quite different from the rights of a similar guild elsewhere. The historical accretion of an immense variety of simultaneous rights in economic resources characterized the property system.

In the United States, there are four main varieties of productive property: (1) "common" or "public" property, especially roads; (2) government property for governmental activity, especially weapons and schools; (3) corporate business property; and (4) family business property, especially in agriculture, the professions, and trade. The common property that anyone can use for specified purposes is secured by positive governmental provision that it be kept free for that common use. (This is legally quite different from the "waste and common land" of unenclosed natural resources of medieval France and England.) Government property is held by national, state, and local governments, administered by the bureaucracy, and controlled ultimately by the law-making bodies at those levels. Corporate business property is legally subject to the decision apparatus of boards of directors, who operate through their agents, the company executives. The stockholder "owners" cannot legally overrule a decision of the board of directors, but can only replace the directors. Family business property is usually considered the property of the active businessmen and to be "individually" owned.

In some contrast to eighteenth-century France, there is extensive provision that all property rights be negotiable and salable. They are evaluated in money terms in internal enterprise administration (in the accounts), in the courts (in damages), and in the market (in price). Historic rights in a piece of land that interfere with its projected use in an enterprise are typically brought out and joined into the enterprise's fund of rights.

THE EMBEDDING OF PROPERTY RIGHTS IN ADMINISTRATIVE SYSTEMS

Usually the person or group that has a socially and legally defensible right to make a decision on the use of the resource does not do so directly. The fund of resources of a large corporation like General Motors consists of rights in millions of different things. The board of directors could not decide what should be done with all rights, even if it wanted to. Instead, the fund of resources is entrusted to an administrative apparatus, of which the property-owning group (the board of directors) is the formal head. Likewise, the fund of animals that constitutes the resources of a Karimojong family may be scattered in different grazing areas, some near the settlement, some far away. At least the moment-to-moment control over the animals is distributed among the boys who herd milk cows and small animals near the settlement and men who herd the cattle at the camps.

That is, the property rights are, in both cases, used to make the activities of an administrative apparatus controlling the resources legitimate. The reason a shop superintendent in a General Motors plant can throw a broken machine part in the junk is that the board of director's fund of resources includes complete rights in that machine part, and they have delegated authority over that right to the superintendent, subject to certain accounting rules and certain authority patterns that they have established. We can say that the property system gives legitimacy to the administrative system that actually produces economic goods. Or we can say that socially defensible right to control goods, which makes up the property right, is delegated to the administrative apparatus under conditions specified by the owner of the property right. Or we can say that the fund of property rights held by an administrative apparatus defines its jurisdiction in the society as a whole—the area and the resources within which the decisions of the administrative apparatus are binding. Except for property rights in goods that are consumed individually and a few productive resources that can be operated by one person, the main significance of a property system is to make the administrative apparatuses that use the resources for some useful purpose legitimate.

It is very hard to give an accurate picture of the variety of administrative apparatuses legitimated by different property systems. Most aspects of the uses of property rights do not appear in court cases, which tell us only about the *challenged* uses of property rights. However, we can broadly differentiate our three examples of societies by their main administrative structures in economic life. Among the Karimojong, the dominant administrative apparatus is the extended family itself. In eighteenth-century France, the dominant administrative form was some form of tenancy, with members of different families having simultaneous rights and simultaneous duties in a farm's activity. In the United States, the dominant administrative form is the bureaucracy of paid officials arranged in a hierarchy.

Among the Karimojong, legal ownership rests in the *elop*, the owner of the family and virtually always a man. He delegates control over his resources almost exclusively to members of his extended family—those who depend on the herd of which he is owner. These may include his wives, his sons, his sons' wives, his grandchildren, and so forth. Only in exceptional circumstances, when he does not have enough kin living with him to make an efficient herding operation, will he delegate rights to control his stock to nonkin, through forming a herding association.

In contrast, the landlord in eighteenth-century France would typically delegate actual control over agricultural land—the main type of resource—to a family of tenants. These tenants were quite often inheritors of the tenancy from the former tenants—sons, widows, or other relatives of the former tenants. The definition of the relative property rights of tenants and lords was one main bone of political contention during the eighteenth century.

In the United States, the board of directors of a corporation, or the legislature and executive branch of a local, state, or federal government, delegate the practical control over resources in which they have property rights to full-time paid officials. These company presidents or cabinet ministers, in turn, set up a structure of salaried officials who control the details of the use of various resources. Instead of a contract, such as that between landlord and tenant, the basis of control is a system of hierarchical authority descending from the board of directors to the person who actually uses the resource. This authority generally has no existence in law and cannot be enforced in the courts.

THE SOCIAL STRUCTURE
OF LABOR MARKETS

Resources are usually used in activities, and activities are done by people. Thus, any administrative system that decides on the use of resources is also a system of authority directing the activities of people. We have to ask how people come to form social bonds with an economic enterprise so that they accept the authority system that gets the work done. We can conveniently discuss this under two topics: How do societies conceive the relationship between the individuals and the economic enterprise? and How do they recruit individuals into the statuses that give them that relation to the enterprise?

Among the Karimojong, the normal relation of a worker to the extended family enterprise is that of family member. This is thought of as a relation of "ownership," in which the head of the family "owns" the family member in somewhat the same way that he "owns" his cattle. People come to be owned by the family head by birth (this is the normal way for males and for young females), or by marrying into the family. Marriage is the main way in which people are exchanged among different economic enterprises—with women moving from the enterprise of their fathers to the enterprise of their husbands or their husbands' fathers. As with other transfers of ownership, cattle are exchanged to validate this exchange of women. That is, kinship and membership in an economic enterprise are conceived of as being two aspects of the same thing—when a woman speaks to her *elop*, she speaks at the same time to the head of the family and the head of the economic enterprise. When one moves from one economic enterprise to another, she changes kinship relations at the same time. (This simultaneity of role relations, and simultaneity of changes of role relations at marriages, is characteristic of primitive societies.)

In eighteenth-century France, many kinship relations had much of the force and significance they have among the Karimojong. But in addition, there were two major forms of relation to economic enterprises that were not based directly on kinship: tenancy and employment. The more important of these two was tenancy. In general, tenancies were thought of as simultaneously a contract and a property right. That is, the tenant was thought, usually in usage and quite often in law, to have a right to continue in the tenancy when the formal term of tenancy came to an end, that is, the tenant had a property right. Quite often the tenant passed these tenancy rights on to his children or to his widow when he died. On the other hand, the landlord had permanent rights to certain rents or other services in payment for the tenant's right to use the land, and sometimes a right to renegotiate the price of the tenancy at the time when it came to an end. In fact, prices (i.e., rents) tended to be quite stable and determined by tradition, especially in areas of *metayage* (share-cropping), though they changed slowly as the supply of labor changed.

Employment paid with wages or a salary was increasing in importance during the eighteenth century with the bureaucratization of the government administration and the growth of urban crafts and commerce. Tenants and employees were legally free, so that the law and the government could not be used to force them into tenancies or employment. In practice, people tended to be recruited to tenancies by inheritance in rural areas, and by free contract to jobs in a somewhat competitive labor market in the cities. In the bureaucracy, higher posts tended to be recruited from among people (virtually all men) who had had experience in lower posts, with some weight given to proper social connections.

In the United States, most people have an "employment" relation to the enterprise they work in. This is thought of as a contract in which they have to give adequate service in return for a wage or salary. If they give adequate service, then (in most of the economy) their seniority rights come into play. These provide, generally speaking, that more senior people at a given rank have a right to be laid off or fired last. The overall result is that enterprises can vary the number of workers they employ with considerable freedom, yet most of the people in the economy have secure employment. Only those with low seniority are likely to be caught in the adjustments of enterprise size except when the adjustments are drastic, as they have been in the automobile industry in the early 1980s and as they usually are in the construction industry. Many of the people of low seniority are women or blacks or young people, so that white male heads of households are moderately secure. Most people in higher positions are recruited from among people working in the same enterprise in lower positions. Recruitment of new people takes place mainly at the lower ranks, among young people. Wages are determined by a combination of three factors: competition in the labor market, ability to pay (determined by the productivity of workers in the industry), and union pressures.

DIVISION OF BENEFITS

The reason people want to control resources is to use them to produce benefits. People furnish effort in economic enterprises in order to get benefits. Benefits provide the motivational force for engaging in economic pursuits, so the organization of the division of benefits is a crucial part of keeping the business going. Furthermore, people take decisions in economic enterprises in the light of their own interests. If the division of benefits changes, their interests change, and hence their decisions change. Class conflicts usually come to focus on the division of benefits. The norms and organizational arrangements for dividing up the benefits of economic enterprises are quite different in the three societies, and this makes both their economic enterprises and their stratification systems work differently.

The fundamental problem of the division of benefits of economic activity is the relation of families to the economy, for in virtually all societies, the dominant consumption unit is the family. Armies, monasteries, men's clubs, and other nonfamilial households are important consuming units in many societies, but only rarely are they more important than families for organizing consumption. The division of benefits, then, is mainly a matter of the relation of families to the economy.

There are three different situations in the three societies in the relation of the family to the economy. In Karimoja the system might be called "family self-maintenance." There is a virtually complete lack of a distributive apparatus that exchanges goods among families on a daily basis (though much exchange takes place on ritual occasions such as marriage). In emergencies there are charitable contributions from one family to another. But normally, the family that runs a herd collects the benefits from that herd and eats them up itself; the benefits are not distributed throughout the society. Since no nonfamilial resources are used, no payment to them is necessary. Since other families produce pretty much the same set of products, there is no advantage to exchange or trade. The division of benefits is, again, part and parcel of the relation of fathers and sons, husbands and wives, brothers and sisters.

Eighteenth-century France was in a period of evolution from a somewhat manorial agricultural economy to a cash tenancy economy. The manorial system had considerable cooperative labor in groups larger than families, often under the active supervision of a local lord. In the cash tenancy economy, each family farmer produced goods and sold them in the market, paying wages for any help he got, then paid the landlord a cash rent for the use of the land. In different parts of France, this monetization of the landlord–tenant relation had reached different levels. It was most developed, naturally, where cash commerce in agricultural goods was most pronounced, in the North and East and in wine-growing areas. The burden of rents and taxes sometimes ranged up to one-half or three-quarters of the total benefits produced by the tenancy. Most of these rents were collected by families of landlords, though the nonfamilial households of the church were also supported from rents and taxes. The economic enterprise, then, yields benefits first of all to the people who work the enterprise, the tenants, who then pay a large part of those benefits (either in money or in kind) to another much richer family because that family historically had property rights in the land the tenants work.

In the United States, practically all goods produced by the enterprise are sold. This creates a flow of money income, usually to a nonfamilial organization. Then there are claims on that flow of money by individuals—workers, stockholders, and pensioners—who take that money and contribute it to a family budget. The income from selling cars, for instance, goes to General Motors as a legal entity. No one can do anything with that income until the board of directors decide who gets what out of it, from a legal point of view. The claims that individual workers, officials, stockholders, or bondholders have against that flow of income are claims against the board of directors, and not (usually) to any particular part of the flow. These wage claims and interest claims and stockholder claims against the flow of income to a nonfamilial organization are the devices linking the individual to the economy.

Families then add up the claims of individual family members in order to construct a family budget. This basic structure of individual claims on flows of income to nonfamilial organizations, which are later summed into a family budget, is also characteristic of the governmental part of the economy, though people do get individual social security rights on the basis of the claims of their kinsmen. The main exceptions to this structure are the familially organized sectors of the economy, especially agriculture, and to some extent trade, and the welfare rolls where there is some claim for a minimum family budget.

In essence, then, all a family gets among the Karimojong is what the family produces. In eighteenth-century France, all the lower-class family got is what it produced. But a system of rents and taxes allowed upper-class families, monasteries, and armies to have budgets made up of economic benefits not produced by themselves. In the United States, families in general do not produce anything, but rather have individuals in them who are productive in other organizations and bring home money to contribute to the family budget.

FLOWS OF INCOME

A second way of looking at the division of benefits is in terms of a division into three different kinds of income: (1) property income, (2) redistributive income, and (3) wage income. Property income is income attributable to ownership and control of resources. Redistributive income is that which is collected by the government or by the church and redistributed to people according to some other criterion than either their property or their work—social security payments, the sustenance of a monk who does not work, or charity are examples. Wage income is that which is directly a payment for work.

In Karimoja the situation is essentially that wage and property income are not distinguished, since the herd and its caretakers both "belong to" the same owner. There is no regular redistributive income flow, though some ceremonial exchanges or contributions of cattle may have a redistributive effect.

In eighteenth-century France, generally speaking, wage income came in the form of the residual profits of the enterprise the worker worked in, after he had paid the rents and taxes to the landlord, the government, and the church. That is, it was the tenant's income that varied most severely with variations in the success of the crops, rather than the rents or taxes on which the upper classes lived. The lower classes were forced into risk-taking so that the government and upper classes could have a steady and predictable income. Most of the income that did not go to the family running the enterprise went to property income. Most taxes went to pay government or church salaries for work performed, or for very large payments of interest on the national debt, but some of it went in a sort of social security for the rich—special pensions for people who had served the king well. Some taxes supported monks.

Compared to the Karimojong and the Old Regime, the most marked characteristic of the United states is the degree to which these forms of income are differentiated. People do not typically work in the same organizations they own. Even if they do have stock in the company they work for they get separate checks for their dividends and their wages, and there is no confusion about which income corresponds to work, which to property. Stock-owning workers certainly cannot, in their role as stockholders, give orders to their foremen. The same is true of redistributive income, mainly Social Security income. This also comes in a separate check and is never confused with salary or property income. Often, in fact, people get only one of these kinds of income. The complete mixing of property and wage income, characteristic of the Karimojong and much of the lower classes in eighteenth-century France, is fairly rare in the United States.

A second distinctive feature of the United States is the amount, and degree of organization, of government redistribution to the poor. The old are the main kind of poor in modern society. Among the Karimojong there is virtually no redistribution between families; in the Old Regime what redistribution there was was mainly to take care of the shabby genteel and the monks and nuns; in the United States, redistribution has been largely substituted for kin group as a means of taking care of the old.

SUMMARY

Every society has to provide some systematic way for making decisions about the use of valuable resources. Because these resources can be used to produce benefits, there is a latent possibility of conflict over the use of the resources. But if the solution of the problem of who is to decide about the use of resources interferes with constructing economic enterprises in such a way that they produce as much benefits as possible, this creates pressures to change the organization of property relations. That is, if the system for arranging for benefits keeps the benefits from being produced, it tends to get reorganized (as G. Cohen, *Karl Marx's Theory of History* points out, this is the central tenet of historical materialism). Thus, property rights, as the socially legitimated part of the organization of the division of benefits, are a central focus of tension between social classes, and also of the tension between forces wanting to reorganize and modernize an economy and the more conservative groups.

But property rights do not of themselves produce anything. Property rights give a person the possibility of calling on the courts or their equivalents in societies without formal courts, but the courts do not produce things to eat. The property rights have to be embedded in a system of authority for running an enterprise. Property rights are generally delegated to others who make the actual day-to-day decisions about the resources. The main forms of delegation among the three societies we are considering are (1) to other family members among the Karimojong; (2) to tenants in the Old Regime; and (3) to salaried officials arranged in a hierarchy in the United States.

But a system of authority is of no use unless it governs someone's activity, and that someone has to be recruited and attached to the enterprise. This recruitment in general involves some participation in the benefits of the enterprise. Among the Karimojong, recruitment is by being born into the enterprise or by marrying into it, and payment is by being permitted to eat out of the common larder. A main form of recruitment in eighteenth-century France was birth into the family of a tenant, though it was no longer the case that the sons of tenants were legally obliged to work for the landlord of their fathers. Payments were a part of the returns from the enterprise, the residual after rents and taxes were paid. In the contemporary United States, a main form of recruitment is hiring young people by free contract, and promotion mainly by seniority within their line of work—often promotion within the same organization; payment is by wages, salaries, and opportunities for promotion. A part of the labor market (agricultural labor, service employment, etc.) is organized as a "free" labor market without seniority rights, nowadays usually called the "secondary" labor market (see, e.g., R. Edwards, et al., *Labor Market Segmentation*), and a part is organized by family enterprises and family recruitment.

The combination of property claims, wage claims, and tax claims on the income produced by the enterprise results in a division of the benefits of the enterprise. This division of benefits must be arranged so that there is sufficient motivation of the resource holders and the workers to continue to participate, or else the enterprise disappears. Any durable enterprise must, therefore, satisfy the resource holders and workers. This is simple when the resource holders, the workers, and the decision-making apparatus are all in the same family, as among the Karimojong. The family simply does not carry out any activities it does not find rewarding. In the Old Regime the main form of division of benefits was payment of rent by the people who ran the enterprise, that is, the tenants. In the United States, the division of the flow of income to a nonfamilial organization is negotiated or bargained out among the various interests involved, who then obtain individual claims to an income. These individual incomes then are summed within the family to make up the household budget.

ECONOMIC ORGANIZATION
OF THE KARIMOJONG

Property, labor, and kinship are so thoroughly interwined among the Karimojong that it is purely a matter of conceptual convenience that we separate the three. One cannot describe the family system without describing the property system, for families are defined by the Karimojong as the group that depends on a single herd. One cannot describe the provision of labor in the family enterprise without discussing marriage and descent, because marriage and descent determine who is within and who outside the family. In order to make the analysis of the Karimojong comparable with the analysis of eighteenth-century France and the United States, I will organize this discussion mainly around ideas of ownership.

The Ownership of Grass and Water:
Men's Natural Resources

There is a sharp division between men and women in Karimojong society in the type of economic activity they mainly do. The men herd cattle, while the women do agricultural work. Two rather different systems of property rights apply to men's and women's resources, both because agriculture is more settled, and because men bear quite a different relation to the family (which uses the resources in common) than do women. Grass and water are the main resources used by the men to keep the herds in good condition, so that herd products will be available. (For this material, see Dyson-Hudson, *Politics of the Karimojong*. Much of the material presented here comes from lectures by Dyson-Hudson.)

Grass and water are not thought of as being individually owned. They are "owned" by the tribe, in the sense that no one outside the tribe has a right to graze cattle in the tribal area without general tribal permission. Such an outsider is subject to raiding and violence if he is caught by

Karimojong, and he has no recourse within the Karimojong legal system. Karimojong cannot attack each other with deadly weapons, nor steal each other's cattle, nor otherwise interfere with each other's use of natural resources for supporting their cattle. Though the territorial boundaries are vague, there is a fairly clearly defined territory within which all Karimojong herds have a right to graze, drink, and walk.

But it fairly often happens that in some particular area there is enough grass and water for one herd, but not enough for two. In that case, there are various bases for individual claims that may hold temporarily. This is not a property right in the modern sense, of a permanent and unequivocal right to deny the use of the resource to everyone else. The general presumption is the opposite, that unless there are exceptional circumstances a man is to be allowed to use what grass and water he needs, where and when he chooses. One cannot give the explanation that he is allowing his cattle to drink the water because he "owns" it and expect to be understood. His claim on the water comes from being a Karimojong, and all Karimojong have, in the abstract, an equal claim.

In the dry season, however, there is not enough water and grass to go around, in terms of being able to keep animals in good condition. There are claims of prior usage, of the "we've always been coming here" variety. There are claims based on "we got here first, and there is not enough here for you too." These claims are not absolute, but are asserted in competition, much as the claim of the right to get into a stream of traffic after a big ball game is asserted in the United States. If necessary, they will solve the conflict by fighting among themselves with sticks, just as we resolve the right to use a crowded street after a ball game by bumping fenders. Spears are not used in such fights among the Karimojong, just as we do not use guns to force our way into a stream of traffic.

A firmer property right is created among the Karimojong by mixing one's labor with a natural resource. For instance, if a man has dug a water hole, it is possible for him to allege that another man has stolen his water hole. He can bring him into court for a judgment (only men can bring people to court among the Karimojong). He could not claim among the Karimojong that the other man is stealing his water, because the water belongs to everybody—to his opponent as well as to himself. But he has put in labor to make a water hole for his animals, and when another man uses the water hole without his permission, it is rather like stealing "equipment" rather than stealing the resource.

Similarly, wood collected for making houses or other utensils is not regarded as anyone's property until it is collected and brought into the settlement. It belongs to the tribe as a whole, in the sense that anyone outside the tribe is likely to be attacked inside the territory, and one is unlikely to collect much timber in an area where he or she will be attacked. But just by being Karimojong, one gets the right to use any such natural resources.

The Ownership of Agricultural Land: Women's Resources

Whereas the herding land toward the outside edges of Karimojong territory is claimed by the whole tribe, the central portion used for settlement and agriculture has a slightly more complex ownership structure. The basic ideas are the same—claims on natural resources only come about when people mix their sweat with the soil. Agricultural work involves the investment of labor in the land as does building a relatively permanent settlement. These investments of labor tend to be done in the same place month after month. And the area used is small enough so that a person can actually survey it, watch over it, and actively interfere in anyone else's use of it.

Thus, although the ideas about ownership seem rather strange to Western people who think of everything as owned by *somebody*, the practices about agricultural land approach more closely the pattern we might call "private property." But this property right does not pertain to the individual who made the investment of labor. In the typical case most of the labor invested in a piece of agricultural land will be the investment of a woman. But women are exchanged between kin groups through marriage. When a woman marries and leaves a kin group, she moves into the household where her husband lives and takes up a piece of agricultural land there. Her right in the land she worked on before lapses and passes to the kin group she lived with at that time.

In order to understand the property system in agriculture, it is necessary to ask how the Karimojong think about the group structure of society in relation to the property system. Individual investments of labor in a garden plot or elsewhere are, so to speak, credited to the account of some group. They establish the property rights of that group. That group, in its turn, has to be recognized in order to be legally permitted to make use of those resources and to establish its claims— a foreigner from an enemy tribe cannot settle and invest his wife's labor and derive a valid claim from it.

The central section of Karimoja territory, where the settlements are located, is divided into sub-areas associated with major social groups, which Dyson-Hudson (1966) calls "territorial sections." These territorial sections are thought of as owning all the land in their settlement area, in somewhat the same way that the tribe as a whole is thought of as owning the herding land near the outside borders of the tribe. The major difference is that people from other territorial sections are not excluded from using the area for settlements or gardens. Instead, in order to use it, outsiders from other sections have to ask permission of people in the section which owns it. The way it operates is that the male of a family that wants to settle in a particular place goes to the nearest small settlement unit that he can see (the nearest "neighborhood") and gets permission to settle. A neighborhood is a handful of settlements scattered over something like a square mile. Implicit in that permission to settle is permission for the women to use garden land, since, of course, they cannot survive otherwise. Any neighborhood can act as an agent of the territorial section, and give permission to settle, and hence allow the establishment of something like squatters' rights in the section's land and gardens. In each settlement within the neighborhood, there would be one or more families with their associated herds and wives and garden lands.

Thus, the property rights in the settlement are all thought of as pertaining to the family group that has been given permission to settle by members of the territorial section. Of course, that group's concrete membership will change, as people die, or as women marry and leave the settlement, or as men bring their wives home, or as children become adults. But the entity that "owns" the resources created by their collective labors is the family that has been given permission to settle. Within the family, particular gardens are thought of as the property of the woman who works them, though she really has more a "right of use" than ownership. She could not defend her right of use of a particular piece of land before a court, because women do not bring grievances to court among the Karimojong. Her rights lapse when she stops working the land, for instance, when she moves to another family on marriage. They will probably be taken up again by a woman who married into the group.

The Ownership of Cattle

Without cattle a Karimojong man cannot act like a human being: cannot marry, cannot worship, and cannot participate in politics. He is civilly dead, without rights or duties, without prospects nor capacity to make promises and contracts. Consequently, the organization of ownership of cattle is central to the total social organization of the Karimojong.

The basic property-owning unit for cattle is the household, and the head of the household is considered as owning the herd and owning the people in the household. That is, no agreement about the disposition of part of the herd would be considered valid or defensible in the courts, unless the head of the household consented. There can be only male heads of households, and so only males are thought of as owning cattle. Sometimes there are women that appear to own cattle, but on closer examination it always turns out that they are thought of as holding the cattle in trust for male children. Sometimes a girl's father gives her cattle to hold for her children—perhaps children born in the father's household before the girl was married. Her husband does not have the right to sell or dispose of these animals, and in that sense she is their "owner." But she is a guardian of the animals.

Of course, as a practical matter, women have to get products from cattle—especially milk and blood. They have, in fact, a *right* to animal products. When milk animals are left in the settlement, they are usually left in the care of a particular woman who has the right to dispose of the products of the animal. The animal is not thought of as belonging to her, but rather to the head of her household (her husband, her husband's father, or, before marriage, her own father).

The herd under a particular ownership constitutes, then, a fund of resources on which the family depends. Just as the fund of resources that constitutes the "investment" of a corporation in the United States may be thought of as creating and constituting the corporation, so the herd can be thought of as creating and constituting the family. When a boy leaves the home of his father with a part of the herd to set up an independent herding enterprise, he is also setting up a family. The animals born into the herd become part of the herd and have the same ownership as their mother.

For certain purposes an independent herd may be considered by the Karimojong to be a fragment of the herd from which it was created. That is, it may be thought of as part of the herd of *the father of* the head of the household. For instance, the bridewealth paid for the first wife of a young man is generally obtained from the various fragments of the herd of the grandfather of a man—what are now usually of course, the independent herds of his father and his father's brothers. Likewise, when the head of a household dies and he does not have sons eligible to inherit his widow (e.g., he may have had only one wife, and his son could never inherit his own mother as a wife), she may pass to the family that depends on any fragment of the herd from which her husband's herd was created. These fragments are the same set of herds from which her bridewealth was paid. In a sense, then, herds have "lines of descent," and for certain purposes are thought of as belonging to a fictional household, which no longer exists, to which their ancestors belonged.

The Ownership of People

Women and children are property among the Karimojong, in the sense that they are considered as being owned. This is an aspect of the interpenetration of spheres of life, so that people who appear in one aspect of life, as for instance, loved ones, appear in the economic context as valuable resources. This means that the word "to own" does not have the purity of meaning that it has in a society in which one never owns his kinsmen. The possessive "to own" has a mixture of meanings, ranging from the possessive meaning of "my" in the phrase "my mother" in English, to the meaning of "my" in the phrase "my spending money." When we say that people are "owned" among the Karimojong, it is important to keep in mind that the relationship of owning among people occurs between men and their wives and children and grandchildren. They love their wives and children and feel themselves to have obligations to them. But there is an aspect of their relation to their wives and children that is sufficiently analogous to their relationship with their cattle (which they also love) that they refer to it as "owning" the people.

The labor group that cares for, and depends on, a given herd is just an aspect of the family. The relationship of each person to the herd is an aspect of his or her relationship to the owner of the herd—the head of the household. The owner of the resources on which they depend is also their husband or father, who is the same as their legal and political representative to the outside world. The word *elop* means, strictly speaking, "the owner." It means, at the same time, head of the household, owner of the herd of animals, and owner of the people who make up the family that depends on that herd.

This conception is reflected in the arrangements for marriage in which property of one kind (cattle) is exchanged for property of another kind (women). When these property rights pass, the children and women become the "property" of the *elop* and his descendants, and the progeny of the cattle become the property of the family who have received them as bridewealth. The basic function of these arrangements is to make it possible to make statements of ownership about women and children—to know for sure who they "belong to." The bridewealth has a role much like the idea of a "consideration" in English and American common law of contracts. If Americans give up something of value in a contract for no "consideration," it is presumed by our courts that the contract is the result of fraud, or incompetence, or of some illegal arrangement not mentioned in the contract itself. Such a contract without a "consideration" cannot transfer property rights in a binding fashion in Anglo-American law. Likewise, in order to carry out a binding transfer of a woman and her reproductive powers to a new kin group—that of her husband—the Karimojong consider it necessary that there be a "consideration." The only thing of "consideration" among Karimojong are cattle.

Bringing the Kin Group and Work Requirements into Correspondence

The Karimojong ideal of an economic unit is an extended family big enough to provide the labor to look after the animals, and a herd of cattle big enough to support that extended family. In fact, this is quite a tricky thing to achieve. What one gets in case of failure of correspondence between labor requirements and family size is a herding association. A herding association essentially consists of a man with a lot of cattle and not enough labor together with a man with too many mouths to feed and too much labor for his amount of cattle. By adding together these two imperfect families, one gets a viable economic unit—a large enough herd for the number of people and enough people to take care of it properly.

But we can, in a way, think of the extended family itself as the preferred form of a herding association. The penchant for forming extended family households can be considered as a very strong preference for that type of herding association made up of a father with his married and unmarried sons. The main difference between extended families and herding associations is that in herding associations, they keep very close track of exactly who has property rights in which cattle and which people. In the extended family household, all the property rights that will later be divided among the sons are held in common as family property.

We can give a rough indication of what is "enough labor" and "not enough labor." Below a certain point, the amount of labor that Karimojong need for economic exploitation has nothing to do with the size of the herd they are looking after. It is, rather, the result of the different elements out of which the herd is made up. A herd contains grazing animals (cattle) and browsing animals (especially goats). These have to be kept in different places to feed, since the goats can live off the vegetation of the overgrazed area near the settlements while the cattle cannot. In the cattle herd there are immature animals, mature animals, and milk cows with suckling calves. Each of these has to be treated in a different way to get the best results from it.

For economic efficiency, even a moderately small herd needs a minimum of about four herd boys and a herd owner directing them. The owner needs a boy of five years of age or older to watch the calves from the milk herd close to the settlement. He can be very small, as much a baby as the animals he is looking after, because he is working in very secure conditions. A boy of eight or older is needed to herd the smaller animals, sheep and goats, in the scrub country close to the settlement. He has to be older and have some sense of responsibility, for he will sometimes be out of sight and hearing and must control more indepen-dent-minded animals, but this is a fairly safe job. The settlement also needs a boy in his teens to take care of the adult animals from the milk herd, to graze them beyond the overgrazed area adjacent to the settle-ments, and to bring them back in the evening. Finally, the herd in the cattle camp can never be left alone, but is too far out to bring back to the settlement. Hence, there need to be at least two people in the cattle camp, so that one of them can visit the settlement at a time. Because this is a most dangerous and responsible position, both of these two herders must be adults or near adulthood. For reasonable efficiency in the wet season, then, a minimum for any reasonable size herd with a reasonable mixture of components is a man and four males of staggered ages. In emergencies, which come fairly frequently in the form of a bad dry season, this table of organization may be quite inadequate to keep the herd going.

The fact that the minimum size of a work group is larger than the small family of the father and minor children, combined with a strong preference for family enterprises and a strongly familial conception of property, creates considerable economic pressure to keep the extended family together.

The Economic Failure of Families

Cattle ownership is the only way to form a Karimojong family, to participate in the religious and political life of the tribe, and to be re-garded as a real Karimojong. But the Karimojong live in an uncertain environment, with raiding on their herds from neighboring tribes, ep-idemic disease, and other catastrophes that can completely destroy a family's herd. In such a case, men cannot contruct social units that are self-supporting, and there are no other kinds of social units to support them except other families. Such men become dependents of other fam-ilies. Families with big herds may welcome them. They usually settle at the cattle camp helping with the more dangerous and unpleasant work away from the settlement in return for enough to eat. Karimojong say that if the owner of the cattle is very generous, he might from time to time give him an animal—he might pay him with a handful of animals out of strict generosity. Such men of ruined fortune are, of course, easily recruited for a raiding party to try to steal cattle from neighboring tribes. They are already socially dead, so the loss to themselves and to other people is fairly small if they also physically die. But, if they get cattle, they can live again and form families and take part in civil society.

Summary

The two primary economic units in Karimojong society are the tribe as a whole, which holds and defends the natural resources of the tribal area for the common use of tribal members, and the family. The key problem of a herding economy that tribal property and tribal defense of tribal territory solve is that in marginal environments, a herd needs access to more natural resources than a family can enclose and defend for themselves. Furthermore, such marginal environments force rapid adaptations to changing conditions. The area that supported the herd last year may not be adequate this year. A common overall policy of defense of tribal resources against outsiders, combined with a shifting and opportunistic organization of rights to use the resources within the herding area, is most appropriate to the technology and the environment.

Cattle, on the other hand, are fairly easy to keep track of, to stay near to, and can be defended and watched by a small group. They are the central resource of the Karimojong economy that can be effectively appropriated by small groups of people and are therefore the main form of "private property." They are, that is, the main resource owned by a group smaller than the tribe as a whole. A family is defined as a unit that owns cattle—that depends on a given herd. The family is owned by the same owner who owns the herd.

Labor is exchanged among these herd–family units by marriage, when young women leave the herd–family of their parents to go to the herd–family unit of their husband. This labor exchange is, in effect, an exchange of property rights in the woman, and these property rights have to be paid for in cattle in order for the transfer of ownership to be considered valid. Labor is also exchanged among herd–family units by the formation of herding associations made up of a family with too many sons and not enough cattle and a family with too many cattle and not enough sons. The requirement for a relatively large minimum labor force to take adequate care of a herd tends to encourage extended family households.

Except for ceremonial occasions, there is no redistribution of income outside the extended family. This general rule is broken in cases of grave emergency, as when a man has lost all his cattle in raids or epidemics. But such situations are considered specifically exceptional and often involve the man helped giving up virtually all his rights and duties as a Karimojong and becoming a secondary member of someone else's family. He has no rights in that family.

THE ORGANIZATION OF WORK
IN THE OLD REGIME

The main sectors of economic activity during the eighteenth century in France were agriculture and government. Commerce and manufacturing were considerably less important, in terms of people employed or value produced. Consequently, the dominant forms of organization of work were those employed in agriculture and government.

The Organization of Agriculture

There were three main types of land tenure arrangements in the Old Regime: *fermage* was similar to what we call renting; *metayage* was similar to what we call sharecropping; and a fair number of plots were held in what was essentially ownership by the peasant.

In *fermage* the tenant (called a *fermier*) paid a fixed rental, usually in money, for the use of the land. He (the tenant was usually male, and texts from the Old Regime speak as if it would always be a male, so we will use "he" for tenants and landlords here) usually provided much of the working capital (seeds, tools, animals for traction, etc.). Since he would not make such an investment without some assurance of being able to stay on the land, the contracts tended to be for a longer period than a year (generally six–nine years). Since this whole arrangement involved a monetization of the tenancy relationship, it tended to be most characteristic of those areas where more of the produce of agriculture was sold on the market, for instance, in the Siene and Loire basins.

The general supposition in *fermage* is that the tenant can take care of himself and is a businessman in his own right. He is not "ruled" by his landlord, and the landlord does not interfere actively in the administration of the farm. Since the obligations of each are stated in money and negotiated explicitly at the time of signing the lease, there is much less vagueness and diffuseness of the obligations of the landlord to "take care of" the tenant, or of tenant to "render service to" his landlord.

Since the landlord did not have to arrange for working capital, nor measure the size of the crop to make sure he was not cheated on his rent, he did not have to keep a close watch on the administration of agriculture. He could easily live in the city away from the land. He is not thought of as the ruler of the peasants with general obligations to see to it that they are all right. Consequently, in *fermage* there is no necessary relation between the landlord and the lord, between ownership of a piece of land and belonging to the governing class. When the bourgeoisie invested in lands (which were usually near cities), they were more likely to rent the lands out in *fermage* than in *metayage*.

Metayage was much more characteristic of the areas of less commercialized agriculture, because when the product was not monetized by entry into commerce, it seemed less natural to monetize tenancy relations. *Metayage* often involved much more landlord intervention in the administration of the agricultural operation, for the landlord provided much of the working capital. Landlords, however, often worked through local agents, petty bourgeois people from local cities and towns, in carrying out this intervention. Generally, *metayage* was more common when there were dispersed plots of land in mountainous areas or small enclosed farms. If the renter is to provide nothing but the labor of his household, the natural size of farm for him is a family-sized plot. (Since the *fermier* is more of a businessman, providing capital as well as labor and administrative talent, he may be able to use a larger farm.)

Metayage tended to be an exchange in kind, where the landlord actually furnished the capital equipment (rather than just paying the bills), and actually took a part of the physical crop (rather than receiving an appropriate payment). In general, exchange in kind leads toward traditionalization and stereotyping of the terms of exchange. Rents tend to be determined (in the short run, at least) according to the status of the people, rather than by market competition. There was considerably less variation in the rents paid in *metayage* than in *fermage*, with tradition giving the appropriate rent as half of the main crop. Since the seed for planting, usually reserved before division, amounted to about a fifth of the crop, and since incidental products of the land (pasturage for cows, a vegetable garden, etc.) were not included in the share arrangements, the rent amounted to somewhat less than half of the net income from the plot. There was considerable variation in the extent of taxes and seigneurial dues paid by the peasant.

Generally, in *metayage* the overall result of the greater physical isolation of the farm, lesser independence of the peasant, traditional and stereotyped rates of exchange, and diffuse relationships of lord to peasant rather than of landlord to businessman, tended to give a more traditional and "feudal" cast to areas of *metayage* as compared with *fermage*.

In eighteenth-century France, there was no legal notion corresponding exactly to our idea of "clear title," or "ownership in fee simple." All land was thought of as being "burdened" with obligations. From the Old

Regime point of view, land merely differed in the degree and amount of various obligations that had to be paid by the man who worked it, rather than being classified into two clear classes of "owned" and "held in tenancy." Consequently, there is no consensus on how many of the French peasants in the eighteenth century "essentially owned" their land, in the sense of being able to sell it, use it as they pleased, and having to pay nothing except "normal taxes." Taxes and rents were not distinguished in early feudal society and were only in the process of becoming clearly distinguished during the eighteenth century.

Estimates of how many peasants "owned" their land range from about 10–40%. These differences in estimates mainly involve differences in the way people treat various seigneurial dues and feudal obligations that were destroyed by the Revolution. If all those people who only owed those types of dues and rents that were abolished by the Revolution are considered to have "owned" their plots during the eighteenth century, the estimate of 40% of peasant owners is probably nearer. If only those who, in the eighteenth century, already paid only those taxes that were paid by a full owner after the Revolution, then the appropriate estimate would probably be nearer 10% of peasant owners. Whichever way it is considered, it is clear that there was a substantial body, probably close to 40%, of the peasantry who had tenures that were quite valuable to them, which they would defend with that sense of self-justification that a countryman feels when he is defending "his own" property.

The principal social feature of this type of agrarian structure is a sharp social division between a land-owning class collecting rents and a cultivating class paying rents. The landlord is typically not an active entrepreneur intervening in the administration of his estate in order to make it as profitable as possible, but a *rentier* passively accepting rents. In general, a landowner need not devote himself to getting rich—or rather, a noble landlord may try to get rich by getting into royal favor, but not necessarily by active agriculture. There were noble "improving landlords," but many landlords lived off their rents. Agricultural rents are often regarded as a source of income on which a person can live comfortably, *vivre noblement*, without having to concern himself with the dirty business of making money.

In the nobility (who made up a large part of the land-owning class), this was a rather explicit code of honor, and the "improving landlord" was not as much a hero in the French aristocracy as in the British. Of course, not all of the nobility lived up to the ideal of not thinking about the sources of their incomes, and agricultural practice did respond, if sluggishly, to changes in prices. With the increase of prices of grain during the eighteenth century, new lands were brought under the plow, with the corresponding investments in drainage and clearing, which were made mostly by landlords. Tenants, especially in the commercialized northern plain, were introducing the more modern forms of agriculture with crop rotation and artificial manuring.

Broadly speaking, whatever the form of tenancy, the basic work group was the peasant family as a whole. This family group did the work necessary for the plot to produce, being directed in this activity by the father. In most cases where there was hired labor, it was incorporated into the household of the family that cultivated the farm as "domestics." Generally, women did more of the work near the house, including household chores, gardening, caring for small animals, and perhaps milking. Men did more of the large-scale activities of cultivation farther from the house (farmlands were not always concentrated near the house of the peasant).

Some of the men's work tended to be performed collectively rather than on a family-plot basis. The extent to which the French peasantry formed relatively tight-knit communities with cooperative work has received contrasting evaluations. Turgot, who became a reforming prime minister and Enlightenment thinker, and whose experience in local administration was in the mountainous regions of south-central France, thought each village was a collection of huts, without the slightest trace of communal life or collective will.

Land held in common and exploited by sporadic individual effort, especially forest and pasturelands, was, in the more advanced regions, tending to pass out of collective property and to become individual property, as it was brought under the plow. There was almost never common exploitation by cooperative tillage of the soil of the common lands. The common lands were what we have called "common" property, similar to our streets or parks, rather than "public" property exploited by the public for specific activity, like our post office buildings. It is also clear that peasant villages and valley neighborhoods formed a locus of public opinion formation about taxation and land tenure questions. These pockets of rural public opinion formation became important during the Revolution. (See Theda Skocpol, *States and Revolutions;* both the sections on France and those on Russia illustrate the point.)

The overall picture, then, is one of a set of families working the land in family-sized plots (often scattered some distance from their house), producing a crop of grain and some other agricultural products, and selling much of this crop to pay rents and taxes to support various landlords, clergymen, and government officials. These latter groups, in general, did not interfere very actively in the administration of the agricultural enterprise, though they were more active in areas of *metayage* than in areas of *fermage*. The degree of commercialization of the farm and the degree of monetization of the tenure relationships varied among the regions of France and generally increased during the century. The historical rights of the nobility were being turned into cash rental transactions, with the cash going increasingly to support a noble life in Paris or other cities rather than in the countryside.

The Organization of Governmental Work

By the eighteenth century, most of the things we now think of as governmental functions were carried on by the formal government apparatus, with the king at its head. Such functions as the upkeep of a military establishment, building roads, inspection, regulation, and taxation of economic activities, welfare measures in disaster, administration of justice, circulation of mail, and protection of travelers on the road, had all become the province of the royal government. They were no longer functions that pertained to the landlord of an area, as had been much more characteristic in the Middle Ages.

But what is striking is the variety of ways in which the government undertook to perform them. (Much of the following is based on a lecture by Sasha Weitman.) Whereas in contemporary France, most of these activities are *bureaucratically* managed by agencies of the central government with salaried officials, in the Old Regime the government experimented with various ways to administer these functions. Each of the various types of social organization of task performance led to slightly different results and generated different problems and by-products.

Administration through Venal Officers

Many of the officers of the Old Regime were paid from the fees they charged for performing the services, the fines they imposed on offenders against the law, by admission fees, rents of stalls in government markets, or similar devices. Many of these offices generated more return in fees than the cost of a person (usually a man) to run them. One way the government had of filling such offices was to sell tenure in the office to a family. In that way, the government received payment in advance for the returns from the office, which was an indirect way of borrowing money on the expected returns from the office. Institutions of credit and money creation were not well developed in the eighteenth century to finance government loans; this was a substitute.

Administration by venal officers had the disadvantage that once an office was sold, the government could no longer determine what was to be done by the official. The official tended, naturally, to emphasize those parts of his functions that brought in fees, and probably to shade his official acts in favor of those decisions that brought him higher fees. Venal officials resisted any sort of administrative reform that would bring their functions more under governmental control, just as the landed aristocracy resisted interference with the tenure arrangements that brought them their income.

Administration through Farmers

Many of the royal taxes were collected by a system of tax farming. The tax farmer "rents" or "leases" the right to collect certain taxes (created by laws of the government) for a fixed rental fee, or sometimes for a share of the proceeds. Then, the government lets him (tax farmers were very often partnerships of financiers) use the coercive apparatus of the state to collect the taxes. After he "leases" the tax, everyone owes the tax to him rather than to the government.

Probably the most famous of the tax farmers in the Old Regime was Lavoisier, the chemist who discovered the functions of oxygen in combustion. He was executed along with other general tax farmers during the Revolution. A primary result of tax farming is public wrath. Probably the reason is that taxes only become legitimate, if they are legitimate at all, by the functions that the government performs with those taxes. If tax collection is done by private individuals, and the taxes go to his private purse (though that individual's payments have made it possible for government functions to be performed), that last squeeze of the tax laws that really hurts is applied for his personal enrichment. This may serve the function of taking the onus for unpopular taxes off the king and the royal government, but it is dangerous for the tax farmers in the long run.

Administration through Grant of Powers

During the Middle Ages, a rather typical pattern of administration was a more or less complete grant of sovereignty to a lord in return for services rendered or for some expression of fealty. That is, a king would administer a conquered or expropriated territory by appointing someone else as permanent "proprietor" of the government of the whole territory. The control of the territory then largely passed out of the royal hands, and the laws applying within the area become those of its new governors. This system was no longer used in metropolitan France during the eighteenth century, but some of the colonies were still administered through this system (as were Maryland and Pennsylvania in the English colonies of North America).

Administration by Tutelage

Crafts and manufacturing, municipal services, and a few other areas were administered by granting a charter of incorporation to guilds or municipal corporations that selected their own memberships and had their own governing bodies. The Crown then influenced their corporate behavior by manipulating rewards and punishments—by defending or interfering with corporate monopolies, by granting or not granting tax concessions, and so forth. In order for such tutelage to work, some of the privileges that the Crown can grant to the corporation need to be capable of manipulation by the Crown—that is, some of the rights must not be guaranteed by a firm charter which the Royal government agrees not to interfere with.

The general effect of such corporate grants of privileges was to create an oligarchy in the corporation that restricted entry into the corporation and restricted "citizenship" in the guild or municipality to a small part of the concerned public. This tended to undermine respect for local and occupational governments and led to clamors on the part of the affected population for direct intervention of the central government and destruction of the *corps intermédiaires* during the Revolution.

Administration by Régie

Direct management of governmental services by salaried governmental agents arranged into bureaus with specialized functions is called *bureaucratic* administration, or administration by *régie*. This form of administration was increasing throughout the eighteenth century, replacing other forms of public administration when they were too inefficient, corrupt, unprofitable, or unpopular. A corps of officials was developing who devoted their careers full time to public service, and who had a professional ethic of technically adequate and nonpolitical service. An example of this development in the royal bureau of bridges and roads was discussed in the previous chapter. This form of administration was also used in the military establishment, national police (*maréchaussée*), secret service, horse-breeding and horse training establishments, and many other areas of public administration.

Thus, the overall characteristic of the social organization of governmental services is its tremendous complexity and variety. This mixture of forms of administrative structure presents problems not only to those who wish to describe and understand them as we do here, but also to those who want to keep them under control, as the King of France. Many of the administrative forms were especially open to officials' insubordination, disobedience, or subversion of the purposes of the King. Difficulties of discipline were caused especially by corruption, but also by open refusal to do what the King wanted. Without a clear hierarchy and without an ethic of service to the state regardless of personal interest, the King was often pushed into sending one officer to check up on the another. Often the King could not remove a corrupt, inefficient, or insubordinate official without creating more trouble than it was worth. He could not easily change the jobs of many officials who had bought offices that later had become obsolete. Many of the administrative arms of the government had problems of legitimacy, especially some of the more profitable local and guild oligarchies and most of the tax farming apparatus. In many cases, bad service to the King was combined with a public feeling of illegitimacy of privileges in the same irremovable and unmanipulable administrative structure. This rigidity of the bad parts of the state apparatus is one of the causes of the Revolution.

The Legitimacy of Rents and Taxes in the Old Regime

In retrospect, after the Revolution, we can judge that the tenure system in agriculture, parts of the taxation apparatus, and parts of the monoploistic guild organizations were thought to be illegitimate by subjects of the Old Regime. It is possible for people to come to opinions that they never held before in an unusual situation like the Revolution. But generally massive and passionate movements—such as those abolishing tax farming, those abolishing certain so-called feudal rents and dues, and those abolishing privileged corporations—have roots in the society before the Revolution.

Alexis de Tocqueville (1856), in his book on *The Old Regime and the French Revolution,* has essentially argued that this extensive illegitimacy of landlords (and hence of the nobility as a class)—of many taxes, and of *corps intermédiares*—was due to the process of administrative reorganization going on in the society as a whole, particularly in the government. He says that when the landlords who served as the local government actively intervened in the managment of their estates and lived in the local area, their status was legitimate. Hence, the returns from the land, needed to support a noble style of life, were also legitimate. When the nobility's local political function was taken over by officials of the central government, when the noble living in Paris had only an interest in the cash income from rents, leaving supervision of agriculture to the peasant, then noble income from the land comes to be seen as mere extortion.

According to de Tocqueville the process of reorganization itself involved the invasion of the ancient prerogatives of venal officers, privileged corporations, nobles, and so forth. The accusations and counteraccusations of officials trying to do their jobs, and privileged people trying to defend their ancient hallowed rights and incomes, undermined the legitimacy of both structures. But the structure of the central government at least had the advantage that it did in fact render services, build roads, and raise armies. Often the venal officers, privileged corporations, and local nobles were only too glad to get rid of the obligations to render the services that supposedly justified their positions of privilege.

What de Tocqueville is suggesting, then, is that the legitimacy of rents and taxes depends on how well the payments are thought to correspond to services rendered. A correspondence between the structure of property rights and the structure of work group authority would tend to make rents legitimate. A correspondence between the agencies of government that collect taxes and the agencies that render services out of those taxes likewise increases the legitimacy of taxation. When landlords for generations make no contribution to the development or administration of a farm, or when tax farmers appear to be collecting taxes to go into their personal pockets, the rents and taxes they collect tend to become illegitimate.

The Organization of Commerce and Manufacturing

In the eighteenth century, trade and urban manufacturing were not as differentiated as they are now. Butchers cut and sold meat, instead of meat-packing companies selling to the stores that eventually sell to customers. Printers sold books and newspapers; cabinetmakers sold furniture; shoemakers sold shoes. There were, of course, merchants who handled agricultural goods or imports that they did not produce, but there were very few manufacturers who did not also sell their products at retail. Most of the pure manufacturing enterprises were in textile manufactures. Shops were generally small. The most common structure was the family firm with apprentices who were often partially incorporated into the family household. This family enterprise made the product, carried on the commerce, and waited on the customers.

Many of these family businesses were organized into local guilds. These had a collective legal existence as chartered corporations, often a collective sacred existence celebrated by eating together and attending services together in honor of a patron saint, and a collective economic existence by having a guaranteed monopoly over licensing family firms to make and sell goods in their line. Guild monopolies concerned end products rather than specific production processes—it is hard to keep someone from doing a particular kind of work, but not hard to keep him or her from selling a particular product in a local market. Therefore, the enterprises the monopolies licensed tended to do all stages of the production of a particular good. There was vertical integration into one firm and guild of production processes from raw material to finished products, rather than the modern form of process specialization where firms do the same work on several different products.

Guilds had political rights over their membership, rights of taxation, discipline, expulsion, and admission. There were three classes of membership: masters, journeymen, and apprentices. Masters were those with rights to have firms in business in the line of work of the guild. Apprentices were supposedly in training to become journeymen. Journeymen were qualified workmen who had to be paid wages for their work, but who were not masters. Political rights within the guild, to play a role in guild decision making, were different for different classes of membership: masters had more rights than the other two groups.

One criterion of membership in the craft guilds was a demonstration of competence. Where this was appropriate—when the guild produced a complete product rather than, for instance, being a craft in the construction industry—this test of competence took the form of a "masterpiece," a product made by the candidate to show that he was thoroughly competent. The master's thesis was a corresponding requirement for admission to full membership in universities, and for the license to teach there, for universities were also divided into apprentices and masters.

The overall effect of this sytem was to give a body of small businessman–workers in an industry a monopoly. Bodies of people rarely vote themselves out of jobs and rarely encourage competition with themselves by new firms with a new organization. In fact, much of guild treasuries were spent in litigation challenging other guilds that had (they maintained) invaded their monopoly. Royal power was too great for these jurisdictional squabbles to reach outright warfare—as they did in some of the small states of Germany and Italy. But such monopoly claims tended to make any innovation in manufacturing a subject of crippling litigation. New forms of capitalist organization, such as the putting out system in textiles, were located in rural areas partly to avoid guild regulations.

Since the post of "master" within the guild was at the same time a position of ownership of a family business, and also a legal qualification to practice a certain trade, there was alternation between nepotistic family criteria for filling openings and criteria of skill. In some cases, for instance, guilds had by-laws which provided that a master's post would automatically revert to his widow, regardless of her qualifications, so that she could keep the business open.

Summary

The basic form of property rights in eighteenth-century France was simultaneous tenancy by a landlord and a peasant in a piece of land. Subordinate forms of property rights in the society included the holding of the right to do business by being a master in a guild, ownership of venal offices, or rights to use common forest and pastureland for the people of a certain village. With a good deal of variation, and some growth of bureaucratic forms of administration in the government, the basic administrative apparatus that made use of a property right was a family, and most of the rural and urban economic enterprises were carried out by a family firm.

People, and families, were free to move into and out of various types of tenancy relations, to take up guild membership, and so forth. There was legal economic freedom in the limited sense that a person did not have to stay in the same business that he or she had been in. But if a person wanted to use the property rights accumulated by his or her family, to use a traditional guild membership, to occupy a venal office owned by the family, it very often had to be done in person. That is, there were many property rights that could not be bought and sold on the open market. During the century, these inalienable property rights (i.e., property rights that theoretically could not be bought and sold) became increasingly monetized and commercialized, thus increasing the opportunities for mobility. Wage employment was increasing during the century, and the increase of salaried government officials was marked. Although the labor market was becoming much more flexible during the century, there were still very major elements of rigidity due to the close identification of a given property right or business with a particular family.

In general, the division of benefits corresponded to the property system. A family, usually a tenant family, ran the business, and paid whatever rents and taxes were laid on that business. Since most of these businesses were agricultural enterprises, the most basic division of income in the society was the division into peasants' income and landlords' rents. The landlords, many of whom derived their property rights from noble titles, which in the Middle Ages had involved both government and landlordship, were often very much richer than the peasants and lived in a completely different style from their peasants in Paris.

THE ECONOMIC ORGANIZATION
OF AMERICAN SOCIETY

The American economy is characterized by two main forms of property rights in productive resources: government property and corporate property. There is one main form of administration of these properties: the bureaucratic administration of salaried officials. There is one main type of relation between the·worker and the economic enterprise: the free labor contract for a wage or salary. And there is an overall pattern of division of benefits so that about a fifth or a sixth of the national income is distributed as property income, about 7% as social insurance, and the other three-quarters or so as wages, salaries, fringe benefits, and government pensions.

The three main types of social units that participate in different ways in the economy are governments (of the nation and of states and localities), private corporations, and families. We will put most of our attention here on the economic role of the government and of the business sector of the economy.

The American Property System

At any given time, there is roughly four times the annual national income in existence in the form of buildings, roads, inventories, durables, land, and so forth. Of these concrete resources, roughly a third are houses and consumer durables used by households for direct capital services to the household. The other two-thirds of the national wealth can be thought of as "productive resources" as opposed to "household resources," though we do not intend to imply that a residence is a less productive building than a factory or store of the same value.

Thus, at any given time, the amount of productive resources in the economy is roughly three times the annual national income. Of this national productive wealth, about a third is held by the government as public property, and about two-thirds is held by private businesses. That is, the government holds title to resources valued at about the yearly national income, while private businesses hold about twice the yearly national income as resources. To put it another way, private business capital is about twice as large as government capital, and about one-and-a-half times as large as household capital.

But the government does not derive its control over the flow of income in the economy from the property it holds. Most government income is, of course, derived from taxation powers rather than from property rights. American governments (federal, state, and local) spend or give away about 40% of the national income each year, while the private business sector spends the other 60%. Much of what governments spend is for wages and salaries of the people who work for the government. Government purchases from contractors or suppliers, of course, appear *both* as government expenditures *and* as private business expenditures (wages, rents, and profits).

The parts of the economy managed by the government fall into three main sectors: (1) defense and foreign relations (federal); (2) government services to the population (mostly state and local); and (3) transfer payments in the form of interest and in social security and related programs (mostly federal). In 1978 about 5% of the national income went for national defense, foreign relations, space exploration, technology, etc. About 20% of the national income went for government services of various kinds: postal, educational, highway, police, including civil service pensions when they do not function as transfer payments, etc. Over two-thirds of these concrete governmental services are administered by state and local governments. About 11% of the national income was collected by the government from some people and paid to other people. Of these transfer payments, about a fifth (about 2% of the national income) are payments of interests on governmental debts (mainly federal debts), and the other two-thirds are mainly federal social security payments. Social security payments and health insurance for the elderly make up about 7% of the national income each year.

That is, of the overall government financial activity, about a seventh was federal national defense and foreign relations expenditure, a little over half was for the provision of governmental services, mostly by state and local governments, and about a third was made up of transfer payments from taxpayers to government bondholders, or from contributors to retirement schemes to the elderly. Of course, much of this government expenditure goes to buy things from private business, and so appears also as profits and wages to private businesses.

Private property rights give their holders command over about a quarter of the national income each year. This private property share is made up of the income of proprietors of small businesses (this income also includes, of course, much payment for the proprietor's own work in the business), corporate profits, and pure *rentier* income of rents and interests. About 7% of the national income in 1979 went to pay proprietors óf small businesses for their work and for profits on their investments. Approximately another 10% of the national income goes to corporate profits. And about 8% of the national income each year is paid to landlords, owners of bonds, or creditors, in the form of interest payments and rents. (These figures are rounded from *Statistical Abstract 1980*, p. 445.) Making an allowance for proprietors' wages, this gives an average rate of return on business property of about 10% per year. In 1980, for example, the median return of equity of the 500 largest industrial corporations was 14.4%. This amounted to about $5107 of profit for each employee (*Fortune*, May 4, 1981, report on the 500 largest industrials).

In sum, about 75% of the national income was paid out in compensation of employees, both government and private; about 16% is paid out to the holders of property rights; about 7% is transferred from the young to the old through social insurance schemes.

Governmental and Private Administration
of Economic Resources

In both the governmental and the private sector of the economy, the major social structure that actually holds and manages resources is a corporate group ultimately governed by a committee. But these groups have very different legal forms, and the governing committees are selected and influenced by quite different processes. In the private corporation, the governing committee (the board of directors) is legally selected by the owners of common stocks in the corporation, with voting in proportion to the number of stocks they own. In a practical sense, they are usually selected by past members of the board from among the salaried officials of the company or from representatives of other corporations with which the corporation does much business.

In the governmental sector, there is a somewhat more complicated structure. The citizens who select the committees (i.e., who elect the legislature and the executive officers) are specified by citizenship laws rather than by property rights in the government. Membership in governing committees or legislatures is much less likely to be mere cooptation by past members of the legislature or executive, but instead is usually the result of party competition at an election. Approximately 40% of the annual expenditure by governments is done by state and local governments, and about 60% by the federal government. As we mentioned above, most of the concrete governmental services to members of the population, such as education, roads, police and fire services, and the like, are administered through the state and local governments.

The Administration of Resources

In the private part of the economy, there are two main control devices that determine how resources will actually be used: bureaucratic administrative apparatuses of particular firms and the market. The market in a modern economy is organized so as to give very rapid information about the results of using resources in a given way. To oversimplify a bit, the activity of a given shop is determined jointly by what the salaried official in charge of that shop says ought to be done, and by what the market says about whether that official said the right thing.

We have already treated some of the varieties of administrative structure in the private sector of the American economy in the previous chapter. But when it is contrasted overall with the overall structure of the Karimojong or French economy, the striking characteristic is the degree to which the family has been replaced as the basic unit of the productive and distributive apparatus. Only in agriculture and in certain parts of trade and services is the family firm a major organizing principle. Most businesses have a corporate form, and the officials who actually administer the resources are salaried people with a defined job, a defined jurisdiction within which they control the decisions, and a defined place in the authority system so that their decisions are only reviewed by their superiors.

But the control system of the market makes these formidable hierarchical systems somewhat less fearsome. It may seem unbelievable that such great corporations controlling the American economy are actually subject to market forces that they cannot control, but which instead control them. For instance, consider the following losses for the year 1980 from among the 200 largest industrial corporations (ranked in terms of sales) in *Fortune's* (May 4, 1981) list. This list obviously shows that 1980 was a bad year for the automobile industry with Ford and Chrysler both losing over a billion and GM losing over three-quarters of a billion dollars. In 1981 it was a bad year for airlines. United Air Lines had an operating loss of near $149 million (they had only lost $66 million in 1980), Pan American World Airways lost even more, and TWA, Eastern, and American Airlines all ran in the red. Overall the 12 major carriers had a 6% drop in traffic from 1980 (*Business Week*, March 1, 1982, p. 92). In 1964 the big losers included a lot of railroads (New York, New Haven & Hartford, Reading, and Erie Lackawana), airlines (Eastern and Republic), a steel manufacturer (Kaiser), a publisher (Curtis Publishing), and a couple of food manufacturers (National Sugar Refining and Ward Foods).

Rank	Corporation	Losses (in 1000s)
3	General Motors	762,500
6	Ford	1,543,300
32	Chrysler	1,709,700
49	International Harvester	397,328
73	Firestone Tire and Rubber	105,900
155	American Motors	197,525
164	Uniroyal	7,842

The point is many large corporations are severely controlled by the market. Of course, actual losses are merely the extreme form of market control of the activities of a business. More often the information that a business is using as a resource in a way that is no longer valuable to the buying public comes to the corporation in the form of *declining* profits, rather than actual losses. When the profit rate on a particular resource falls below the rate of about 10%, pressure is exerted on the administrative system that controls that resource to put it to another use (often by selling it to someone who can use it better).

In the governmental sector of the economy, the salaried official with a defined jurisdiction is the same, but the network of controls over him or her has a different structure. The central economic control device in public bureaucracy is budget making. There is a great deal of continuity from year to year in the amount budgeted by the political process for the use of a particular agency of a government. Each agency tends to have a fairly stable characteristic rate of growth in its budgetary allocation (see Aaron Wildavsky, *The Politics of the Budgetary Process*, 3rd Edition). Over the long run, then, agencies that are "popular" with the legislature and the public grow more than agencies that are "unpopular." But the popular one is not boosted to ten times its original size in a year, nor is the unpopular one abolished. The other main control device is the creation of new agencies, when a traditional function is thought to be badly served by its present administration or when the government decides to render a new service.

The main departures from the pattern of gradual change through differential rates of growth of agencies come in times of crises, especially wartime. For instance, the federal budget grew very rapidly with the onset of the Second World War and was radically reorganized to give more support to military and foreign policy agencies. Then at the end of the war it was radically decreased, and radically reorganized, to give more emphasis to veterans' benefits and to peacetime services.

The ultimate determinant of the direction of evolution of the government budget is some combination of conceptions of the public interest and the interests of various interest groups. For example, in the federal government most of the money goes for defense and foreign relations, once we deduct Social Security and other transfer programs. Yet the interests of the American economy are only marginally involved in foreign affairs. In 1979, only about 8% of the American national wealth was in foreign assets (and about 6% of the wealth in the United States was foreign owned). About 9% of the net product of the United States was exported, and about 11% of final sales was imported. Although a few companies with large export markets (Boeing, General Motors, General Electric, Ford, Caterpillar, and Du Pont are the largest exporters in the *Fortune* list of August 24, 1981) do form an important foreign affairs interest group, all have larger sales in the United States. These interests are too small to account for the massive defense budget; conceptions of "the national interest" clearly dominate budget making for defense. At the opposite extreme, rivers and harbors development is almost entirely directed at serving the immediate economic interests of corporations concerned with shipping.

In general, agencies with a clear clientele to agitate for their budgets grow faster than those which depend on conceptions of the public good. Conceptions of the public good tend to be very unstable, as shown by wide fluctuations in the percentage of national income devoted to defense.

In both the government and private sectors of the American economy, then, the immediate control over resources is generally vested in a salaried official. But the system of economic controls under which he or she works is different in the private and government sectors. In the private sector, the ultimate source of the standards that he or she applies in decisions is the market evaluation of the output of the activities in his control. In the government sector, the ultimate source of standards is the government budget, as approved by elected officials, who in turn must face periodic election in an electorate defined by law.

The Supply of Labor

Most labor in the United States is done on a free contract in a labor market. The contract is with individuals, rather than with families or any other social unit. People are hired and fired as individuals, not as families or work crews. There is, further, a great deal of mobility; people are hired, fired, laid off, and quit at a fairly high rate. That is, the labor contract is surrounded by an environment of contingencies that limit it. These contingencies are the possibility that workers will quit to take another job, or that they will be laid off or fired if business goes down or they do not work as promised. People take advantage of these contingencies when the labor market is favorable to them. If people are earning more where they are than they could earn anywhere else, they are less likely to quit. If employers are getting more work for their money than they could get from other people in the labor market, they will not be as likely to lay off or fire workers. The point at which these two forces come into balance—the point at which workers get as much pay as they can from the employers, while the employers get as much productivity as they can for their money—is determined broadly by competitive conditions in the labor market.

These forces of free equilibrium in the labor market are modified by four main forces.

1. A government supply of education and a family supply of genes and motivation for school determine the supply of skills in the labor

market. People coming from states with better educational systems, or from families with greater capacity to get children to take advantage of schooling, get higher wages. This relation will be studied in more detail in the following chapter.

2. Experience on the job makes people more valuable at that particular job, and also generally gives them some moral, legal, or trade union right to prior consideration at the time of firing, laying off, or promotion. Hence, people are generally paid more, and paid more regularly, if they have held their jobs for some time.

3. Trade unions provide a collective monopoly over certain types of jobs, and make collective bargains on the terms on which such jobs are held. Collective bargaining is generally constrained by the same forces of competition that constrain individual wage bargains, and consequently has a small effect on wage rates. But if a trade union monopoly on labor is used to limit the supply of people in the labor market, as is done by the American Medical Association and some craft trade unions, then wages are increased.

4. About 8% of the labor force is held to their jobs by property rights which their families hold in the firm. This is especially true of farming. In general, farm income is low, since there are too many people in it (held there, presumably, by property rights and by public policy). The average income of workers in family enterprises is therefore smaller than people who work in a free labor market.

Probably at least 75% of the American labor force has some of one of these types of advantages, which raises their income above that which would be competively expected.

A second major characteristic of American labor arrangements is that work is done outside the home. It is outside in two senses. First, it is physically outside the house, in a separate building, usually at some distance. Second, work is done outside the moral and reward system of the home, and this makes it impossible to carry on family roles at the same time one is working. This physical and moral separation of work from home life encourages the growth of impersonal work institutions, applying criteria of merit rather than of need in determining rewards. Families tend to distribute to each according to his or her need; employers to each according to his or her seniority, rank, sex, and productivity.

A third major characteristic of the American labor market structure is that it is heavily organized by age. People start work late in life, around age 20, and stop working around age 65. Much of this is due to the fact that socialization for the labor market now takes place mostly in schools, which do not finish preparing people until they are about 20. Perhaps this also influences the retirement age, because one of the ways to get rid of people who were educated in the 1940s (when the amount of education was generally less and the content was less modern) is by retirement so that they can be replaced by people educated in the 1980s.

A final important characteristic of the American labor market is its "urbanization." That is, work takes place in cities, towns, and suburbs where it is highly concentrated, rather than spread out where the natural resources happen to be. Furthermore, this characteristic of the labor market is increasing, because fewer workers work in agricultural or mining enterprises, and more jobs can be carried out in urban areas.

Actually, we can make a more precise statement about the general structure of movement in the labor market, of which urbanization is a particular aspect. In general, as people get richer, they spend a *higher* proportion of their income on some goods and services (e.g., education, products of the chemical industry, cameras, government services, and "luxuries" generally), *about the same* proportion on some other goods (e.g., clothes), and a *smaller* proportion on some others (especially starchy foods, grains, and home-grown and homemade products). As the economy as a whole becomes more efficient (and the people in it therefore get richer), there will be a net movement of demand away from the goods that make up most of the budget of poor people, and toward the goods that make up most of the budget of rich people. Other things being equal (particularly, supposing technical progress is equal in all branches of the economy), the industries that grow with an increase in income will be those that dominate the budgets of rich people, and those industries that decline will be those that dominate the budgets of poor people.

Generally, industries that particularly decline with increases in income are those producing raw materials, including agriculture, mining, and forestry. Those that increase most are the industries providing highly sophisticated products and highly sophisticated services, such as the chemical, educational, or financial industries, or government. The overall movement of the economy, then, will be to move people out of mining, agriculture, and forestry, and into the chemical industry, education, government, or finance. These growing industries are urban, even metropolitan, industries, because they depend so much on communication to get their work done. Consequently, the overall trend in the labor market is to move people's jobs into metropolitan areas. The people themselves, as we saw in the chapter on ecology, tend to move to within commuting distance in the surburban fringes of these metropolitan areas.

This overall movement of the labor force into more sophisticated industries has had substantial human costs. In general, the educational institutions of a community are designed to give an education appropriate to the labor force of the industry that dominates the community. A large proportion of the population in each generation is raised in communities dominated by agriculture or by industries that produce for poorer people's budgets; but they end up working in communities dominated by more sophisticated industries. Thus, there are many people in cities who were trained in the educational systems of rural areas, such as the South or Appalachia, who are now ill-fitted to work in the labor market where they find themselves.

The structure of the labor market as a whole, then, is strongly differentiated from the family structure and reduced to a wage and salary basis. The structure is, broadly speaking, competitive with some "balkanization" due to seniority, trade union organization, or the petty bourgeoisie holding property rights in the firm where they work. People are employed outside the home and by an organization which has very little to do with the family except paying something to one of the family members. People enter the labor force in their late teens or 20s, and generally leave it in their 60s. During the time they are in the labor force, their careers are quite often organized heavily by age and seniority as embedded in promotion systems.

The Division of Benefits

The primary way the American society arranges the division of the benefits of economic activity is to arrange for individuals to have claims on the flows of money that go through the corporate organizations we spoke of earlier. It is convenient to divide these claims on flows of income into three main groups:
1. Wage and salary claims
2. Property income claims, which in turn can be divided into two main groups
   a. Proprietorship income, involving returns from a business of which the owner is also the director
   b. Other property claims, such as corporate profits, rents, or interest payments
3. Social security and other trust fund claims.

Wage and Salary Claims

The main determinants of the distribution of wage and salary income in the United States are race, sex, education, and experience. The racial differences in wage rates, and consequently in family income, are probably greater than those due to any other single cause (except the differences between men and women—female-headed families are on the average much poorer than families with both husband and wife). In 1979 the median money income of black families was about 60% of that of white families. In 1978 black husband–wife families in which the husband alone worked had about 71% of the income of comparable white families; if both husband and wife worked, black families had about 88% of the income of median white families.

Sexual discrimination in wage and salary income is also very substantial. Aside from sheer discrimination, so that women get paid less for the same work and are disproportionately recruited into occupations paying lower salaries, women also suffer the disadvantage of having more disorganized careers. Generally, they leave the labor market or take up part-time jobs while they have small children, and they move when their husbands find it strategic to male career advance rather than when it is strategic for female careers.

Provided people are of the same race and sex, there are marked educational differences in wage and salary income. Education is an explicit criterion for hiring and for promotion to higher jobs in many bureaucracies. Many professions grant a monopoly of certain jobs or of selling certain services to people with a specified education. The highest paid occupations are physicians and lawyers. They earn their positions by education.

It is not very clear how much of the wage differences that we find between people of different education is due to the education itself, and how much is due to the fact that more intelligent people get more education, and also do better at most kinds of jobs. There is certainly a great deal of variation in the incomes of physicians and lawyers, all of whom presumably have the same education and the same license to practice. Some of that variation may be accounted for by differences in abilities. But Jencks and others in *Inequality* find very little effect of measured intellectual ability, once education is controlled.

There are also large differences in incomes received due to different number of hours worked in the market. On the average, married men work more for wages than women; however, the difference is balanced by the greater amount of household work done by women, so the total working hours of the two sexes are about equal. But since this means that married men work about 25% more hours per week for pay than married women do, they get more income (men also get higher wages per hour). Because upper middle-class people usually get longer vacations, the fact that they often work more hours per week does not mean that they work more hours per year. In fact, very few of the occupational differences in income can be explained by different numbers of hours worked. Farmers and ministers, for example, work very long hours for low pay, while physicians work very long hours for high pay.

This wage and salary income, besides serving as family income for the families of wage earners, is a major control device in the labor market. People are moved from the country to the city by differential wages, and then redistributed among cities by wage differences. When the relative wage rates of scientists increase relative to the wage rate of physicians, there is a quick drop in the number of applicants to medical schools and an increase in the number of applicants to graduate science departments. When universities and science-based industries are in relative decline, applications for medical schools increase again. Thus, at any given time, aside from the gross differences in wage income due to race, sex, education, and experience, there are also differences that may be called "adjustment differences" or "motivational differences," reflecting an undersupply of people in particular newer lines of work.

Property Income Claims

Property income, as it appears in the statistics, is partly wage income, since it is impossible to separate that part of the profits of a proprietorship which are payment for the use of the proprietor's property, and that part which is payment for the proprietor's managerial efforts and labor or the efforts of his family members. About 7% of the national income goes to proprietors, who make up about 8% of the labor force. Thus, their property holdings as a class do not cause inequalities; they just get a little less than their share. However, within the class of proprietors, there is a large subclass of quite poor people, many of them farmers, and a smaller subclass of quite rich people. There is more inequality within the class of proprietors than there is in the class of wage earners.

Something like a sixth of the national income is distributed each year to owners of property rights that are not in their own business. About 10% each year goes into corporate profits, and about 7% is paid in interest and rentals.

This property income is very unequally distributed. For instance, Gabriel Kolko in his book *Wealth and Power in America* gives a figure that 7.9%, or about a twelfth, of the population owned some stocks. But 58% of all the holdings were owned by only 2% of the holders. That is, two-tenths of 1% of the population own some 58% of the stocks. In 1956, the Du Ponts, the Rockefellers, and the Mellons *each* owned more stock than *all* of the wage earners in the United States put together. Property income is much more unequally distributed in the United States than is wage and salary income.

A second feature of the distribution of property income is that it really does go, to a surprising degree, to widows and orphans. *Statistical Abstract 1980*, p. 547, gives the percentage of women among owners of stock as 49.6%. Women apparently own many of the property rights because it takes considerable time for a man to accumulate property. But since women live longer than men, a man who gets rich in late middle age very often dies soon after, leaving the accumulation to his wife.

Another way to look at this property income is to consider the profit per employee for some major companies. For General Motors in 1980, the loss per employee was $1,022; for Exxon the profit was $39,991 per employee; for Mobil, $15,376; for Texaco, $39,592; for Standard of California, $59,700; for Ford the loss was $3,617. For comparable figures for nonindustrial corporations we find in 1978 that the profits per employee for the Bank of America were $6,495; for Citicorp, $9,549; for Sears, $2,143; for K Mart, $1,611.

Social Security and Trust Fund Claims

Most of the widows and orphans do not, of course, inherit very much property income. Instead, they live on social security, (as do men who are too old to work and too young to die). Relatively few of the widows live off their half of society's property income (which would be about 10% of the national income). Instead, the immense majority of widows live off their share of the social security insurance payments, which amounts to less than 5% of the national income. Social security income, and the income of other trust funds administered by the governments, is essentially distributed by age.

Summary

American economic institutions have to manage an economy of quite a different scale and character than those of the Karimojong or of the Old Regime. Most products are consumed by different social units than those that produce them; most social organizations use a variety of property rights in a variety of different types of resources.

The dominating institutions in the large-scale organization of the economy of the United States are the government, the corporation, and the competitive market. Governments own about a quarter of the nonhousehold resources of the society, and their expenditures amount to about two-fifths of the national income. The other three-fourths of the productive resources, and the other three-fifths of the annual income, constitute a "purely" private business section, where the dominant institutions are corporations, great and small. Relatively few of the productive resources, and only about 10% of the national income, are the property and income of a family business, the dominant form of income of Karimoja or of eighteenth-century France.

The allocation of money among firms is carried out by the market, and resources used in business are generally judged (with more or less error, confusion, and sentimental distortion) by the return they bring in the market. The allocation of money to the government is determined by governmental decision, by the budget-making negotiations between the executive and legislative branches of the many governments in the United States. The single most powerful force in the allocational system is, of course, the federal government, which spends about a fourth of the national income each year, determines the quantity of money by its fiscal and monetary policies, and regulates both the conditions of citizenship in subordinate governments and the conditions of doing business of subordinate corporations. Much of that regulatory power is used to make sure that the conditions of market pressure on business is preserved, as for example, the deregulation of the airline industry seems to be pushing much excess capacity out of the industry.

Both governments and corporations administer their resources with hierarchies of paid officials, each with a defined jurisdiction. These bureaucratic administrations are controlled by quite different structures, and hence, respond to different criteria in deciding what to do. Essentially, corporations have self-preserving oligarchies, not legally responsible to anyone except those who have bought voting stock, and not actually very immediately responsible to them. Only social control through market mechanisms keep them using their resources "for human betterment." Governments have elected legislatures and elected executives (except for some cities with professional city managers), and the elections take place in an electorate defined by law rather than by property rights. In fact, most of the adult population is legally in the electorate. This electoral competition is made effective by the general existence of competitive party organizations.

Over the long run, the structure of control provided by governments has been winning out in the competition with private businesses. That is, over time the proportion of the national income that the people choose to spend or distribute through governmental agencies increases, and the proportion they spend or distribute through market and private business agencies declines. The big increases in the size of government came near the beginning of the Great Depression in the early 1930s; and in a failure to go back to the 1941 level when World War II ended. That is, the increase in government has not been constant, but instead had come mainly in two steps, a depression step and a Cold War step.

People's movement in the labor market is constrained very little by their other institutional ties. National citizenship has become the most important limitation on migration; however, once a person becomes a citizen, he or she can move anywhere. A person is unlikely to be tied to a present job by property ownership of the business or by ties of a noneconomic kind.

The division of benefits is determined by three master processes: the determination of property income, the determination of wage income, and the determination of governmental pension income. Property income, amounting to about 25% of the national income each year, is distributed roughly in proportion to the amount of property owned, at a rate of about 10% of equity. But property is very unequally distributed, because it is primarily owned by a small number of the middle-aged or elderly men and by a few widows. Wage income is also unevenly distributed, but not as unevenly as property income. Race, sex, education, and experience seem to be the main determinants of differences in wage and salary income.

SOCIAL RELATIONS OF PRODUCTION

Perhaps the most remarkable feature of this account of the economic institutions of the three societies is the degree to which, in any one society, the same institutional arrangements appear as the answer to all the questions one asks.

Among the Karimojong, the answer to almost every economic question is a family and herd matter. The family holds resources, insofar as they are held as private property. The family provides labor and recruits new labor. The family divides up the benefits. The administrative apparatus of the firm is the family authority structure. And what the family mainly does is all intimately connected to the family's herd.

In eighteenth-century France, almost every economic question comes down in the end to a tenure question: on what condition does this family hold the resources it uses in the family enterprise? The appropriate answer to such a question described fairly well the structure of the rural economy, of guild arrangements for urban commerce and manufacture, and of that large part of the government managed by venal officers of tax farmers. Only for the growing bureaucratic apparatus of the royal government was the question of the conditions of family tenure in the enterprise wildly inappropriate, and even there it was the right question to ask of the Royal House itself. Who the King should be was determined as a tenure question.

In the United States, almost all questions come down in the end to one of what controls there are over the bureaucratic apparatus that administers resources. Such apparatuses may have their decisional premises controlled either by elected officials in a budget-making process, or by a self-perpetuating oligarchy sensitive to market pressures. Almost everything important in the economy is ultimately decided either by passing a law in a legislature, or by the play of supply and demand in the market. Amounts and prices of labor are determined by an interplay of legislation and government subsidized education, and the growth of different industries with different labor requirements. Benefits are divided by competition in the labor market, and by competitive determination of the direction of investment in the capital market, as modified by government regulation and government provision of subsidized services for general use.

Worker Incentives and the Mode of Production

> Whatever the social form of production, laborers and means of production always remain factors of it. But in a state of separation from each other either of these factors can be such only potentially. For production to go on at all they must unite. The specific manner in which this union is accomplished distinguishes the different economic epochs of the structure of society from one another. In the [capitalist] case, the separation of the free worker from his [or her] means of production is the starting point given [from Karl Marx, *Capital*, vol. II, Moscow 1957 ed, pp. 34–5, as quoted by G. Cohen, *Karl Marx's Theory of History*, p. 78].

Broadly speaking, the social form of the "union" Marx tells about involves (1) some sort of "property" right in the means of production; (2) some incentives such as profits or rents or goods and services for the property holder; (3) some supply of labor power from some designated "workers"; (4) some incentives for the supply of labor and for actually producing the goods and services efficiently; (5) some division of the actual practical decision making about what has to be done to produce the goods and services; and (6) some set of socially defensible claims on the incentives for the property holder, on the incentives for the workers, and on the rights to take practical decisions, so that the whole structure of the "unity" has a solid social existence.

The "unity" then is actually a complex system of mutually dependent incentives and rights, occurring in abstract form in laws and rules of formal organizations, and in concrete form in the latest efforts of an airline company to avoid bankruptcy by paying its workers only half their pay for one pay period, or in the latest gift of a sacrificial animal by a Karimojong herd owner.

The structure of norms and administrative arrangements has to be arranged so that both the provider of the property and the person who provides the labor are better off if goods and services are produced and worse off if they are not produced. For example, both the herder who walks a long distance with the cattle, and the owner who provides the cattle to be walked, have to be better off if the cattle get enough grass and water. This congruence of incentives is easily achieved if the herder and the owner are the same person, and are within fairly easy achievement if the herder is the son of the owner. But similarly the owner of an automobile parts wholesaling firm and a parts salesperson must both be rewarded if the parts inventory is adequate and if a repair garage gets prompt delivery of exactly the right part. This is "easily" achieved if the parts salesperson has a believable career in the firm, is paid a commission according to his or her sales, is supervised so that an adequate computer record of inventory and sales can be maintained, and if the owner can charge enough more than the salesperson's income to yield a profit.

What justifies calling both these systems by the same concept, "social form of production," is that they accomplish the same end, the "unity" of labor and the means of production. The institutional aspect of economies, the "social relations of production," are structures of incentives for the laborer and incentives for the controller of capital to bring about that unity, to decide what should be done with that unity, and to implement those decisions.

Comparative Class Relations and Incentives

The incentives are derived from the benefits produced, either directly or indirectly. The origin of economic oppression is that the total incentives necessary to get all the work done need not add up to the total benefit produced. For example, the total cost of worker incentives for refining oil in a refinery that will last 20 years is the wages of the construction crews and suppliers of steel and materials, the wages of the workers who monitor the machinery in production, and the salaries of the necessary supervisors, record keepers, and the like. The total benefits are these worker incentives plus the profits of the oil companies, the interest on loans, and other property income.

For example, the eighteenth-century French peasant who owned his own work animals had to combine his labor (and that of his animals) with land in order to produce food and fiber. He and his family might own that land (subject to a few feudal dues, the *dîme*, and royal taxes), they might sharecrop it, or they might rent it. The total benefits to the peasant would, of course, be large if the peasant owned the land. But the incentives to cultivate the land and to produce food and fiber were sufficient in all three situations to motivate hard work. The difference between ownership and tenancy of the land, then, was a difference in the "class situation" of the peasant. The core of the class situation is the relation between worker incentives and the total product (this immediately implies that it is also a relation between the incentives of property owners and the total product).

One of the reasons that sharecropping (*metayage*) usually involves more intervention by the landlord in the administration of a farm is that the incentives for labor are less than in ordinary cash renting (*fermage*). The last hour of labor (say an extra weeding) that increases the yield by a bushel only brings the *metayer* a half bushel, the other half bushel going to the landlord. But since the *fermier's* rent is fixed, that same last hour brings him a full bushel.

The implicit wages for that last hour are therefore twice as high for the *fermier* (in fact, for the *fermier* they are just as high as the implicit wages for the last hour by the peasant owner). One would expect the *metayer* to decide the extra yield is not worth the extra effort at an earlier point, so that sharecropped tenancies would receive an undersupply of labor if the *metayer* is left to himself. The extra landlord supervision therefore partially substitutes for the effectiveness of the peasant incentive system of *fermage* or full ownership. The arrangements of property rights and the arrangements of decision rights are interdependent.

The dimension from *fermage* to *metayage* has a further extension in hourly wage or salary labor, in which the incentives to the worker do not vary with the amount of product at all, but instead with hours worked or months worked. (Piecework wages, such as those paid to weavers who worked in their homes in the eighteenth century, are similar to *metayage* in that the returns for the last hour of weaving go partly to the capitalists, partly to the weaver.) We would expect then that still more supervision would be supplied to wage workers than to *metayers* or pieceworkers.

The bureaucratic apparatus for supervising wage and salary workers thus appears as a substitute for paying the workers according to their product. The iron discipline of the early factory had as its purpose making the workers work as hard as they would if they worked at home and received the full product of their last ounce of effort. The reason for substituting supervision for measurement of and payment for the product is partly that the division of labor used in factories makes the measurement of individual productivity very difficult.

Thus the "unity" Marx speaks of between labor and the means of production can be brought about by different combinations of incentives and supervision. The simplest case applies to the Karimojong *elop* and the French peasant who owned his own land. The full benefits of labor *and* the full benefits of improving one's capital are both returned directly to the supplier (or rather, to the family of the suppliers). The incentive system, if we ignore conflicting interests within the family, then rewards the last hour of effort (and the last sacrifice of present meat consumption to the size of the herd next year) with its full product. No supervision by an "outside" owner is theoretically necessary.

Monopoly over the land by eighteenth-century landlords brought with it the opportunity to create incentives for workers that were less than their full product, so that "surplus value" could be created in the form of "rent." There developed a range of incentive systems from *fermage* (fixed rents, full marginal product to the tenant), *metayage* (sharecropping, partial marginal product to the tenant), to wage labor (common only in a few highly commercialized areas in the Seine basin and in some wine-growing areas). The inefficiencies of the incentive systems entailed variations in the intensity of supervision, with the *fermier* being an autonomous businessman, the *metayer* a feudal dependent, and the *journalier* (day laborer) closely supervised by the landlord, peasant, or *fermier*.

In the United States all these varieties of incentive systems still exist. Much of the farming and service sectors are organized by full ownership and undifferentiated worker–capitalist (or "petty bourgeois") roles. Farming in more fertile areas and part of real estate are organized by cash rentals. Sweatshops, much of wholesale trade, and small contract construction are organized by a sort of "piecework" payment, with part of the product going to the capitalist, part to the worker or petty bourgeois subcontractor. And most of the economy is organized by wage or salary labor with intensive supervision. The proportions of each incentive system have changed since the eighteenth century, but the legal forms and social arrangements of the modern extraction of surplus value from workers all existed in eighteenth-century France.

The primary innovation of the modern system is the supplementing of the wage-or-salary-with-supervision system by a system of *career bureaucratic incentives.* The basic function of promising a person a career in return for responsible performance over the long run is that supervision can then be reduced to a broad judgment of the overall quantity and quality of output. This is particularly important when one wants to hire people to supervise workers. Operatives in a factory will report that they are supervised more than once a day, their supervisors will report that they are supervised and their performance examined about once or twice a week, on the average, and higher executives may be examined and supervised once a month or less. Thus, to make a modern factory run, one has to motivate a high level of performance (backed up by infrequent inspections) for the higher levels of the hierarchy. Career incentives can substitute for profit incentives for the supervisory and managerial staff.

Further career incentives are important for motivating highly skilled performances by professionals and craft workers. Both the intelligent reading of blueprints by the craft worker or foreman, and the intelligent drawing of blueprints by the engineer and draftsman, require frequent use of good judgment. If that good judgment has to be applied by supervisors looking over the craft worker's or engineer's shoulder, it leads to great inefficiencies. Career rewards tend to be found wherever a modern organization must hire people whom it would be very expensive to supervise in detail, because their work involves too many detailed decisions requiring intelligence and experience. The amount spent on career rewards and promotion guaranties is usually, of course, smaller than the value of the total benefits produced by the use of supervisory loyalty or professional and craft skill.

Property Income and Surplus Value

The possibility of setting up an incentive scheme in which one of the participants gets less than the full product of his or her contribution brings up the question of who gets to set up the incentive system. Marx's basic argument was that this was ultimately a political question.

For example, profits in the United States are usually about a third of total private sector value added while investments are about a sixth of private value added. A socialist government with the same efficiency and the same objectives on the rate of growth could therefore manage to pay for the investment in the economy for about half what it now costs, and the extra sixth of private income now spent "to reward capitalists for saving" could be spent instead to reward workers (or to reward pensioners and the needy and to provide income for the widows who now live on property income). The yearly payment of a sixth of national income for capital-saving functions could be sustained by expropriating capitalist rights and substituting government investment. Thus, the present pattern of a third going to capitalists is a "political choice."

This does not mean that the issue came up in the last election—it only means that the present overall division between worker incentives and capitalist incentives is embedded in the structure of the legal system, as this system is brought into concrete reality by the administrative and incentive structures we allow capitalist corporations to build.

Similarly, most of the value of land in the eighteenth century was not the result of the capital investment of clearing lands, but instead land had "monopoly value" from the capacity of landlords to deny peasants access to it. The ultimate origins of most landlord tenancies were military and political. The fact that it was a landlord rather than a working peasant who got to set up the incentive system on a given piece of land was a historical outcome. But the ancient events that created the claim now defended in law were largely political and military events, and the legal preservation of those rights was also political.

A number of systems with extensive landlord income have been turned into small peasant-owner systems in land reforms, for instance, in nineteenth-century Serbia or in post World War II Japan and Taiwan, without damage to productivity. This shows that land does not produce because it is owned by a duke, but because it is worked by a peasant.

The power to set up the incentive systems under which others will live to one's own advantage, is the core of the system of *class relations* of a society. We can therefore say that class relations in Karimojong society are dominantly within the family. The *elop* has the right to set up incentives for his sons, his wives, and his sons' wives and children. Class relations are, like almost everything else in Karimoja, aspects of the relationships between men and women within the family and between the generations within the family.

Class relations in eighteenth-century France were dominated by property rights of individual landlord families, which gave the power to set up tenancy relations in which the tenant collected only a part of the benefits he and his family produced. But some 40% of the peasantry and some urban artisans worked under a system much like the Karimojong system, and a few day laborers, a few government servants, and some of the clergy, worked under more "modern" bureaucratic or wage labor structures.

Class relations in the United States include examples similar to the dominant Karimojong structures, although relations are controlled by market forces in a way the Karimojong are not. They also include tenancy relations and piecework systems similar to those of eighteenth-century France. But the dominant structure is the "capitalist" one, in which a corporation uses invested money to give incentives to construction workers and machinists to build a plant, then uses working capital to manufacture goods or produce services that people will buy. The legal capacity to set up such incentive systems for one's own benefit does not exist (on any large scale, at least) in the Soviet Union or China. It is the frequent use of that legal capacity to set up businesses for profit that marks the United States as an "advanced capitalist society." Bureaucratic supply of the supervision necessitated by wage payment (in place of piecework or cash tenancy) is typically motivated by career incentives, but such bureaucratic incentive structures are also found in the Soviet Union and China.

Hegemony, Incentives, and Class Relations

Michael Burawoy argues in Chapter 5 of *Manufacturing Consent* that preoccupation with the incentive system (in the "Allied Corporation," a modern type of partial piecework system) obscured the question of the overall division of the total income of the corporation into wages and profits. The thing one could manipulate as an individual on the shop floor was "making out," increasing one's pay without endangering the piecework rate. Concentration on this visible "game" one plays with management diverts attention from the larger structural game that allowed the corporation rather than the workers to set up the incentive system in the first place. In particular, it obscured the fact that, if Allied Corporation profits were at the societal average, in an average year the corporation would take out twice as much surplus value as they would invest. Societal bargains can be made about such profit rates, and in several European capitalist societies the corporate profit rate on capital is only about two-thirds as high as it is for American corporations.

The feudal "structural bargain" similarly disappears in the concrete life of the eighteenth-century economy. A "fair landlord" offered his tenancies at the traditional nominal rate of about one-half of the net produce, although the rents were often lower in other societies at the time (for instance, they were lower in the United States and Canada). Western French peasants who paid these structural rates came to be fierce defenders of the privileges of the church and nobility (see Charles Tilly, *The Vendée*). The fairness of the landlord under the incentive system obscured the privilege of setting up the incentives.

But the hegemony of an overall division of income among the classes is facilitated also by the fact that there are multiple systems of incentives in all complex societies. In America, career incentives motivate loyalty to a bureaucracy in ways that hourly wages cannot. Millions of hard-working farmers and small business owners do not experience their profits and wages as distinct, and their whole work lives are wrapped up in their property. These groups do not therefore derive their politics from the dominant capitalist wage labor system. Whereas the dominant form of unity between the laborer and the means of production is land rent and tenancy in the Old Regime in France, corporate profit and wage or salary payment in the United States, there is great variety within those main forms, and many people who fall outside them.

The unit that has a "mode of production" is the unit that sets up the incentive system—the agricultural holding or the factory or the municipal government or whatever. Societies do not have modes of production, but rather have various mixtures of the units that do have them. The best Marxist thought pays attention to the details of incentive systems that create the unity of labor and the means of production.

5

Peopling the Social Structure

POPULATION THEORY

The topics of this chapter are conventionally called population and labor force and are studied by demographers. But the conceptual tools needed for studying the matching of people to roles in primitive societies are different enough that we must go behind the categories developed for advanced societies. For example, there is no significant sense in which an eighteenth-century French farmer was "in the labor force." The fundamental phenomenon we are interested in is that a given generation of parents produces a set of children whose social composition at birth is defined by their relation to those parents. The set of adult statuses and roles that they will eventually fill is normally defined partly by reference to the same social composition. Every society has to create more roles for some families than others. Complete determination of the role of adults by the family position of children is impossible.

In modern societies the mechanism for adjusting the social composition of a new generation of children to the social composition of the roles they must manage as adults is the labor market. A person "enters the labor force" when he or she is "seeking work," that is, when looking for an adult role. Within certain limits one takes what role one can get. There are numerous characteristics of schools that are designed to make it more likely that people entering the labor force will take what they can get. The central device by which we teach children what to expect is the school. (See my review of Robert Dreeben's *On What is Learned in School* in the spring 1970 issue of *Sociology of Education*. Also Burton Clark, "The 'Cooling Out' Function in Higher Education," *Am. Journal Sociology*, May, 1960, 569–576.)

These institutions of "free choice" and schooling do not exist in most societies. The question "Are you seeking work?" would make very little sense to a Karimojong or to an eighteenth-century French peasant. Schools do not exist among the Karimojong; they were relevant to occupational placement only for the urban population in eighteenth-century France. Roles among the Karimojong for the rising generation are defined by relation of the child to the herd–family unit, and by relation to the age-set, which will be discussed later. Neither of these roles is in any significant sense chosen by the child. In eighteenth-century France most adult roles were created by inheritance of peasant property, of government position, or of social status as noble, bourgeois, or commoner. But only one man (and at least one man) could be king, however many princes there were, so birth alone could not determine the kingship. A noble inheritance did not always allow all the sons to *vivre noblement*. The inheritance of a peasant might not allow him to live at all in a bad year (which would leave more peasant positions open for the next generation). These societies do not allocate roles through a labor market.

The Social Distribution
of Births and Deaths

We can think of each birth or death as filling or vacating a virtual social role. When a disproportionate number of virtual social roles are vacated by the death of the heirs who have preference as occupants, or are left unfilled by failure of births of heirs, a set of virtual openings are created for other people to move into.

Before modern sanitation the death rate was generally higher in cities than in rural areas. The death rate in the cities was especially high among those most subject to infectious diseases, namely children. The death of children, of course, has much the same effect on the population as does lowering the birth rate. The upper classes more often lived in cities than did the lower classes in eighteenth-century France. In addition, it seems that the upper classes, but not the peasantry, used some form of birth control. Certainly the kings' mistresses had fewer pregnancies than one would expect from the nature of the position.

Thus we have several grounds to expect that the upper classes would tend not to reproduce themselves in premodern times, and that particularly the urban upper classes would show a proportional deficit. We would expect that a large proportion of the residents of cities would be migrants from rural areas, and that a large proportion of the merchant, governmental, and religious upper classes would be new people.

Among the Karimojong, polygyny generally results in richer men having many more children than poorer men. Furthermore, since all children that depend on a given herd "belong to" the owner of that herd, many children who have a poor genitor will be counted as the social children of a rich *elop*. Thus, there is a systematic tendency for rich men among the Karimojong to more than reproduce themselves. Upon division of a large herd, the children of rich men more often end up with a smaller herd than their father had. The smaller number of children of a poorer father each inherit a larger proportion of their father's wealth. Thus, the Karimojong reverse the Western phrase, "The rich man gets the pleasure; the poor man gets the blame." By assuming social fatherhood of the children of a larger number of wives, a richer Karimojong sets up a reverse flow, or "downward mobililty." A large proportion of the men with small herds will have inherited from a man with large herds.

Generally speaking, the smaller the set of parents whose children would be defined by birth as the virtual occupants of a given role, the greater the chance that the virtual occupant will die or fail to be born. The probability that a firstborn son will have a son is obviously less than the probability that one of a set of brothers will have a son. The probability of extinction of a given social group is therefore larger when only the firstborn son can pass the family position on.

Furthermore, this probability of the failure of having heirs is higher the more chancy life is. Death is a great deal more variable from year to year and from place to place than is birth. A population regime of high birth and death rates is therefore much more variable in its inheritance results than a population with low death rates. That is, more small groups will die out in each generation, and more roles with a small set of children who are virtual role occupants will fall vacant. It is harder demographically to construct an ascriptive system, in which people are assigned to virtual roles at birth, in traditional societies with high birth and death rates than in modern societies. If traditional societies are more ascriptive, they must work harder to achieve it.

When there is a great deal of variability in the rates of growth of different family groups from one generation to the next, due to chance fluctuations in the birth and death rate between groups, the sizes of groups whose membership is defined by inheritance tend to become more unequal. That is, if in a given generation a group has a good chance of having a high growth rate, and a good chance of being wiped out by such things as plague, famine, or cattle raiders, then a run of good luck will produce a very big group, whereas a run of bad luck will produce a very small or nonexistent group.

For example, suppose that upon setting up a village community on new land, families are given equal-sized plots. If there is a great variability in the rates of growth of families, and if families divide inheritances within families equally, then in a short while there will be great inequalities between villagers. Likewise, the ten sections of Karimojong society are structurally and ritually equal. They may have once been fairly equal in population, though we have no evidence of that. If they were once equal, we would expect the chancy environment of sporadic local warfare, local epidemics, local cattle epidemics, differential rainfall and local famines, all would produce a wide variability in the death rates of different sections. This in turn would produce the wide variability in the present size of sections. The two largest sections, *Ngibokora* and *Ngipian,* are about 20,000 people apiece, or about two-thirds of the tribe together. The Ngimaseniko section is about 10,000, or another sixth of the tribe. The other seven sections together are about 10,000, or about a sixth of the tribe. Such small sections have a much larger chance of being wiped out completely than do the larger sections, by fluctuation of local conditions.

Such fluctuations in the size of groups, even in the existence of groups, and fluctuations in the vacancy rate of structural positions, create recurrent strains in the allocation of positions. They create strains also in the performance of social roles.

The Birth and Death of Social Roles

We can distinguish two broad types of role creation, which I will call the *status creation* method and the *role accretion* method. By status creation I mean that a job description for a role is worked out in the abstract, with corresponding rights and duties. That is, a set of *jural relations* of the role to other roles is created first. Then the status becomes a *vacancy* in the structure, and this vacancy is filled by recruitment. The activities of the person who fills the vacancy make up the role that has been created (see Harrison White, *Chains of Opportunity* for extensive use of the idea of vacancies).

In the role accretion method of creating roles, various rights and duties are added in small bundles to the "estate" of a given person. A Karimojong man may get a few cows in various ways: as a gift, a bride price, or a herd segment on his father's death. Similarly, he may get a wife in marriage negotiations carried out by his father, by the death of a brother, and so on. Corresponding to this gradual growth of the set of rights and duties that constitute the man's estate is a gradual change in his activities. His activities adapt at the margin of his role, gradually, rather than suddenly on the assumption of a new job or a new overall jural status. The status system changes by increments rather than jumps. Statuses do not exist as vacancies, but as new obligations or rights to be attached to existing people in roles.

Broadly speaking, traditional societies create new roles by the role accretion method, whereas modern societies do so by creating vacancies by jural means. There are no real vacancies looking for recruits in rural France; there are no families without heads or "positions vacant" as herdboys among the Karimojong. When people discuss jural matters, they very often talk as if the present status structure (i.e., the complex of jural relations) is fixed and immutable—that rights and duties could be divided in no other way, and that when rights are not exercised there is a vacancy. The motto *Nulle terre sans Seigneur*, "no land without a lord," was a case of such idealization of jural relations in the eighteenth century. In fact, many pieces of land, especially in the Midi, the south, had not had lords within living memory. Such jural ideas then do tend to create vacancies. The rigidification of contractural provisions in land rentals into immemorial rights of the seigneur in the motto turns an accreted role into a vacancy, and the position of seigneur then becomes a separate social object from the individually variable rights that make it up.

There were, however, roles in French society that were so thoroughly institutionalized that there were special institutions of vacancy. The leading case was the Regency. When Louis XIV died in 1715, the heir was a rather sickly infant. Louis XIV tried to set up the government under the Regency by his will, leaving the care of the infant king to his bastard son, the Duke of Maine. To back up the claim of the regency to the throne, Louis tried to give control of the palace troops to the Duke of Maine. He also tried to organize a regency council that would decide by majority vote, rather than being advisers to the temporary King. The Duke of Orleans, however, persuaded the *Parlement* of Paris to recognize him as Regent, and to disallow the provisions of the will about the control of the troops and majority rule. Here we have a clearcut debate in the institutional centers of the society about how to handle a clearcut vacancy. The kingship was not only the property of Louis XIV and of his heir, Louis XV, but also a continuing status in a well-organized jural system. When Louis XIV tried to treat it in his will as his own absolute property for which he could change the rights and duties, he could not make it stick.

Role-Creating Structures

Modern societies differ from traditional societies by having institutions of innovation. That is, everyone expects the formal social organization to change and be rearranged in order to carry out new activities, to correct grievances, and to adapt to new environmental conditions. This rearrangement of jural relations of multitudes of roles is formally decided on, for the most part, by the boards of directors of corporations and legislative authorities of the government. But these role creating jural mechanisms are so closely tied in with market mechanisms that the government typically manipulates the unemployment rate (i.e., a departure of role creation quantities from population quantities) by manipulating the money supply. For instance, if one wants to increase unemployment one pursues a "tight money" policy. To understand how role creation and allocation work, then, we must review again the interrelation of organizations and markets.

A market is an institution for transferring jural relations from one social unit to another. A simple market transfers jural relations to objects (i.e., transfers ownership): commodities, land, houses, and so on. A capital market transfers claims to flows of income from going concerns, especially flows from firms and the government. A labor market transfers claims to roles in going concerns, with their associated income. All of these markets depend on a set of legal institutions that allow such jural relations to things, going concerns, and roles to be easily transferred from one organization or person to another. But neither the total quantity transferred nor the prices or exchange rates of the transfers are determined by the jural mechanisms as such.

This transfer of jural capacities allows the component organizations participating in markets to increase or decrease the number and kind of statuses they create. Control over the resources used in roles, and control over rewards for roles, are then *the same thing* as the capacity to create statuses. The activities one is capable of causing to be carried out in roles in an organization are therefore dependent on the market situation of the organization.

The reason for emphasizing the obvious point that unless an organization can pay workers and provide them with tools, it cannot create worker roles, is that it is not, after all, obvious. In fact, it hardly applies to societies like eighteenth-century France and the Karimojong. The general state of the economy in the eighteenth century affected *the returns to* the property and activities that were the undifferentiated roles of peasants, craftsmen, merchants, or office holders. The state of the market affected very little *whether or not the roles existed* in the first place. In the same way a drastic decline of production among the Karimojong in times of famine does not produce unemployment, that is, does not produce people without status rights in the productive system. It merely means that status rights do not produce enough to eat. The reason, then, for using an opaque language to describe the relation between market situations and the creation of roles in the previous paragraph is to take the obviousness and inevitability out of the connection. It is exactly the fact that role structures do vary rapidly and easily in response to market forces that distinguishes the adjustments of American role structures to demographic facts.

The core institutions of modern society for the creation of roles are the institutions that facilitate the transfer of resources among organizations and that allow organizations great powers to reorganize the status system in response to such transfers. These core institutions are the legal personality of corporations and civil contracts. By legal personality we mean the right of an organization to change (1) its status system, (2) its complement of roles, and (3) its rights and rewards and their mutual obligations. These rights, in turn, are almost the same thing as the right to sue and be sued, the right to hold property, and the right to hire people for a wide range of purposes under a wide variety of labor contract arrangements. All these rights can be summed up as the right to make contracts that will have legal existence.

This set of arrangements means that the role-creating mechanisms of modern societies generally are not adapted in detail to the demographic facts of the succession of generations. This is reflected in the much higher unemployment rates of young people than of middle-aged people. It is also reflected in unemployment of people who have worked in organizations that have gone out of business, or whose business has declined (e.g., because of a cut in defense contracts). Modern organizations do not have to provide jobs for people they do not need and can create jobs for which no one is prepared. The extensive existence of vacancies without occupants and people without appropriate roles is a by-product of free, market-oriented creation of status systems.

The Social Control of Fertility

In all premodern societies, the main way fertility is controlled, if at all, is by the control of sexual intercourse. First, societies vary a great deal in the relationship between marriage and sexual intercourse. Marriage involves the formation of a contract between husband and wife, and generally between their families, in which in many societies legal authority over the woman is transferred and the family membership of the children of the woman is fixed. This creates a set of rights by the husband over the wife and children, a set of rights over inheritance and social position by potential children, and a set of rights and duties of the two families with respect to the new marriage. In many societies it also creates rights of the wife. One of the rights that is almost always involved is sexual access to the wife by the husband. But this allocation of sexual rights to husbands may or may not be the only normative circumstance under which sexual intercourse takes place, and these rights within marriage may or may not be limited by extensive sexual taboos, for instance, taboos against sexual intercourse while the woman is nursing a baby.

The simplest case is when sexual intercourse is almost exclusively limited to marriage, and when unlimited sexual intercourse can take place within marriage. The very low rates of illegitimacy and of premarital conception in eighteenth-century France, combined with childbearing at approximately the natural fecundity of women within marriage, indicates such a system. In this case the main social determinants of fertility are the marriage practices of the culture.

If sexual intercourse is confined to marriage, there are three main aspects of marriage practices that then determine exposure to sexual intercourse: (1) the age at marriage of the women, (2) the proportion of women remaining unmarried, and (3) the average length of time that widows (or divorced people) remain unmarried. The fertility of the population will be lower if the age at marriage is older, the proportion of women remaining celibate is higher, and the rate of remarriage is lower. As we will see, the fertility of the French population was substantially reduced by all these marriage practices.

The restriction of sexual intercourse to marriage is not an especially common institution, however. Among the Karimojong, unmarried women freely take lovers and bear children. The illegitimacy rate for blacks and whites in the United States is above that found in eighteenth-century France (even though contraception is certainly more frequently practiced now). The abortion rate in the United States indicates substantially less regulation of sex by marriage practices than in the eighteenth century. About 24% of all conceptions among white women in 1977 were aborted; about 41% among black women were aborted (*Statistical Abstract* 1979, p. 68). Many of these abortions are for pregnant single women.

Even if societies with relatively free premarital sex were to have a late marriage age, or many celibate women, or little widow remarriage, the exposure to sexual intercourse would not decrease much. But at any rate, late marriage, celibacy, and widow celibacy are not common institutions in societies with much premarital sex. Late marriage, celibacy, and widow celibacy seem to be most characteristic of Europe after the Middle Ages. Thus, for most of the world, marriage practices have relatively small effects on exposure to sexual intercourse.

When sexual intercourse takes place, it may or may not result in pregnancy. If no contraception is used, the probability of conception varies with the natural fecundity of the women, which varies with age. Data from rural France in the eighteenth century indicates that for women in their 20s, about 50 children will be born in 100 woman-years of exposure; for women in their early 30s, about 40 children per 100 woman-years; for women in their late 30s, about 33 per 100 woman-years. Since women who have a child every other year are either pregnant or newly delivered (hence sterile) half or more of the time, these figures mean that a woman in her 20s conceived, on the average, after about a year of nonpregnant sexual intercourse. Roughly speaking, then, these figures should be about doubled to be comparable with the contraceptive effectiveness figures in Table 5.1.

Table 5.1 shows that the birth rate of women regularly using contraception is generally much lower than natural fecundity, even with ineffective techniques. This does not mean that individuals who do not want babies are not running serious chances of pregnancy. Instead it means that they will have many fewer children than women not using contraceptives. Abortion is, however, very nearly 100% effective, as is surgical sterilization of either the man or the woman. Except for those who have moral objections to abortions, fertility is now under nearly perfect control in advanced countries.

The ability to control conception changes the causes of lowered fertility. Instead of exposure to sexual intercourse, the main causes lie in the knowledge of contraceptive methods, in the disciplined and regular use of those methods, and in the number of children desired. Freely available abortion makes the number of children desired into the most fundamental determinant of fertility.

When contraceptives are widely used, the pattern of fertility changes to one in which fertility depends on the number of children a family already has. As a couple reach the number of children they want, their fertility drops dramatically. Thus, the dominant causes of fertility change to those that affect the number of children people want. The central variable that we want to explain in modern societies, then, changes from the fertility rate per year, which is the important variable in traditional societies, to the completed family size, for completed family size is the core variable that determines people's contraceptive behavior. The conceptual framework appropriate to modern fertility studies, then, is that

TABLE 5.1

Relative Effectiveness of Popular Contraceptives [a, b]

Intent and method	Percent failing R	Monthly conception probability p	Contraceptive efficiency e	Expected time to conception M	Cumulative probability of conception in 10 years Y
Delay pregnancy					
Pill	7	.0058	.9708	171	.504
I.U.D.	15	.0125	.9375	80	.779
Condom	21	.0175	.9125	57	.880
Diaphragm	25	.0208	.8958	48	.920
Foam	36	.0300	.8500	33	.974
Rhythm	38	.0317	.8417	32	.979
Douche	47	.0392	.8042	26	.992
No Method	NR	.2000	0.	5	.999
Prevent pregnancy					
Pill	4	.0033	.9833	300	.330
I.U.D.	5	.0042	.9792	240	.394
Condom	10	.0083	.9583	120	.634
Diaphragm	17	.0142	.9292	71	.819
Foam	22	.0183	.9083	55	.891
Rhythm	21	.0175	.9125	57	.880
Douche	40	.0333	.8333	30	.983
No Method	NR	.2000	0.	5	.999

[a] Based on observed failure rates per year for married women with between one and four previous births.

[b] NR means not reported. R is calculated from pregnancy histories by Ryder (1973, *Fam. Plan. Persp.* 5: 133–143). Michael Hout carried out these calculations for me.

$p = R/12$

$e = 1 - p/.2$ (.2 being the estimate of p for couples using no method)

$M = 1/p$

$Y = 1 - (1 - p)^{120}$

we study social causes of ideal family size, and then perhaps ask what social causes (ignorance, norms against contraception, lack of discipline in the use of contraceptives) or the causes of failure to procure an abortion may cause people to fail to fulfill their ideals.

Generally, ideal family size is larger in rural populations of industrialized societies and in underdeveloped countries. Ideal family size in most poor countries is in the region of four or five children. In urban areas of advanced countries, the ideal family size varies in the region of two or three. Rural populations in advanced countries have an ideal family size between these two. Rural populations tend to carry their family size ideals with them into the city, so that rural migrants (especially uneducated rural migrants) to the city have more children than people born in the city.

Within thoroughly urban populations (i.e., urban populations not counting the rural migrants), the dominant determinants of ideal family size seem to be economic, residential, and cultural. Generally, richer people in cities want more children than poorer people. But this generalization is modified by requirements for economic investments, so that small businessmen generally want fewer children than professional people. (Note however that farmers are also poor small businessmen in most of Western Europe, North America, Japan, and Oceania, but they want more children than urban workers). People who live in apartments generally want fewer children than those who live in houses, though this may reflect a choice of housing in accordance with family ideals rather than determination of ideals by housing. And finally, ethnic and national groups have variations in ideal family size that are hard to explain on economic grounds. For instance, Mexican urban people want more children than Brazilian urban people; Jews want fewer children in the United States than Protestants or Catholics (Jews have also lived in apartment houses more often, which may be a partial explanation).

But if richer people want more or the same number of children than poorer people, why have poorer people had more children? The first explanation is that more of the poor people have been migrants from rural areas. These are the poor people who have more children. Urban-born workers have fewer children than rural-born workers, though the difference is decreasing in recent years as rural areas become more urbanized. They have no more children than urban-born middle-class people. The second explanation is that the urban poor historically have used contraception less. *Among those who use contraception regularly,* urban workers have had *fewer* children than the urban middle classes. Thus, with the spread of contraception and abortion, the differential fertility of urban populations tends to reverse itself. The more diffused contraception is, the lower is the working-class birth rate as compared to the middle-class birth rate.

What then has explained the slower adoption of contraception among the urban poor? Contraceptive practices require people to enter on a plan of action that will have consequences only in the long run. This is reflected in Table 5.1 in the different rates of contraceptive failure among those who are only trying to postpone births than among those who are trying to prevent births. The greater discipline of the latter results in a lower rate of failure among almost all contraceptive techniques; sterilization, the contraceptive technique with the lowest failure rate, is only available for preventing births. This pattern of action has usually required people to enter into relations with professional people or service bureaucracies. Until the development of the pill, this pattern of action only worked a relatively small part of the time. Furthermore, until recently, successful contraception required a high degree of continuously exercised self-discipline. This is obviously true of withdrawal and the safe period. But all older methods required a continuous supply of contraceptive materials, which means a continuous supply of money to buy them or regular visits to public clinics. The methods all required the decision to use them every time sexual intercourse took place.

Such long-term planning in the face of uncertainty and disciplined continuous regulation of behavior is undermined by the attitude of fatalism. The conviction that people cannot control their fates, that the best laid plans often go astray, that luck and impulse determine outcomes, undermines rational self-discipline. The central determinants of the nonfatalist conviction are education and occupational experience with controlling the world. Education and control of the world are more common experiences of the middle class. The skills of getting what contraceptives they want from physicians and service bureaucracies are the skills of middle-class urban life. Thus, the social determinants of being able to reach family size ideals by contraception are more common in the middle class. Abortion is more equally accessible to people with both impulsive and disciplined life-styles than is contraception.

In the urban population of urban origin, the distribution of contraceptive practice has in the past been opposite the distribution of family size ideals, with the poor wanting smaller families but getting larger ones. As contraceptive practice becomes easier and more widely diffused and abortion becomes available, failure to reach family size ideals becomes a less important cause of fertility. Then family size ideals become a more important cause, and the birth rate of the poor tends to decline below that of the rich.

If a child is conceived, then the next question is whether or not it is aborted or results in a miscarriage. We do not understand very well the natural causes of the probability of carrying a child to full term. But it seems that aside from a few known infectious diseases that kill or damage the fetus, the main cause of variations nowadays in the rate of fetal death is induced abortion. The birth rates of urban areas of countries that have legalized abortion go down rapidly. Japan and the Soviet Union at some periods have shown especially sharp effects. In general, abortion seems to be an alternative to effective contraception, and legalized abortions have less effect on the birth rate in populations with widely diffused contraception. Nevertheless about a third of all conceptions in the United States are artificially aborted.

Social Determinants of Mortality

Medicine has had very little effect on noninfectious diseases such as cancer, circulatory disorders, aging, and degenerative diseases. The main effects on mortality have been effects on infections by bacteria and to a lesser extent viruses. These have come about in four main ways: sanitation, the control of insect carriers, the control of infections from wounds (of war, surgery, and accidents), and vaccination.

The effects of these on the overall death rate are shaped by the nature of the mechanisms of immunity to diseases. Many diseases largely kill children, because they are the main population without developed immunities. Children infected with diseases for which there are immunity mechanisms either die or develop antibodies. Thus, the adult population consists largely of people immune to the most common infectious diseases, if they are diseases to which there is a human immunity mechanism. Infectious diseases therefore largely produce an increase in the infant and child mortality rates.

Probably the main exception to this generalization is infections of wounds. Warfare is one of the main killers of adults. The death rates from wounds have been drastically reduced by aseptic procedures and by aseptic surgery. Antibiotics also have a major effect on the death rate from wounds.

The main effect of vaccination is to make the child population as immune as the adult population, for those diseases for which there is an immune mechanism. Vaccination is not a danger-free method, but ordinarily has a much lower death rate than the disease itself, at least with modern technology. Where the disease is almost absent (as, for instance, smallpox now is and rabies is in Scandinavian countries) vaccination is more dangerous than the disease.

The effects of sanitation and control of insect carriers (especially of malaria and bubonic plague) are similar to each other. They decrease the probability that an infected person will infect another. Human and animal wastes from infected people carry the germs of some diseases, especially of the alimentary canal and the respiratory tract. Exposure to such infected wastes causes infections, which in turn increases the degree of infection of the wastes. The sewage and garbage of healthy populations is reasonably healthy. (For example, modern garbage workers do not have the high rates of infection of garbage workers of former times.) But wastes not properly disposed of produce sick populations, which in turn produce infected waste. In much the same way, malarial populations produce mosquitos infected by malaria, which produce malarial populations. By breaking the cycle by sanitation or by control of insect carriers, the infections tend to die out rather than become endemic.

These cycles of infection and reinfection in premodern populations tended to be carried from place to place by groups of people who were mutually exposed to each other's wastes or each other's insects. War brings the mutual exposure cycle of the army into new populations. Shipping brings crews who live together into port. Famine moves populations in the search of food. Disease cycles in one population move to another population largely by moving social disease cycles, not by moving individual infected people. The rats and lice of a ship, infected in their turn by sick crew members, carried plague into Marseille in 1720, not an individual person sick with the plague. Thus, formerly epidemics were spread much more by war and commerce than individual migration.

The breaking of disease cycles by sanitation, insect control, and vaccination had its main effect by decreasing infant and child mortality. This has the same effect on a population as increasing the birth rate. That is, modern sanitation and preventive medicine increase the ratio of children to adults. Thus, with decreases in the death rate, the average age of the population *decreases*. Populations become *younger* as the average life expectancy increases, unless the birth rate also declines.

The first improvements in sanitation were probably not introduced for reasons of health, but for the amenity of the environment. Sewage systems and garbage collection make the environment of cities more pleasant, as well as healthier. Before the germ theory of disease was popular, well-organized cities decreased the germ population for aesthetic rather than health reasons.

Under a premodern sanitation regime in rural areas, about half of all children die before reaching adulthood. About half of these, or a quarter of all children, die in the first year. At the other extreme, in 1977 about three males and two females in every 100 died before reaching 20 years old among whites in the United States (about four males and three females in 100 among nonwhites died before reaching 20 years old). Approximately half of these die in the first year among whites, but about two-thirds of the nonwhite deaths before age 20 are in the first year.

In 1900, premodern mortality of one in four deaths in the first year, and another one of the three remaining before adulthood, still characterized the black population of the United States. The white death rate by 1900 already was halved by preventive medicine, with about one out of eight children dying in the first year, and one of the remaining seven dying before 20 years old.

We can therefore see the small effect of preventive medicine on older age groups by comparing life expectancies of older people between 1900 and 1966, for whites and nonwhites. In 1900 the black male population, under a primitive sanitation regime, had a life expectancy at age 65 of 10.38 years. The white male population under semimodern sanitation had a life expectancy of 11.51 at 65. The 1977 white male population has an expectancy of 13.9 years, the nonwhite of 14 years at 65. The control of infection between 1900 and the present only made a two and one-half to three and one-half year difference at 65. Life expectancies at birth were very different for these male populations: blacks in 1900, 32.54 years; whites in 1900, 48.23 years; whites in 1977, 70.0 years; nonwhites in 1977, 64.6 years. (All figures in this and the preceding paragraph were taken from *Statistical Abstract* 1979, pp. 70–71.)

Broadly speaking, then, medicine does not save the lives of old people, though it may make their dying more comfortable. It does save the lives of children, mainly by sanitation, vaccination, and control of insects. And it makes wounds less deadly to the soldiers of advanced countries. Most of these effects on mortality are effects of public health measures. Individual medical care when people get ill has very little effect on mortality. Probably with the advance of medicine, private practice (excepting perhaps surgery) is not positively harmful, which it seems to have been up to about 1900.

Thus our three societies have very different ways of bringing the population into adult roles, and creating the roles to induct them into; and they have very different population dynamics, very different patterns of births and deaths, to produce people for those roles. The structure of matching people to positions therefore differed greatly among these societies.

SOCIAL CONTINUITY
AMONG THE KARIMOJONG

Karimojong Demography

The Karimojong population is characterized by very high and variable death rates, and birth rates near the limit of human fecundity. (In addition to *Karimojong Politics*, especially Chapter 5, Neville Dyson-Hudson has let me use materials from his lectures in this section. Without access to this material this section could not have been written.) Virtually all of the life of all of the women in Karimojong society is spent exposed to sexual intercourse; a woman's reproductive powers are used to their fullest. The "normal" death rate is so high that more than half of all children born die before two years of age. Epidemics and warfare kill many of the adult population, and famine conditions are frequent.

There are three institutional practices that combine to make full use of the reproductive powers of a Karimojong woman: premarital lover relationships, polygyny, and widow inheritance. All of these depend on two cultural themes that make the Karimojong attitude toward child-bearing very difficult from those of either eighteenth-century France or the modern United States: the differentiation of biological fatherhood from sociological fatherhood, with a consequent differentiation between sex and marriage, and the general postulate that the more children, the better.

The premarital lover relationship is one that might be called "semi-institutionalized." That is, it is a socially recognized relationship for which special provisions are made, but on the other hand, it does not have the ritual and economic complexity of true marriage relationships. The first component of this relationship is the specification of who the *sociological* father of a child is by the present lineage membership of the mother. An unmarried woman is a member of the lineage of her father and brothers, and the Karimojong say of her male child, "He is taken by the brothers and becomes as a brother." Thus, there is no real concept of "illegitimacy" of children, nothing problematic about how the child will be supported, about who will take care of it, or about what group is, in the last instance, responsible for its social placement. For this reason pregnancy before marriage is not irresponsible or shameful.

Very often when the girl does marry, her husband will adopt her children by premarital relationships into his own family. But in order to do that he has to "clear his title" to the child by the payment of a price of a cow for a girl or an ox for a boy to her father or brothers, who are giving up something valuable in giving up the illegitimate child. The father and brothers are happy to have another child and are institution-ally assumed to have obtained something valuable when the "illegiti-mate" child is born. When they give up this valuable thing, they must be recompensed. Far from being shameful and a serious disadvantage upon marriage, then, a child conceived before marriage is thought of by everyone concerned as a valuable thing, for which a prospective husband should be sufficiently grateful to pay an adoption price.

The second element of the semi-institution of the premarital lover relationship is the social recognition of its temporarily monogamous character. Someone besides the lovers is supposed to know who an unmarried girl is sleeping with. This allows them to know who it is that should pay the fine or support payment when a child is born. The lover has obligations toward the child without rights toward him or her, and is supposed to contribute to the child's support by giving the mother's family a few goats and sheep. A girl would be considered promiscuous if she slept with a number of men at the same time so that the genitor of her child was unknown, or if nobody knew who the father was. Thus, there is a lesser version of the extensive social recognition of a marriage relationship for the lover relationship. The relationship, so to speak, exists in the eyes of the community as well as being a private arrangement between the two lovers.

The family of the girl itself makes provision for the relationship by providing a special hut for adolescent girls to meet their lovers in. The principle is the same as family recognition of the dating relationship in American society, except that there is more explicit recognition of what is likely to happen on dates.

Because this semi-institutionalized lover relationship exists and is approved of, and because the problem of who is to take care of and have rights in the child is arranged in a satisfactory way, the age of marriage among the Karimojong does not regulate the ages of sexual exposure. The reproductive powers of women before marriage are utilized by the society, or more precisely by her "owner," the owner of the herd on which she depends before marriage. Her sexual powers are used by whoever is lucky.

The institution of polygyny means that women would not fail to be married because of lack of husbands. This is important for two reasons. The first is that the death rate of men is probably somewhat above that of women due to the practice of raiding and warfare. The second is that polygyny facilitates the practice of widow inheritance. A woman once married becomes the property of the lineage into which she has married. If she had to look for an unmarried man to remarry, she might have to go outside the lineage, involving the difficulties of marriage prices and the transfer of property rights. Since she can be added to the group of wives of other members of the lineage, there need be no difficulties.

The institution of widow inheritance immediately transfers the reproductive powers of a widowed woman to some other member of the lineage (never her own son—typically the new husband is a brother of the man who has died). Thus, there is no body of unmarried widows who are left without exposure to sexual intercourse for an extended period. The demographic effect of widow inheritance mainly applies to women who are still young when the husband dies. Widow remarriage also provides social security for older widows, and guarantees that any children of the widow have a herd to depend on and a family to manage their social placement. The institution of marriage then has as its crucial element the passing of sociological fatherhood of all the children of a woman for all her remaining reproductive life to the lineage of the husband. Which member of the lineage will be the sociological father and the owner of the woman may change with the death of members of the lineage, but the institution of fatherhood is permanently arranged at the time of marriage.

The cultural theme of the differentiation of sociological fatherhood and biological fatherhood clearly shows up both in the arrangements for premarital lover relationships and in the inheritance of widows. Whoever is or becomes the "owner" of a woman becomes the sociological father of her children. The fact that the genitor is a lover, or a dead brother or uncle, rather than the owner of the woman himself, does not affect the social responsibility for the child nor the rights in the child.

The cultural proposition that the more children, the better, also permeates the institutional arrangements for ensuring continuous reproduction by fertile women. It is reflected, for example, in the treatment of what we would call an illegitimate child as an object of value, for which the husband who married an unmarried mother should be expected to pay. It also informs the institution of polygyny, because the central institutionalized purpose of having more than one wife is to have the children of more than one woman become children of the lineage. As we have mentioned, the availability of sexual services of a woman is not necessarily restricted to marriage. What one gets by marrying a woman, institutionally speaking, is the right to her children. The reason for marrying rather than carrying on an affair is to gain the right to the children. Widow inheritance again reflects the wish not to waste a resource of reproductive capacity owned by the family. In addition to these institutional reflections of the desire for children, Karimojong people show in many informal ways that they love children.

This maximization of the birth rate goes on in an environment in which it is very hard to stay alive. As we discussed in Chapter 2 on the ecology of Karimojong society, famine is frequent. Epidemic disease spreads easily, especially through uncontrolled insect carriers. The general probability of infection of children, even in times of no epidemic disease, is very high. In addition to death by famine and infectious diseases, wounds often result in death from infection, even if the spear of the raiding or defending enemy misses its mark of a vital organ. Thus, the high rate of warfare and brigandage contributes to a high rate of death among the adult male population. The combination of these factors apparently makes for an even higher death rate than that we find in eighteenth-century France.

Because there is so much variation in the death rate from time to time, the overall tendency of population growth is rather difficult to determine. It appears however that after the disasters near the end of the nineteenth century that decimated the population of all of East Africa, the Karimojong population has probably grown. They seem to have expanded the territory that they occupy southward, and there seems to be on the one hand a history of general tendency for the cattle herds to expand, and on the other hand a present situation in which the herds support the maximum number of people possible. Since the statistical materials on Karimojong population and vital rates are virtually useless for detailed study of population growth, we have to make precarious inferences from this territorial expansion to population growth. It appears, then, that in the absence of disastrous situations combining human epidemics, cattle epidemics, and famine, the general tendency of the Karimojong population is slowly upward.

The Reproduction of Roles and Statuses

The general idea behind the creation of roles for the upcoming generation of Karimojong is that they ought to reproduce the preexisting structure of society and that the structure that has to be reproduced consists entirely of the roles of men. Women's roles are created as an adjunct of men's roles. The principle is that the grandfathers are reproduced in their grandsons. There is a kind of structural amnesia of all social rights beyond the third generation, in the sense that no particular rights are justified by a mythology going back more than three generations. But this succession of grandfathers by their grandchildren is embedded in a general picture of a kind of cyclical time, in which the present generation of grandfathers is a reproduction of their grandfathers, and that in reproducing the organization of present grandfathers in this generation of children, we are implicitly bringing the cycle back around to regenerate the fourth generation ascending. Thus, among the age sets, there are two generations of dead people, two age sets in limbo so to speak, who come back on the scene as their grandchildren take up their names and age-set membership when a new age set is opened to replace the presently existing grandfathers. History disappears, because the present generation of children replace their grandfathers, who replaced one of the latent dead generations; the present children are new creations of the latent generation.

We can organize our discussion of this process of cyclical replacement by distinguishing the following aspects: (1) individuals are regenerated by *repetition*, (2) families are regenerated by *proliferation and splitting*, (3) political classes are regenerated by *succession* of age groups, (4) territorial groups are regenerated *by absorption and by proliferation* of their component families, and (5) political communities, or tribes, are reproduced by *replication*.

The Karimojong have the convention that, when somebody dies, one does not mention his or her name any more beyond the necessary period of mourning. Mentioning a dead man gives offense by distressing people who were close to him. Bereavement is considered a very extraordinary state in which, for example, one has to take very serious care that the bereaved person does not commit suicide. Continuing other people's bereavement by continuing mention of the dead person is therefore inducing people to enter into a dangerous and painful state, which no decent person would do. However, the Karimojong convention in naming children is that children are named after people in their grandparents' generation. Thus, the distribution of names is the same, and in principle each person in the grandparents' generation has an individual in the grandchildren's generation who carries on his or her name.

But perhaps a more indicative practice is the one by which a man continues his own name (this practice is not reported for women). Besides the name he has from his grandparents' generation, he takes up a more individualized name, which refers to his favorite animal. The name for giving the maximum honor and individuation to a man is to add the word for "father" to a description of his favorite animal. The name that is most bound up with a man's self image, then, is a name like "father of the spotted ox," or "father of the ox with horns like a gate." The problem of the individual's continuity in being "father of the ox with horns like a gate" is that oxen on the average have a much shorter life span than do men, at least under Karimojong conditions. Thus, in order to ensure that a man is the same man, he must always have one ox with horns like a gate.

When the ox gets old or otherwise looks as if he might die, he is speared by a good friend of the man. A big ritual is set up in which the favorite oxen of a large number of men are speared by their good friends; it is one of the central exchanges of ritual services by which good friendship is manifested. A man could not be expected to kill his own favorite ox. Then another young ox with exactly the same characteristics, so that exactly the same description applies, becomes the favorite ox of the man. A young ox with horns like a gate becomes the favorite ox of the man, so that he continues to be the father of the ox with horns like a gate. When exact repetition of individuals is possible, which of course only applies when you can kill the individuals at an appropriate time and replace them at the same time with another (i.e., it only applies to cattle), there is, in fact, a deliberate ritual repetition of individuals which reproduces exactly the social relation which has been destroyed.

But the dominant status rights in Karimojong society are not attached to individuals but rather to families. They are exercised on behalf of the family by the "owner" of the family and of the herd on which it depends, but he occupies his position because he is the owner of the family rather than because of his individual rights. Consequently a more crucial aspect of the creation of roles and statuses in Karimojong society is the creation of families.

By the terms *proliferation* and *splitting* I refer to the fact that the solidarity of the group of descendants of a given family disappears after the third generation. This continual disappearance of structural ties between remote descendants means that there will typically be many corporate descendant groups of any given corporate family. There are means for producing enough of the central corporate groups of the Karimojong status system for all the people.

In any one generation, upon the death of the owner of the family, each of the sons takes a part of the herd (and, if relevant, part of the wives) that has previously constituted the corporate group and sets up a separate family. In this one generation, then, the family splits into as many groups as there are sons. Since in general, the larger the herd, the larger the number of wives and the larger the number of sons, more new corporate groups are created from larger families and larger herds of the previous generation. The new family head takes his share in his family of orientation, that is, the family of his father, to endow his family of procreation (which will probably already have been started) with separate corporate existence. He becomes an owner by splitting the owner role of his father with his brothers.

In case the owner dies without male issue, the herd and the wives are, in a way, reunited with the "latent herd–family" of *his* dead father, and divided again among the brothers. The structural position of inheritor is then typically occupied by a son, but may be occupied by a brother or nephew or in extreme cases by an uncle of the dead owner. It is the structural position of inheritor that joins together the corporate groups of different generations, and it is the multiplicity of inheritors that provides the possibility of proliferation of families.

The names that families carry from one generation to another are called *atake* (plural *atakerin*) among the Karimojong. Each new family and herd created from the family and herd of the owner when the owner dies has the same *atake* as the father. The *atake* then is inherited like the surname in American society, through the male line. There are 19 distinct *atakerin* in Karimojong society. This may or may not indicate that at some time in the very distant past there were only 19 distinct families that have had descendants in every generation (since one would expect that in an environment like the Karimojong live in, many families would die out).

But the Karimojong also say that there are hundreds, many many *atakerin* more than you can count. What they mean by that is that the set of recognized groups that have inherited a common name from a *known and recognized* ancestor, so that there are some residual solidarity and some residual mutual rights of inheritance between them, are very many. These are the groups of families that are tied together by having common descent from an ancestor less than three generations away. The structural ties between descent groups whose common ancestors are more than three generations away have completely disappeared, and no longer have structural existence in the society. The Karimojong then change their descent reckoning every generation, in the sense that the ties between corporate families change in each generation by the disappearance of those ties that now become too distant to be remembered. The Karimojong are aware that there must have been similar processes in previous generations, and that the present set of *atakerin* in the narrow sense have been produced by forgotten processes of inheritance in distant generations. They describe this process of endless splitting and the creation of new families from old by a phrase which, literally translated, means "people proliferate." Herds must by the same token proliferate as well, except that they refer to this as dividing the herds rather than as proliferation.

Political classes in Karimojong society regenerate the previously existing structure by succession. That is, the status of elder continues to have the same attributes at all times. This status is held by a group of people, who were initiated when they were young men into the age group which is now the elder age group. When the age group of elders starts to empty, by death and incapacity of very old men, individuals are not recruited to replace the dead or incapable men by being inducted into the age group of elders. Instead the whole age group of mature men is promoted en masse to the status of elder in a succession ceremony, and a new age set is opened for initiation of young men.

The succession ceremony is arranged by the elders who are to be replaced. There is undoubtedly some ambivalence on their part because it means that they pass out of social existence; their roles as ritual leaders and as members of the group of judges that deal with disputes are taken from them by the ceremony. There are various informal pressures that the age group of mature men can bring to bear when the population of the elder age group is depleted and the men in it start to become incompetent in their multitude of leadership roles. But the formal initiation of the process belongs by right to the elder age group, and they use various devices of delay. For example, an age group about to be promoted to the elder age group tries to initiate as many very young men as they can, so that the age group will maintain its competence as long as possible.

Again the ideology behind the succession is that grandsons replace the grandfathers. The newly opened age set wears the ornaments of their grandfathers, and take the place of the grandfathers in the cyclical alternation of age groups. Only two age groups can exist at the same time, and since the younger newly opened age set replaces the grandfathers, the grandfathers' age set become latent. The grandfathers, the few former elders who are left, have no official place in the age system. The relations between the elders who are just leaving power and the age group of the mature men are recreated in the relations between the new group of elders and the age set that is newly opened, so that the formal political constitution remains the same, but with new bodies (and in particular many more elders) in the set of roles.

Clearly, demographic variations in the elder age group, once it is closed to new recruitment by becoming the elder age set, will cause variations in the numbers of people who hold the status of elder, and the numbers who hold the status of subordinate age set. These cyclical variations over the course of a generation in the absolute size of different structural groups is adjusted in part by variations in the relationships of the smaller age sets of which the generation age group is composed. Just after succession of a new group of elders, the youngest members of the new elder group will be adolescent boys. While the overall ideology is that there is an elder age group and a younger age group, and to some degree all the elder age group have the ritual and political attributes of elders, the Karimojong do not, in fact, give equal leadership functions to adolescents and to elderly men who own a herd and a family. Because except in a few ritual situations, most of the leadership functions are exercised in an *ad hoc* fashion, depending on what the problem is at a particular time and place, rather than as continuous ritual, judicial, and political officials exercising their roles full-time, these informal adaptations to the realities of age heterogeneity within the age group of elders are easily managed.

The ritual congregations of Karimojong society are territorial sections. The elders exercise their ritual roles as an age group throughout the society, but an elder of a given territorial section exercises his ritual role, in particular, at the ritual ground of his section. Membership in a territorial section is theoretically inherited and determined at birth by the section membership of the owner. In fact, especially near the edges of the territory dominated by a given territorial section, section members are interlarded with members of neighboring sections. In these cases it is inherited section membership that determines a man's ritual congregation, rather than the fact that his nearest neighbors are of a different territorial section.

But there is a good deal of migration in Karimojong society, and people quite often move into the midst of territorial sections of which they are not members. Then the situation becomes more complicated. For the first generation the fact of territorial section membership by birth is definitely dominant, so that a man continues to be referred to as a member of the foreign section. There are no particular disabilities attached to being a member of some other section. A man does not have less right as a Karimojong and as a herd owner or an elder because he is living out of his section. It is only, so to speak, a fact of natural history that a man is from a different section, in much the same way that it is merely a fact of natural history that a person living in Michigan is a Californian. If a Karimojong goes to his home ritual ground on important occasions, when it is convenient, it does not mean much more than going from Michigan back to California for Christmas.

But after about three generations, the general structural amnesia of Karimojong society for all facts that derive from inheritance above the third generation takes hold, and the dominant fact becomes territory of residence. There may be some lingering memory for a while that the family was once different, but they become absorbed into the group they live with. Territorial sections keep their populations in balance with the resources of the territory in part by absorption of families from other sections, over a long period of time.

The same general process of gradual absorption applies to foreigners who become Karimojong. During the 1920s the Karimojong tribe fought and defeated a number of weaker groups who lived nearby and took them over. Thus, there are families among the Karimojong who are now Karimojong who have knowledge of a time when they were not Karimojong. By living with Karimojong for a sufficient period of time, they become Karimojong, and the structural amnesia of different origins above three generations ago wipes out any remaining differences between them and their neighbors.

Finally, we address the question of how tribes are created. Generally speaking, the answer is that we do not know. We do not have accurate histories of any of the politically independent units that now inhabit the general area where the Karimojong are. But we can perhaps get some hint of how it might come about by the development of the section Ngipian, who have moved to the south of the main concentration of Karimojong population. Recall from Chapter 2 on ecology that the section seems to be developing internal structures of ridges similar to the territorial sections of the tribe as a whole. Its social life seems to be progressively differentiated from the collective life of the tribe, as it becomes more difficult to maintain ritual practices at the ritual grounds far to the north, and as they come to depend on different sets of resources, for which they compete with different sets of neighboring tribes. It is conceivable that as the social and political life of such a section becomes progressively detached from the tribe's social life, and as their political objectives are differently oriented, and at times in conflict with those of the rest of the Karimojong tribe, they might develop a structure with the features that make the Karimojong themselves a separate tribe with a more or less integrated political policy.

Such developments would produce a new set of social relations that had a similar structure to that of the Karimojong tribe and that were informed by a similar set of beliefs and ideas, which would have autonomous existence. No doubt cultural and structural drift over time would produce differences in the cultures of these now-divided tribes. But the different tribes in a cultural area might well be replications of the tribes from which they split at the time of division, to go their separate evolutionary way afterward. Perhaps the reason that families of neighboring tribes easily become Karimojong when they are conquered is that culturally and structurally their lives were very similar to the Karimojong the time of conquest. Their tribal customs may have been an evolutionary variant of a main stem of ancestor tribes, of which the Karimojong are also a variant.

The Karimojong, then, create new roles for upcoming generations, adapting the structure of roles to the demographic facts, by a set of processes that are all informed with the ideology that nothing is being done but to maintain things as they are. These various devices take place in what is to the Karimojong an ever-continuing present. They have very few words to refer to the past, and even fewer concepts to describe how the past is different from the present. They have few words that suggest structural reform or a different future from the present. Events happen, and in order to maintain things as they are in the present people have to adapt to them. These adaptations are, to be sure, changes—they involve the creation of roles and structures to respond to the exigencies of the situation. But these changes are not integrated into an ideology of progress or of decline, nor even that kind of enthusiastic conservatism that is produced in advanced countries in response to a radical challenge. The change in the number of families by proliferation is merely preserving the family under the conditions that obtain. The development of a separate social life among the *Ngipian* is merely continuing the social life of the section. The absorption of immigrants into a territorial section is not population growth, but merely a response to people who have been in the section for so long that the memory of the tribe runneth not to the contrary.

Many of the actual changes are made compatible with the ideology that nothing is changing by a fundamental cyclical conception of social life. This is particularly marked with the age system, with its clear cycle of grandsons succeeding grandfathers, and two latent age groups (the grandfathers of the presently existing age groups) which come into existence again when their time comes around. The recreation of individuals in a cyclical fashion, particularly clear in the case of the replacement of a favorite ox so that a man may remain father of the ox with horns like a gate, also adapts the idea of continuity to the fundamental flux of events that tend to disrupt it. To the Karimojong, the idea that a social group like a family, or a structural arrangment like the relations between age groups, could ever disappear or be fundamentally transformed is offensive. The ideology of the Karimojong is well summed up by the French tag, *Plus ça change, plus c'est la même chose;* the more it changes, the more it stays the same thing. But when a modern Frenchman says it, it is a statement of despair and a comment on the futility of effort, for it is said against the background of an ideology of progress. If a Karimojong were to say that the more it changes, the more it stays the same, he would be summing up a philosophy of a timeless cyclical present, with no idea of progress to produce despair over the slowness of change.

AGRARIAN POPULATION ORGANIZATION IN EIGHTEENTH-CENTURY FRANCE

Births and Deaths in Eighteenth-Century France

Most of the French rural population of the eighteenth century was under a regime of uncontrolled conception within marriage, but with conception almost entirely confined to marriage. Consequently, the dominant determinant of the birth rate was the practice of late marriage with relatively many women remaining unmarried. The high birth rates of such a fertility regime were compensated for by high death rates, especially of children, so that the overall tendency during the century was relatively slow growth of the population. This slow growth had been checked by periodic famine and epidemic disease up to about 1740 (see Chapter 2 on ecology). But these disasters were almost absent for the second half of the century, leading to a growth of the population of about 40% (see Louis Henry, "The Population of France in the 18th Century," *Population in History,* eds. D. V. Glass and D.E.C. Eversley (London: 1965), p. 444).

The birth rates for married women were those characteristic of full use of the reproductive powers. Women in their 20s had an average of about one child every two years; women from 30–34 about one child every two and one-half years; women from 35–39 about one child every three years; women from 40–44 one child every six years. (Much of our knowledge of the population dynamics of eighteenth-century France comes from the work of Louis Henry and Jacques Houdaille, especially as represented by their studies of samples of villages in each of the quadrants of France: the southwest in *Annales* for 1972, the northwest in *Population* for 1973, the northeast (by Houdaille) in the *Annales de démographie historique* for 1976, and the southeast in *Population* for 1978. The general picture is the same in each of the regions except that there is some evidence of contraception from around midcentury in some places, while mostly the lowering of marital fertility takes place starting about 1770 or 1780; there are some variations in premarital conceptions especially in the northwest outside Brittany, and there were a few early marrying villages in the southwest. In what follows we will ignore these variations among localities.) This declining birth rate with age mainly reflects a higher proportion of older couples who apparently become sterile, having no more children. (In a monogamous situation, such sterility of the woman may often be physiologically sterility of the man, who ages at the same rate as his wife; or it may indicate that in a few marriages, sexual intercourse ceases; in modern times about 40% of the sterility of couples is due to the male.) If it were due to contraception upon completing an ideal family size, we would expect lower birth rates among women who had already had more children, for instance, those who had married earlier. But fertility rates were almost unrelated to family size or to age at marriage among the peasantry. There was some evidence of contraception among the upper classes.

Thus, if a woman married at 20, we would expect a total cumulative fertility of about nine children if she lived to the end of her reproductive life. If she married at 25, the actual average age at marriage, this would reduce her total cumulative fertility by about two children, to about seven by the end of her reproductive life. There would usually be a good deal of variation around this average, with women who become sterile early having many fewer children, and those with exceptional fecundity having many more children.

Eighteenth-century France was characterized by the "European mar-

riage pattern" of late marriage and high celibacy rates. It seems that
Western Europe in the early Middle Ages had had a pattern similar to
Eastern Europe and to most of the modern underdeveloped world, of
early and nearly universal marriage (this summary is taken from J.
Hajnal, "European Marriage Patterns in Perspective," *Population in History*, pp. 101–143). The percentages of women at ages 40–45 who are still
single in such cultures range under 5%. More than half of the women
are typically married by age 20. Such "non-European" patterns then
have almost no permanent celibacy of women, and marriage typically
takes place in a woman's teens.

For reasons that are obscure, almost all of Roman Catholic Europe
apparently underwent a change in marriage patterns between the early
Middle Ages and the sixteenth or seventeenth century, so that about
half of all women were still single at 25 years old, and proportions
ranging from 10 to 25% of all women never married (Hajnal, 1965; see
also Henry, 1972, 1978; Henry and Houdaille, 1973; Houdaille, 1976).
Thus, compared to the theoretical average family size of nine per sur-
viving woman, about two births per woman are avoided by late marriage
and one per woman is avoided by permanent spinsterhood, for a total
expected completed fertility of about six rather than nine children.

As we have seen among the Karimojong, the age at marriage need
not reflect the age at which people start to have sexual intercourse. But
the rates of illegitimacy in rural France seem to have been below 1% of
all births (see Louis Henry and Claude Levy, "Quelques données sur
la region autour de Paris au XVIIIe siècle," *Population* 17, 2 (1962), pp.
297–326). The rates of premarital conception (birth in the first eight
months of marriage) in the Henry–Houdaille survey range from about
3–17%, with the higher rate being localized and more common in the
latter part of the century. Thus, it seems that generally there was very
little sex outside marriage in rural France, and that little mostly resulted
in immediate marriage.

Of the children born, about half survived to the age of marriage.
(Many village studies give mortality rates for children up to age ten or
15. For instance, at Boulay, for each 1000 births there were 622 who
survived 15 years; figures given by Henry for various villages range from
703 survivors per 1000 births by ten years old to a fantastically low 382
per 1000 for Ingouville from 1720–1790). About 25% of all children died
during the first year, another 20% between ages one and five, and another 5–10% between ages five and ten. We read of the election of two
promoters in the student association of Avignon "whose essential function was to summon the society's members to students' funerals and to
organize the admission of freshmen" (Philippe Aries, *Centuries of Childhood* p. 242. The document is from 1441, but the problem remained in

the eighteenth century). Thus the total number of living adult children of an elderly couple would be on the average about three and one-half.

But the variations in the incidence of death were even greater than the variations in fertility. The dominant causes of child deaths were infectious diseases, which tend to be concentrated in families. It is not uncommon to read of families losing three children in one year. There were therefore great variations around the average of three and one-half survivors of a couple, with many couples having none, many having ten or more. The experience of Louis XIV of writing instructions to the Dauphin, his son, only to have three successive heirs die within a year, leaving no mature heir for the throne, is characteristic of the chancy nature of inheritance in a regime of high birth and death rates. The tendency of high birth and death rates to produce greater variation in family size is still seen in attenuated form in the greater standard deviation of the size of black households than white ones in the United States.

The overall result of these processes was that the crude birth rate in the eighteenth century seems to have been about 40 per 1000. This compares with maxima from today's underdeveloped countries of from 45 to 50 per 1000. The crude death rate outside famine years or epidemics seems to have been about 30 per 1000, for an average life expectancy of about 30 years. This balance between births and deaths should give an average increase of the population of about 1% per year. It should take such a population about 70 years to double in size. This compares with a growth rate of around 3% per year for equally developed countries in the modern world where infant mortality from infectious diseases is under much better control. This theoretical rate of growth agrees well with the observation given above that the population of France grew about 40% from 1750 to 1790.

This also gives a rough estimate of how many years' population growth would be wiped out by famines or plagues. If we accept the overall figure that a famine like that of 1710 caused about 10% of the population to die, this is an elevation of about 7% over the usual death rate. Thus, it should normally take about seven years to make up the loss, unless the sparser population after the famine decreased the death rate or encouraged earlier marriage. On the other hand, those hard-hit villages that experienced deaths of 25% of the population might expect to show clear signs for a quarter of a century, if there were no migration.

The death rate in cities seems to have been higher than in the country. Cities had the disadvantage of more medical care and worse sanitation. As late as the last quarter of the nineteenth century, the mortality following all forms of amputation in England was between 35 and 50% and the rate of maternal mortality in Europe was about 34 per 1000 deliveries if performed in a hospital, 4.7 per 1000 if performed at home (both figures from McKeown and Brown "Medical Evidence Related to English Population Changes in the Eighteenth Century," *Population Studies* 9 (1955–1956), pp. 120–121). One in 30 women died in delivery in hospitals, one in 200 at home.

Though it seems probable that medical services were on balance bad for you up until the turn of the twentieth century, the same is not true for sanitation. But the development of effective sewer systems and systematically organized garbage collection and street cleaning was primarily an achievement of the nineteenth century. In the eighteenth century the practice of isolation of sick people was practiced especially for the plague (for example, the people of Marseille were forbidden to leave the city in the plague of 1720); however, for a disease transmitted by fleas, this practice did little good. The larger degree of mixing of the population in cities therefore led to higher rates of infectious diseases. The vaccination practiced in the late eighteenth century against smallpox was quite dangerous, and reached very few people anyway.

It is hard to estimate how much higher the death rate was in Paris than in the countryside. The best data come from foundling hospitals, where childhood diseases must have spread with exceptional rapidity. It was sufficiently noteworthy to contemporaries that they put their children out to board in the country (*nourrice*) if they could.

The birth rate of the city population was probably also lower because more of the population were single. Much of the immigration into Paris was of young unmarried men and women. A position as household servant or apprentice, then as now, tended to depress the marriage rate. A large proportion of the poor of Paris were servants to the relatively large Parisian upper class. Finally, the only class for which there is reason to suspect contraception, the rich, were more numerous in Paris.

Thus, Paris and other cities may have had a much lower rate of natural increase than the provinces. This combined with the growth of cities must have set up pressure for a relatively large net immigration into the cities.

Property and Accretion of Roles

When people are used to thinking of a man's status as an *occupation* that occupies his full time and more or less completely determines his social standing, they tend to be bewildered by systems in which most rights are marketable property. An entirely disproportionate amount of attention has been paid to those few rights, like noble titles and entailed estates, which passed by inheritance in a congealed lump. Such congealed lumps of rights were permanent places in the social structure, which stayed more or less in the same place from generation to generation. But most of the status structure of eighteenth-century France was not nearly as frozen as this.

Thus, an optical illusion has been created by looking with bureaucratic eyes at the Old Regime system organized around property. *Insofar* as there were permanent positions in the organization chart of French society, these were quite highly congealed and rigid, and passed by family inheritance. But that does not mean at all that the overall system of legitimate rights to decide what to do with resources was rigid. Authority was dispersed in bits and pieces of negotiable property, rather than in an orderly hierarchy of permanent positions.

A typical modern student looking at class structure during the Middle Ages (serfdom did not exist in eighteenth-century France, except for a very few remnants) might ask whether *a man* occupies the *status* of serf. A medieval man more typically asked whether *a piece of land* to which he had tenure rights *was held* in servile tenure. A man might hold one piece of land in servile tenure, another piece in freehold tenure.

It is even easier to make such a mistake in the eighteenth century, because there had, in fact, grown up an appreciable set of statuses that were permanent, which pertained to the individual person rather than to property, and that carried a whole set of rights and responsibilities. In the political realm these were the status groups of the clergy, nobility, members of privileged municipal corporations, and so on. In the occupational realm there were some full-time royal officials and certain professions and crafts which certified journeymen and masters.

These institutions were the seeds of future developments of universal jural statuses and bureaucratic organizations. Furthermore, they were near the powerful center of French society. Even here royal politics changed the structure rapidly, creating new nobles, legitimizing and delegitimizing bastard sons of kings as princes of the blood, creating and selling offices. But it still looks at the center more like a permanently organized status structure through which people come and go, rather than like a stock market in which people build up and tear down positions of "owner" at a high rate. The situation in the provinces is perhaps better communicated through an example.

> According to the available documents, the Marquis d'Escouloubre (of Toulouse) purchased thirteen pieces of land between 1767 and 1784 by the application of this right of option [to buy any piece of land sold within his seigneurial domain] on his seignories of Viellevigne and Montesquieu–Lauragais. . . . Between 1756 and 1790 the Marquis . . . acquired thirty-seven scraps of land valued at 37,891 livres plus the seignory of Montesquieu–Lauragais (500 arpents [or 695 acres])

for 349,000 livres. The "scraps" of land were very small, often less than . . . 0.35 acre. Nevertheless, by such small purchases and exchanges the seignory of Viellevigne increased by . . . 66.72 acres in the forty years before the Revolution. . . . The Marquis . . . used [black vetch, a new forage bean plant highly resistant to the Mediterranean droughts of Toulouse] to great advantage on his fallows at Viellevigne and Montesquieu–Lauragais. . . . [He] planned an artificial rivulet at Viellevigne to tap water from the Canal du Midi. . . . Escaloubre cleared less than an acre [of forests] working alone at Viellevigne; by contrast, at Montesquieu–Lauragais, thirty-two proprietors cleared about [139 acres] in five years. [Robert Forster, 1957, p. 224–244]. "The Noble as Landlord in the Region of Toulouse at the End of the Old Regime," *Journal of Economic History* 17 (1957), pp. 224-244).

We see from all this account that the position of the marquis was constantly changing. He added to his estate by foreclosing debts, buying land, clearing forests, irrigating land, and making other permanent improvements. It was quite a different thing to be the Marquis d'Escaloubre just before the Revolution than in 1750. This constant piecemeal change of the set of rights pertaining to a person through market exchanges, exercises of long-dormant rights, strategic use of new legislation, and so on, changes the status system.

The same sort of conception also applied to offices, especially those offices whose holders became nobles and which carried feudal traditions, such as positions in the *parlements*. For example we find Montesquieu buying an office for his son.

A sale contract of 1736 in the Gironde archives [involved] Montesquieu, who is fulsomely described as "chevalier, baron de la Brède et de Montesquieu, ancien président à mortier au Parlement de Bordeaux, un des quarante de l'Académie française." The philosopher is here seen buying an office of councilor in the Parlement of Guienne for his son, Jean-Baptiste Secondat, and promising to pay to Dame Charlotte Rose de Sacriste de Tombeboueuf, widow of the former holder, the sum of 27,000 livres during the next three years [John Rothney, *The Brittany Affair and the Crisis of the Ancien Regime* (New York: Oxford University Press, 1969), p. 46]

This did not necessarily mean that Montesquieu's son would spend his full time in this office, nor that he gave up claims to other economic and political roles as *seigneur*. He even might hold other governmental offices. The office was a property added to the estate, a set of rights to be exploited for what it brought in rather than a "recruitment" to a "position" in a social structure.

The bundle of rights and privileges a person owned at a given time could be called his or her "estate," in keeping with common language. A master craftsman's estate consisted of the right he had to practice his trade in a given city, his business properties such as a shop and tools, his clientele, and so on. A peasant's estate consisted of the various pieces of land he owned or had tenure rights in, minus the obligations (rents, tithes, taxes, seigneurial dues) that are attached to those tenures. A noble's estate consisted of seigneurial dues on some pieces of land, rents and dues on other pieces (the *domanine proche*), tax privileges, and perhaps governmental offices. The point about all of these is that they could be bought and sold as well as inherited or received as a *grace* from the King. Consequently, the status a man occupies does not stay stable during his lifetime.

The overall consequence of such an arrangement is that activities are closely connected with property rights rather than with occupational positions. A man's role (property rights were almost exclusively attached to men's roles in the eighteenth century), what he did and what he exercised authority over, depended on the bits and pieces of property rights he held. The market and inheritance system for property rights thus took the place of the creation of vacancies by bureaucracies as the central status-creating mechanism. If a person could not use his property right productively, he or she sold it to someone who could. If a man left a status (i.e., an estate) vacant by his death, his heirs might be direct replacements in the role (as when a son takes over the farm of a father) or they might divide up the rights, sell some of them, recombine their share with other parts of their own estates, and create quite a different role structure.

For example, a farmer with a number of sons who married late in life had about ten years of adult labor from each son before they married at about age 28, without a corresponding drain on the family budget. This time might be used to increase the productivity of his own farm, to farm additional rented land, to work for wages, or to enter apprenticeships. The added income could be used to add to the estate of the family. When he died, the estate inherited by his sons might be smaller than that inherited by a single son, but the total to be divided might be larger because of their additions. The sons at the time of their marriage, and especially after his death, might add to their cumulated estate by saving, by renting other farms, etc. Conversely, a profligate father might drink up the estate or lose his crops for enough years to waste the estate.

In either case there was a good deal of adjustment and change of the quantities of property rights and their distribution over a generation. This flexibility tended to work out so that all the valuable rights and resources available in the society got used by someone.

It is very hard to get an estimate of what proportion of people did not get roles that would support themselves and their families—the eighteenth century equivalents of the unemployed. People complained about vagabonds, but the complaints of the rich are rarely accurate information about the poor. It is clear that the numbers of people who left their home villages increased in times of famine. It is also clear that there was much of what we would call "frictional unemployment," Dick Whittingtons who had left their villages to seek their fortune in the capital, but who had not yet been taken into an urban household. But also new lands were being opened up under some combination of influences of demographic pressure and the high price of grain. More intensive agriculture, specifically growing fodder crops in rotation with grain, was spreading. In short, the total quantity of work done on the land was increasing during the last half of the century.

Scattered evidence indicates that some adjustment of labor to opportunities was taking place by migration. For instance, in Boulay the proportion of all men who married in the town who were known residents of the town fluctuated around 45% (see Houdaille). In the village of Sainghin-en-Mélantois, about half of the *growth* in population between 1740 and 1800 emigrated from the village, the other half being incorporated within the village. About 10% of all people born in the village migrated. This village was in a region with generally high urban contact. The net growth of cities during the period must have involved the creation of new urban jobs or small businesses.

The Role of Schools in Occupational Placement

Schooling in the eighteenth century was under the control of the church. This means that its connections were generally not to labor market institutions such as the professions, the royal bureaucracy, the judicial system, or the military officer corps. Nor was it governed by the body of scientific investigators and humanist scholars in the way American universities are. Thus, there was little institutionalized responsiveness of the schools to labor market demands, except for the demands of the clergy for theological training and for training in canon law.

The principal achievements of schools in preparing people for the labor market were two: literacy in French and literacy in Latin. Both medicine and law, as well as the church, still had much of their intellectual resources written in Latin. Humanist and scientific scholarship was internationally available partially in Latin. Thus, although most of the intellectual production of these professions was written in French (with the exception of clerical writing) literacy in Latin was still a requirement at least at the top of the professions. Both the intellectual sources and production of the royal bureaucracy and of commerce were almost entirely in French, and Latin was not generally required in those occupations.

The general parish schools therefore served a function much like elementary schools today. They prepared people for apprenticeship in commerce or the bureaucracy where literacy in French was required. The *cultural content* of these occupations was not, however, the subject of scholastic preparation. Secondary schools (*collèges*) served the function of producing literacy in Latin, as a preparation for university training or apprenticeship in the church, medicine, and law. But people read law in the offices and homes of lawyers, and served apprenticeships to experienced physicians. Only training of theologians was exclusively in the hands of the university.

Thus, the overall situation was that schooling had become a virtual requirement for entry into the middle classes. But education itself was not organized in the light of the social function it in fact performed. The subjects of the secondary schools were the traditional trivium (grammar [in Latin], dialectics, and rhetoric) and the quadrivium (geometry, arithmetic, astronomy, and music), with the addition of philosophy and physics (i.e., Aristotle). Consequently, the culture of occupational life had to be learned largely within that life by apprenticeship.

POPULATION AND THE LABOR FORCE IN AMERICAN SOCIETY

The problem of filling social roles with new people in American society is quite distinct from the kind of problem posed among the Karimojong or in eighteenth-century France, because the roles that have to be filled are changing all the time. That is, as mentioned in the chapter on technology, the structure of the labor force has changed quite drastically during this century. There are many fewer farmers, many more professional people, and many more middle-class people generally in today's labor force than in the labor force of 1900.

Likewise, in the government during the course of the passage between the previous generation and this generation there has been a great expansion of services, and the government is doing different things now than it was a generation ago. About two generations ago, the government was fighting the Second World War rather than this one; it had a different internal organization; welfare was a local responsibility.

This is reflected in the kinds of qualifications that people are supposed to have for their social roles. There has been during this century a very substantial increase in the proportion of the population that has completed high school, a very substantial increase in the proportion that has completed college, and this is especially marked among young people.

Obviously, in one of the main employers in government service—the Department of Defense, young people have a different set of roles than old people, but this is true also in the economy as a whole. It is also true that the group of men of 60–65 years old have a very different educational preparation for their economic and social roles than the group of men between 20 and 25.

But the adaptation of the roles of individuals to the productive possibilities does not take place by accretion, but rather by shifting recruitment to "full time" positions.

Cohorts and Social Structure

In order to get a grip on this sort of problem of preparing people for constantly shifting social structure, the most useful pair of concepts are *cohort* concepts: first, cohorts of people, and second, cohorts of roles. By a cohort of people we mean a set of people having a birth date within a certain interval, so that the people born from 1930 to 1935 will be a five-year cohort of people. They will be between 45 and 50 in 1980.

Likewise, a cohort of roles can be conceived of as the set of roles created in any given period: a set of roles to which young adults are disproportionately recruited. From a point of view of social replacement, the crucial cohort of people is the cohort of young adults, and the crucial cohort of roles are the set of new jobs that are created during a given period when a given cohort of young adults are entering the labor force or entering their adult roles.

Another way of saying the same point that we made earlier in the chapter on technology about the changing structure of the economy is that the new cohorts of people entering the economy (a group of people now between 20 and 25, say) are having a different set of roles allocated to them than the cohort of people born between 1930 and 1935. The change of the structure of society is reflected in the change in the roles that are available for people to fill, and consequently, the people who fill them will have to have a different mix, or different composition of roles. For example, between 1975 and 1980 schools declined and did not create many teacher roles. The people born between 1955 and 1960 will therefore have many fewer teachers among them than do those born from 1930 to 1935.

Given this difference in the roles that people are going to be asked to fill and the difference in qualifications for the jobs opening up, the new cohort tends to be quite different from previous cohorts. In the age distribution of education, one finds that the oldest cohorts presently in the labor force are considerably less educated (have spent fewer years in school, at least) that the new cohorts that are just entering.

The Creation of Cohorts of Social Roles

One way that we can conceive of this problem of social replacement, then, is on the one hand as a set of processes for creating roles and on the other a set of processes for determining the characteristics of new entrants into roles. Let us consider, first of all, the structural problem of the processes of creation of roles and then return to the problem of getting enough people for them.

New technologies demand new technical roles. Fluids engineer, for instance, is a role that was not very well developed a generation ago. This role has been created both in schools and in industry by creating appropriate mechanisms for seeing to it that a certain proportion of the cohort entering the labor force are fluids engineers. The central problem of American society is not so much to see to it that all of the roles occupied by the previous generation are going to keep on being filled. The crucial thing that distinguishes American society is the process of creating new roles for new purposes or new technologies.

In the creation of new roles we can see two processes that are more or less distinct in American society: one the creation and destruction of organizations, and the other the change in role structure of organizations.

There are laws about the chartering of corporations and about the legal creation of a business. These laws are so set up that it is relatively easy to create or destroy an organization from a legal point of view. In the second place, we have investment banks and the capital market (e.g., the stock market) that allow the sale of bond issues and the sale of new issues of stock. Both the legal system and the economy, then, have a set of devices by which it is relatively easy for the legal powers of the state to be conferred (in certain limited respect) on corporations: they can sue and be sued and use other powers of the state; they can enter the market for resources in a fairly easy and well-understood fashion; they can enter the labor market, advertise in newspapers, and hire new workers. In short, resources in the society are quite highly mobile, not bound up with organizations that already exist, and it is relatively easy both from a legal point of view and an economic point of view to collect and commit the powers and the resources necessary to run a new economic organization.

Likewise in the government there is a systematic procedure for passing the appropriate laws and making the appropriate appropriations to create new agencies of the government, such as poverty programs and urban renewal programs, and to concentrate resources so that people can be hired and roles created.

There are also recognized devices for destroying or "deorganizing" an organization. In the economy an extreme form of this is bankruptcy proceedings. This is not the only way to deorganize a business, however; a company can also merge with another organization or redistribute its capital after the death of its founder, for example. But then organizations internally change their role structures.

In all organizations in modern societies there exists a legal authority, the locus of the legal personality of the organization, either the proprietor or the board of directors. This authority has the legal privilege, which will be defended in the courts if necessary, to create and destroy roles within the organization. There are various kinds of impediments to change within organizations: unions, professional organizations, tenure rules in universities, and the like, because people do not want their roles destroyed. But the legal authority is well defined, and there are, in fact, defined mechanisms in all organizations (e.g., budgetary procedures) by which new roles can be created or old ones destroyed.

In addition, a great many organizations in modern society have what can only be described as a sort of deliberately shifting role structure, for example, in universities. Universities are in some sense quite stable organizations, and they do not very often either get created or get destroyed. But their basic task is a constantly changing one because the state of knowledge changes, and they are organized with a very flexible mode of defining people's roles. In a typical case, if one reads the current college or university catalog, it is already a mistaken description of the actual role structure of the college or university. Some of the courses listed will not be offered, and some other courses not listed there will be offered. Students have a considerable amount of freedom to shift around among roles (the central roles for students are defined by "majors") and to define, within limits, their own set of role obligations in a given major. Probably there are not more than a dozen people in an average sociology class who have the same student role in the formal sense: that is, not more than half a dozen pairs of people have the same student role in the sense of the same schedule of classes. Likewise, the faculty role structures are quite easy to redefine: one can introduce a new course or destroy an old one with very little trouble.

This shifting and adaptive role structure is increasingly characteristic of other kinds of organizations. For instance, the big research and development laboratories are organized on a project basis rather than a departmental basis. The whole notion behind a project basis of organization is that *of course* next year the organization will be doing something different than this year, and people's roles will have to be redefined to do that new thing.

Both in the role structure of society as a whole in the creation of organizations, and in the role structure of a particular organization, we find a plethora of mechanisms for defining roles. In some sense the basic social units in modern society can be conceived of not as sets of roles so much as sets of role-creating mechanisms. The most successful organizations in the society, General Motors or Du Pont are really not so much industries as they are industry-creating organizations. That is, for General Motors or Du Pont, the profits are made not so much by running a business as by the continual creation of new businesses. In essence, then, the role structure of modern society, rather than being organized or bound by concrete roles, is organized around role-creating mechanisms like registrars' offices, boards of directors, legislatures, industrial engineering departments, and the like. These mechanisms are set up through the capital market, through governmental appropriations, through the budgeting of the federal and state governments. The creation and destruction of "organizations" is mainly productive of *role-creating* mechanisms rather than of rigid structures of roles.

Socialization for Roles

Given the rapid development of American technology and the shifts development entails, these role-creating mechanisms give different results in each generation. The cohort of people to fill these constantly created roles needs to have a shifting set of socialization practices imposed on them to prepare them for this shifting set of roles. The device that is used in American society for socialization of people for roles in the economy can be conceived of as a kind of branching tree. The socialization within the family, before school, and the socialization in elementary school is fairly uniform (but not uniformly successful) in what it tries to do for the whole population of the society; it forms the common trunk of socialization. In secondary school there is a division of the socialization process into two or three different streams or branches, or sometimes more: a potential professional stream, a potential clerical stream, and a potential manual worker stream; young women in high school are mostly in the clerical and professional streams. Some of the men are in the professional stream, hardly any of them in the clerical stream, and many in the working-class stream. Generally only the professional branch goes to the four-year colleges; parts of the clerical and working-class streams go on to junior colleges or technical schools.

Upon entry into college the stream again branches in the first couple of years into mainly technical areas (all the people who take calculus), administrative areas (business administration), and arts and social sciences, in which people have somewhat different socialization experiences. Then, of course, each one of these streams branches into considerable detail in the last couple of years of undergraduate education and the first years of graduate education. The preparation for specific economic roles is defined in detail fairly late in a person's career, so that one cannot, in elementary school, usually distinguish the potential aeronautics engineer from the potential computer programmer. Fifteen years ago when new labor market entrants were in elementary school we did not have a very clear idea of how many aeronautics engineers and how many programmers we were going to need. But the socialization in the general elementary stream went ahead, and the adjustment to developing labor market requirements could take place just before entry into the labor market.

The Keying of Socialization to Structure

The structural provision for the constant shift in the roles that adults have to carry out has, then, the first component of the organization of socialization into branching streams, and a second component of relatively tight interrelation at the top end between the curriculum and the required composition of the next cohort. The demand on the part of the people who want to create a new set of roles, for example, to build supersonic airplanes, is transmitted primarily to the last end of the socialization process. For working-class jobs this last end is usually inside the firm itself. After people have been hired, *then* they are trained for the particular kind of job they are needed for. What this does is to allow people to be socialized at the end of their socialization experience for the particular kind of job for which they are needed. The articulation for the middle class is a relationship between labor market requirements and the detailed curricula in the last two years of undergraduate school and graduate school.

Usually, these adjustments take place by a very efficient communications mechanism of the changing salary rates of the different occupations. When one needs more accountants (as apparently the economy does in the early eighties), the relative wage and salary rates of accountants versus other professions increase. This communication by means of money influences the individual decisions of people who are at the stage just before professional choice and who might choose to be either computer engineers or accountants. If "the economy" needs more computer engineers, then it pays a little bit higher rate for computer engineers; if it needs accountants, it pays them more. If the university system "needs" more sociologists and fewer classicists, it pays sociologists more for the same number of IQ points.

The information about different salaries reaches people who have gotten to the branching points, and they choose which final twig of the socialization tree to study at the end. This is combined in American society with a high degree of responsiveness by the socialization mechanism: colleges and universities respond quickly to the shifting demands of the labor market. This is partly because in the United States there is a great deal of local control and local support for most of the universities; in addition, the university administration adheres to a kind of populist ideology that students should learn what they want to learn. The curriculum adjusts relatively rapidly to shifting labor market demands in the United States as compared, for instance, to England or France, or some of the more advanced South American countries. In these countries the schools know what an educated person ought to know, and if he or she wants to learn about hotel management, for example, that is just tough luck. In the United States, if there is a demand for more hotel managers, some state university feels the pressure and sets up a school of hotel management.

By and large, the American university system is very responsive to labor market pressures, and there is almost immediate adaptation. For instance, during the 1950s and 1960s there was a large growth in demand for arts and sciences Ph.D. graduates; the universities responded practically immediately by creating new graduate programs. The graduate programs are now turning out people for whom there are few jobs, and while they have not disappeared, they have fewer students and few resources for expansion. This combination of free choice by the student, salary motivation for choosing one rather than the other of the various branches, and the high degree of responsiveness by local university administrations in the United States to the demands of the market, is a central set of devices by which the socialization of the cohort is adapted to the new demands created by the fantastic rate of creation of new roles.

In the period previous to specialization (which, roughly speaking, goes up to about the second year in college), the socialization in the schools tends to be organized around general basic principles. For instance, there is a good deal of pressure on the school system not to teach medicine in the high school in order to prepare students better for medical school; instead high schools teach reading and writing, what the significance of an experiment is in science, and elementary mathematics. This creates a special vested interest on the part of teachers in these general bodies of knowledge. The systematic development of the basic principles of various fields of practice is very heavily concentrated in the United States in educational institutions, and the public for generalized new knowledge tends to be concentrated in the educational community.

Basic scientific research is disproportionately conducted in universities rather than in industries or in the government. Basic research in the humanities is more likely to be done in universities than among the people who write for popular magazines or do announcing on television.

The family's impact on social placement is neither teaching specific skills nor even in influencing the specific occupational choices of children and young adults. Rather, the family creates a generalized pressure for success, a generalized pressure by mothers and fathers for children to stay in school and to learn to think enough like high school teachers to get good grades. What people essentially hope for their children is that they will do *something* that is successful; they are not very definite about what exactly that should be. People are not in their childhood socialized for specific roles either by their parents or by the school. They are socialized to be ambitious, socialized to be more or less prepared in reading and writing, in the basic outline of history, and in the basic outline of sciences. Educated parents then give their children advantages not by helping them learn electrical engineering, but by encouraging and helping them to learn algebra, to be applied later on to whatever jobs require algebra when the child enters the labor market.

The crucial overall demographic determinant of how the system of recruitment for adult roles works is therefore not the numbers born into particular families, but the overall size of the cohort. For example, the college age cohort 20 years ago (calculating from 1982) was about 60% as large as the cohort some of whose members are in college now. The cohort that is in the grades from kindergarten to fourth grade in 1982 (which will therefore be in college in about a decade) is only about 75% as large as the present cohort. This means first of all that the size of the educational establishment is likely to decline over the next decade: the *Occupational Outlook Handbook* for 1978–1979 warns, for example, that the supply of secondary teachers "will greatly exceed anticipated requirements if past trends of entry into the profession continue" (pp. 214–215) and for college teachers it says "the numbers of master's and Ph.D. degree recipients is expected to greatly exceed all openings resulting from growth and separations from the profession" (p. 216).

This size of cohort effect in its turn means that the education schools are contracting as fewer people enter on the hopeless quest for teaching jobs. From the 1970–1971 academic year to 1978–1979, the number of bachelor's degrees in education *declined* by 28.6% (National Center for Educational Statistics, *The Condition of Education, 1981*, p. 158), while the overall number of bachelors degrees awarded *increased* by 9.7%. Many of the students who used to major in the social sciences and humanities also used to go into teaching and into other fields in which demand is weak, such as social work, or into doctoral programs in the social sciences hoping to work in now-nonexistent college teaching positions. The number of social science bachelors degrees has shown a similar decline of 30.2% from 1970–1971 to 1978–1979.

In contrast to these fields with weak demands, business schools have been booming. A sampling of occupations in business and management shows that accounting employment is expected to increase "about as fast as the average for all occupations through the 1980's" (*Occupational Outlook Handbook 1978–1979*, p. 132); advertising, "faster than average" (p. 134); buyers, "more slowly than the average" (p. 137); credit managers, "more slowly" (p. 142); industrial traffic managers, "about as fast" (p. 145); marketing research, "much faster than average" (p. 150); personnel and labor relations workers, "faster" (p. 152); public relations workers, "faster" (p. 155); and purchasing agents, "faster" (p. 155). As the opportunities shift from education to business, people learn their social science in the context of business and management schools rather than in liberal arts or education schools. Business and management bachelors degrees increased 49.7% between 1970–1971 and 1978–1979, or about five times the rate of growth of all bachelors degrees. Similarly, the number of master's degrees in business and management increased 90.3%. Even though the overall increase in masters degrees was much higher than the increase for bachelors degrees (30.6% compared to 9.7%), the rate of growth of business degrees was about three times the rate for all master's degrees (rates of growth are from *The Condition of Education, 1981*, p. 158).

The growth of business schools is apparently very responsive to demands on the labor market. Business school enrollment approximately quadrupled between 1940 and 1950. But in 1951 we find that the employment situation predicted for accountants was "competition likely to be eased" (*Occupational Outlook Handbook, 1951*, p. 116); for advertising workers, "stiff competition" (p. 33); for marketing research, "increasing competition for jobs" (p. 119); for personnel and labor relations, "expanding" opportunities (p. 107). This soft demand situation was reflected in a substantial drop of about a third in the number of bachelors students graduating from business schools between 1950 and 1960. Then again during the 1960s business school graduates more than doubled (the category for 1960–1961 was "Business and Commerce," the one for 1970–1971 was "Business Management"). Thus, the 49.7% growth from 1970–1971 to 1978–1979 was actually a drop in growth rate compared to the 1960s.

The important point is that the socialization for business school and for a social science degree is very close to the same up through the sophomore year of college. If we imagine that something like 55,000 students per year who would have gone into social sciences in 1970–1971 were going into business and management in 1978–1979, nothing really needs to be changed in the socialization system from kindergarten through the second year of college—parents can urge the same behavior in their children, algebra teachers can cope with somewhat reluctant students, freshman composition teachers can fight in vain against the tendency toward jargon that would later show up either in social science writing or in business writing. Although few students who chose degrees in the light of labor market prospects have ever heard of the *Occupational Outlook Handbook,* they surge obediently from one school to another to fit their socialization to the occupational composition demanded of their cohort. They switch regardless of the fact that the social class composition at birth is very similar from one cohort to the next. The sources of the small variations in the social composition of different cohorts are the subject of the next section.

The Social Organization of Birth

Most birth in the United States takes place within the family system. The births are relatively highly planned. By no means do we have the ideal that the Karimojong have of using up all of the fertility of the women. Births are highly planned to take place within marriage rather than as the result of teenage sex (e.g., in 1979 among unmarried teenagers there were 124 abortions for every 100 births; that is, about 55% of all conceptions of teenage women are terminated by abortion; see Andrew Hacker, "Farewell to the Family?" in *New York Review,* March 18, 1982, p. 43). Births are also planned to be concentrated in the first few years of marriage in the early and late 20s.

The typical pattern then is for the fertility of teenagers and the fertility of women in their 30s and early 40s just before menopause not to be used. The birth rate in American society has usually been somewhat higher than it is in most other modernized industrial societies, but quite a bit lower than it is in most agricultural and primitive societies. American infant mortality is considerably higher than in other advanced countries, partly because of the primitive organization of medical services, but not high enough to offset the higher fertility rate. Compared to primitive or agricultural societies, however, the United States clearly has a low birth rate and low death rate.

A large social determinant of differential birth rates in the United States (i.e., higher birth rates in one group than in another) is rurality. This means that people who live in the countryside have more births than those who live in the city, and that families of city dwellers of which the male was born in the countryside have more births (see "The Two Generation Urbanite Hypothesis Revisited," by Nancy McGirr and Charles Hirschman in *Demography* for Feb. 1979, pp. 27–35). For a great many years sociologists thought that the working and lower classes in general had considerably higher birth rates than the middle and upper classes. It turns out that much of this effect was (up until recent times) due to the fact that when people moved from the countryside into the city, they moved into the bottom part of the occupational structure of the city, and they carried with them high rural fertility. Rural people who passed through college on their way to the city have apparently adopted urban fertility ideals by the time they marry. In recent years it appears that the urban–rural fertility differential has almost disappeared, and that the difference in total children of white women college graduates and white women with only elementary educations only amounts to about half a child. The black birth rate is considerably higher than the white rate (about one and one-half times as high), but black education in the childbearing years is almost the same as white education; therefore this differential does not reinforce the educational differential. The overall result then is that the different social classes have very near to the same birth rates at the present time.

A second major influence on the birth rate is ethnicity and religion. Blacks have a much higher birth rate, Catholics have a slightly higher rate than Protestant whites, and Jews have a somewhat lower birth rate than Protestant whites. The racial differences are quite substantial as the black birth rate is very substantially above that of the whites (see *Statistical Abstract 1979*, p. 61). This creates, of course, a younger black population so that in 1978 27.7% of the black population were of school age (five–17 years old), while only 21.2% of the white population were of school age. In general, the higher birth rate of the blacks creates an age structure with more people in the young age groups, whereas the low white birth rate tends to create a relatively narrow age pyramid in which relatively fewer of the population are in the young age groups and relatively more of them in the old age groups.

Death and the Labor Market

About a quarter of the males who enter the labor market in the United States will die before they reach 65 (about a sixth of the females entering the labor market will die before 65), but roughly three-quarters of those vacancies in "normally male" occupations that are created by the aging of the working population will be created by retirement rather than death. Very little of the reorganization of the labor force takes place on the occasion of the death of a labor force member. Furthermore, part of the advantage of a corporate form of organization of capitalism is that the *operative* part of the property system—namely, corporate ownership of the means of production—does not have to be reorganized on the death of a property owner. One result of this detachment of ownership institutions from the life of the owner is that widows can become the dominant inheritors of wealth even though elderly women may not be socially eligible for the roles of running national corporations. Because women live longer than men and because men (especially rich men) tend to marry women younger than themselves, roughly one out of eight adult women is a widow who has not remarried. Roughly a tenth of these widows in 1972 were estimated to be wealth-holders holding more than $100,000 (an average suburban home in 1972 was worth around $23,000, so this means that these widows held the equivalent of about four suburban homes). That is, the extent of wealth-holding by widows is probably an indication of the degree to which wealth-holding is detached from positions of authority and management in the economy.

What is mainly redistributed on the death of the owner of capital is claims to the benefits and profits of the capital, and not actual management rights. Similarly, there are usually no labor market positions to be redistributed when a person dies, because usually he or she retired first. The death of an owner or of an active occupant of a social role among the Karimojong or in eighteenth-century France involved substantial reorganization of work and managerial roles. In the United States deaths are a minor contingency for the economy.

Families and Cohorts in Occupational Placement

The link between the social composition of a cohort beginning its life and the occupational structure they move into as adults is almost entirely mediated by the school system. There is a large effect of the social class of origin on years of education attained: there is, in turn, a large effect of years of education on both the prestige and the wage or salary rate of the occupation one gets (more particularly, the occupation one ends up in at age 34–45). But there is very little difference between the occupational prestige or the income of people with identical years of education but from different social classes (see Christopher Jencks, *et al., Inequality*). Almost all of the advantages of being well-born are transmitted through the school system.

Years of education alone do not determine the detailed job one will get. That is instead determined to a large extent by what one gets a degree in. Since women with 16 years of education are very likely to have degrees in English literature, whereas men are likely to have degrees in engineering, the women are likely to be found in teaching whereas the men are likely to be found in engineering or managment. There is a set of options of about the same prestige level (and to a lesser extent the same salaries) available to people who get about 16 years of education—they choose the option in that set of options by choosing how to specialize in the last part of their college years. Similarly, when high school graduates enter the labor market, the detailed job they get will depend on what their employer trains them for—after some shifting around to get as good a job as they can, people settle into the detailed job that their employer has found it useful to train them for and sufficiently valuable to pay them a wage that will keep them from looking further.

POPULATION AND ECONOMY

Although the Karimojong explicitly organize their system of succession to adult roles by cohorts (or "age sets"), only roles above the level of the family in the ritual and political system are allocated by cohorts. But since occupation and livelihood are organized dominantly at the level of the family rather than of the society as a whole, cohorts are in fact less important among the Karimojong than in the United States. This is because many economic roles in the United States are "full-time" roles, so that one cannot gradually ease into them. The discontinuity in roles when one leaves school and takes up a full-time role in the economy forces the problem of succession of generations in modern society into a cohort mold.

At the same time that occupations have become full-time and differentiated from other roles (in particular other roles that a child might have), they have also been differentiated from property institutions. Except in rare cases of herding associations, a Karimojong man does not become a herder without either owning the herd or being the son of an owner. While a French peasant might not own the land he worked, he almost always "held" it in some kind of tenure recognized in the property system of the Old Regime. Obviously, a Karimojong herder's role changes size and scope as calves grow into cows, bulls, steers, or as a successful raid from another tribe wipes out his capital. Similarly, we saw the size and scope of the roles of the Marquis d'Escouloubre and of Montesquieu's family changing by bits and pieces, as they picked up new pieces of property. The shifts in the property system, losses and gains of capital stock, "accumulation" of capital, are differentiated from roles as workers and managers in the modern American system—property pertains to organizations, and organizations create roles for propertyless people.

This detachment of roles from property by corporations (or by the government as employer) clearly facilitates the creation of full-time roles for beginning workers just out of school. The worker does not have to wait for the property to be detached from his father's role before he can take it up. No doubt one of the factors in the decline of the French marriage age for men from an average of around 28 in the eighteenth century to 24 nowadays is that few Frenchmen have to wait for the role attached to the property they will spend their life working on to fall free by the death of a parent. Among the Karimojong a herd–family group stays together until the death of the *elop* who owns both the herd and the people, and his sons (though they may marry earlier) do not become *elop* until he dies and the herd is split. There is no such dependence of roles in the labor force on property accumulation in most of the American economy, because the corporation or the government provides the capital equipment.

Thus, alienation from the means of production, with capitalists (i.e., corporations) owning the means of production for private goods and governments owning the means of production for public goods, means also freedom from the constraints of having to come into the ownership of the means of production before getting a role in the economy. This in general makes for earlier adulthood (e.g., earlier marriage and earlier age at first child). The cruel method of contraception of the Old Regime, abstinence until the male is nearly 30 and the female around 25, tends to disappear for the urban working class even before the Industrial Revolution. Middle-class roles were still tied to property, so abstinence stretched longer for them—until the twentieth century.

The differentiation of capital ownership from worker roles, that is, the development of modern capitalism, is therefore the central creator of the dominance of cohorts in modern social placement, replacing the family through which property was inherited. In modern capitalism the family determines the amount of education of the children instead of supplying capital for a role. Almost all of the effect of social origins on later social placement of children takes place by influencing the number of years of education, as we pointed out above. But this is because the crucial link between father's property and son's work role has been cut by expropriation of workers (even middle-class workers) from the means of production. This in its turn means that it is not so much the wealth of the father that counts in social placement of the children, but instead the education of both the father and the mother. It is owning encyclo-pedias, not owing businesses, that is a favorable sign for success of children in the labor market. Of course, there is a small proportion of the population who pass substantial amounts of property by inheritance between generations (what this means, in effect, is that when the father dies, he leaves enough to support his widow for an average of a decade *plus* a substantial inheritance for his children). But usually these now pass to the new generation at a time when they are already established in a labor market position, and they pass equally to sons and daughters (which they do not, in general, when they are attached to roles in the economy).

The educational system and the expropriation of the workers from the means of production are thus flip sides of the same coin. Both reflect the fact that families no longer create roles for their children out of their own resources. And both are intimately tied to the structural fact that adult roles are "finally" determined just after entry into the labor force for working-class roles, and just before entry (in choosing what sort of college degree to get) for middle-class roles. Success after entry in the labor market depends in large measure on the type of degree one has (one of the main reasons women receive lower salaries than men for professional work is that their degrees do not qualify them for well-paid professions), and on the size of the cohort with whom one entered the labor market (which is why people graduating now do not have their pick of jobs the way people graduating 20 years ago did).

Boundaries around Population Groups in the Economy

After a cohort settles down in a modern economy, say after age 30, they are very likely to spend most of their working life with the same employer. The probability of mobility is different in different modern societies even in the urban economy: from ages 36–45, for example, about 3% of workers in Yokohama (a Japanese automobile manufacturing city) change employers each year, while in Detroit about 8% of workers of the same ages change employers each year (Robert Cole and Paul Siegel, *Work Mobility and Participation*, pp. 70–71). That is, Japanese work-ers are much more cut off by the boundry around the firm from move-ment into different lines of work—they work much more in an "internal labor market" inside the firm than do American workers. But even 8% per year for the relatively mobile American economy still means that about 43% of the workers who worked for a given employer at age 36 would still be working for the same employer at age 45 ($.92^{10} = .43$).

There are multiple social and economic reasons why an employer does not want to get rid of an experienced worker and why the worker may well prefer to stay with the same employer. These forces are of different size in different industries (see my "Social Mobility in Industrial Labor Markets," in *Acta Sociologica* 1979, pp. 217–245), but the basic fact is that once a worker is placed in a position during the first decade or so of his work life that is likely to be his lifetime placement, unless he or she gets promoted within the firm.

The boundaries around the firm (for people with some seniority) in modern labor markets are probably the strongest labor market boundaries around population groups. They correspond to some degree to the firm ties that held an eighteenth-century French peasant family to the land they cultivated, or a master in a guild to the city in which he was licensed to practice his trade. That is, in both types of societies, the strongest boundary is closely connected to property institutions—tenancy in the eighteenth century and "job rights" within the firm in a modern economy. One can have a normatively defended claim to a position connected with a particular firm in a modern economy, or to the tenancy that one's family has held for generations in an agricultural economy. Once one leaves a job in which one has seniority job rights, one may have *advantages* in searching for another job, but one usually has no *normative claim* to that other job.

Beyond the boundary of the firm, there are more permeable boundaries in a modern economy around both *industries* and *occupations*. That is, having worked in, for example, the construction industry gives one experience that is likely to be valuable to a new employer. In particular, having had experience as a painter is likely to give one experience that will be valuable to a painting contractor. Once inside the boundary around the construction industry, or the boundary around the craft of painting, one has an advantage in getting jobs as they come up in that same industry and that same occupation. Sometimes the boundaries around occupations are stronger (as, e.g., in most of the construction crafts and the professions of medicine and law), while sometimes the boundaries around industries are stronger (as social science professionals may change occupations, under pressure, to become professors in business schools, but remain in the education industry).

From the point of view of labor market stratification, what these boundaries around firms, occupations, and industries do is to preserve whatever stratification was produced in the cohort when they entered the labor market. If black people were permitted to enter cement finishing 30 years ago but not permitted to enter plumbing, then plumbers

of 40–50 years of age will be mostly white, whereas many cement fin-
ishers 40–50 years old will be black. Thus, social boundaries such as race
and sex, which have permeated schooling and placement in entry positions in the labor market, are preserved as stratification principles
without active racial or sexual discrimination, by the operation of the
"natural" boundaries of employer, occupation, and industry.

The same arrangement was explicit in eighteenth-century France. If
one reads the oaths or the discussions of *ordres* in the eighteenth century,
it would not be entirely clear that one had to wait for the capital before
one could play the role specified in one's guild, one's "estate," or one's
status as a member of a rural peasant community. Once a member of
the clergy or nobility or goldsmiths or village by oath, one was ideolog-
ically a permanent member of that estate. The boundaries on recruitment
were thus boundaries around permanent positions in the economy.
Mobility did take place—many people were ennobled, many people
made their way into guilds without inheriting the position, and outsiders
bought into village peasant communities or married an inheriting daughter of a local peasant. But the idea of permanent boundaries around all
positions was much more pervasive than in modern economies (see
William Sewell, "Etat, Corps, and Ordre: Some Notes on the Social
Vocabulary of the French Old Regime" in Hans-Ulrich Wehler, ed., *Sozialgeschichte Heute: Festschrift für Hans Rosenberg zum 70. Geburtstag*).

The chief distinction between the modern United States and eighteenth-century France in the nature of the ascription (ignoring any force
that a more explicit ideology may have brought to the Old Regime system) had to do with the way families helped create the roles for their
children. From Montesquieu buying a position with the *parlement* to the
peasant giving over the control of his farm to his son in his old age,
family elements were explicit parts of the process of recruitment into the
bounded occupations and industries of the Old Regime. Blacks and
women do not get their laborer or secretarial positions because their
fathers provided them with small capital, but because the educational
system and discrimination in early placement gives them worse jobs as
the cohort enters the labor force.

It has become popular to describe these processes of boundaries
around firms, industries, and occupations rigidifying early disadvantages as the existence of a "secondary labor market." That is, jobs near
the minimum wage, which are disproportionately held by blacks,
women, and teenagers, generally do not get one a position behind the
boundaries that will protect one's access to a good job for the rest of
one's life. Consequently the high mobility into and out of these jobs

does not add up to any kind of career, but is like Brownian motion, from one hopeless position to another. These jobs are systematically concentrated in the low-wage sectors of the economy, in farming, retail trade, services which serve clients without professional credentials or government monopolies (such as dry-cleaning establishments and laundries) and the "classical capitalist industries" such as food and drink manufacturing, textiles, apparel, shoes, wood products and furniture, plastic goods, and most ceramics and glass products. All these industries hire the cheapest labor available, and do not give that labor any claims on valuable jobs behind labor market boundaries.

All this analysis of boundaries in the labor market is somewhat irrelevant to eighteenth-century France, and without meaning among the Karimojong. The only boundaries of any significance are those between Karimojong and foreigners (within that boundary all men are Karimojong herders, barring accidents), and between Karimojong men and Karimojong women. All get their roles through tribal institutions *and* through inheritance within families, there being no occupational or industry boundaries below the tribal level.

Mechanisms of Role Accretion

Because the change in property is so obvious in the Old Regime, and because it leaves behind records while daily occupational activity does not, the accretion mechanisms of the Old Regime are especially obvious. When there is a market for pieces of authority over particular things or for particular legal rights, which jointly make a given role possible, then it is clear that the role can grow by accretion.

But there are quite similar mechanisms in some of the most advanced modern technologies. The business school ideal of a "matrix" organization is oriented to a shifting set of projects within an organization such as a research and development laboratory or an engineering firm. An expert in, say, numerical methods and their programming on computers may then be in a computer services section, and receive "assignments" to develop programs for various projects that need numerical solutions for various sorts of differential equations. At any particular time his or her role will consist of the assignments that have accumulated from the various projects. Normally as his or her competence grows, the role will "accrete" various responsibilities. As the role expands under the influence of the increased competence of its occupant, it will come to be paid more, without changing organizational position.

A similar process takes place in a modern legislature, as a person's committee assignment and developing competence in a specialized legislative subject makes him or her more valuable for particular legislative problems, and increases his or her power in that specialized area. The differentiation of roles of formally equal legislators by committee assignments and seniority takes place by accretion. In other types of organizations similar processes operate, as, for instance, a graduate school professor's assignments to dissertation committees accrete over time, the most skilled craftsman in a shop gets the tough assignments, a wholesale salesman's territory becomes a more valuable job as he or she develops more contacts, a physician's practice grows, and so on. The things that cumulate are not usually property, but resources or competences valuable in the performance of the job. Rewards may or may not be closely tied to the scope of the job.

However, our three societies clearly differ in the importance of such accretion mechanisms as compared with role creation mechanisms. The job of the numerical methods computer specialist was undoubtedly recently created by a formal role definition and the liberty to develop a clientele within the organization was part of the original job description. Sales territories are divided up by the organization, before a skilled salesman makes one more valuable than another. Positions on the agriculture committee are much more likely to be assigned to representatives from Iowa, while positions on the interior committee are more likely to go to a representative from Arizona, because party chiefs want to give representatives a chance to defend the interests of their own constitutents. Organizational role creation dominates even our modern examples of role accretion. But the *only* way to become a more important herder among the Karimojong is to get more cattle.

Marxist theory is often formulated in terms of the "empty places" in a mode of production. The above discussion shows that this is an oversimplification obtained by projecting the characteristics of modern economies on the world at large. For example, E. Le Roy Ladurie has shown that the number of empty places in the agriculture of Languedoc (and their composition in terms of the quantity of capital they involved) changed with the overall growth and decline of the population. Small peasants simply had smaller peasant roles when the population increased, because there was not enough land to go around. The role of landlord in turn was much more favorable to the landholder in times of population pressure, because this pushed down the price of labor and increased the rents that could be demanded for a tenancy (see *The Peasants of Languedoc*).

Marxism and the Labor Market

The moral interest of Marxism has always depended on the identification of those who are disadvantaged by a given economic system. Marxists are more likely than other social scientists to be interested in the "secondary labor market" of bad jobs occupied by teenagers, women, and blacks, more likely to be interested in the fate of the peasant as the agricultural population grows in Languedoc, more likely to notice the sad condition of women in herding societies dominated by large patrilineal lineage groups (see Karen and Jeffery Paige, *The Politics of Reproductive Ritual*). The identification of population groups subject to oppressions generated in the economic system is, however, more complicated than naming the roles in the system. If there is free mobility among roles, then the fact that a person now occupies the relatively oppressed role of herd boy does not identify one who cannot become an *elop*. On the other hand, identifying the role of a woman in the same herding society may well identify an oppressed person, because there is no mobility of women into the roles of men.

Consequently, the exact mechanisms of the matching up of roles and people, the creation of roles for a new generation, have to be specified. Then the preservation of oppression in the social placement process in the lifelong social status of a person depends on the character of boundaries between population groups occupying roles in the economy. It is the boundaries around firms, and to a lesser extent around occupations and industries, that preserves the initial disadvantages of women and blacks in the American economy. It is the fact that the son of a peasant will rarely inherit the capital to set up as a landlord or a member of a high court that constitutes the practical boundary around the social class of peasants. A prosperous prolific peasant, all of whose sons have the misfortune to live to marriage age, may create a large number or roles of misery for his sons' families, though his own position in the petty bourgeoisie is secure.

How far particular positions in the American economy show the features of differential recruitment and tough boundaries around firms, occupations, and industries, depends on the details of their mode of production. Some of the occupations that show the toughest boundaries for minorities and women to penetrate show clear signs of their descent from medieval guilds, as do the crafts of the construction industry. Others show all the signs of having been born of the latest innovations in solid-state physics, as do many dominantly male jobs designing computers. The details of allocation of oppressive or privileged positions to particular population groups has to be investigated in detail, at the level of the concrete ecology, technology, and economic organization of particular industries.

The same is true of eighteenth-century France. Positions as nobles were being created, mostly in the state bureaucracy, but to a lesser extent in wholesale trade and colonial expansion. "Ascription" of noble status thus varied considerably between branches of the economy. And the rate of accumulation, the rate of "accretion" of roles, was clearly generally greater in the urban part of the economy in the eighteenth century, and was greater in agricultural areas subject to rapid technical change (as in the western part of the Northern plain) than in more backward areas in western and central France.

Thus, the central point of this chapter is that the sociology of the organization of industry in its ecological, technological, and economic aspects does not yet solve the problem of economic sociology for Marxist thought. It is an additional and complex subject to specify how the advantageous and oppressed roles in an economy are allocated to advantaged and oppressed population groups.

6

Toward a Theory of Modes of Production

WHAT SOCIAL UNIT HAS A MODE OF PRODUCTION?

Marx was interested in the causes of political behavior and class relations in whole societies—France, Germany, and England were his usual units of analysis. When he analyzed the spinning factories in Manchester and Glasgow, which did less than half of all the work in the textile industry (which in turn was roughly half of the work needed to produce clothes), he was therefore interested in England's future, not in these two cities alone. Within Manchester he was interested not in the quarter or so of the labor force who worked in the mills, but in the whole class system. Marx saw that the factory system was the wave of the future (although he may have expected it eventually to employ more than the quarter of the labor force that it did), and that new dynamics of class relations were being worked out there, so he analyzed capitalist society by mainly analyzing an industry that now occupies about three tenths of 1% of the American labor force.

Marx was very conscious of the fact that at that time English agriculture was organized very differently from factories and that weaving was still much influenced by the putting out system. He was not so conscious that English steel making, forging, and machine manufactures were small-scale skilled trades; that English canals, railroads, and docks were largely built by migratory, often foreign, casual labor employed by contractors with little capital; that butchers and bakers and candlestick makers were petty bourgeois manufacturers. In short, the English mode of production was a mixture of "stages" of the development of the forces of production, or technology, and of the relations of production, or economic organization. Furthermore, the branch Marx studied was neither numerically nor economically dominant. It consequently did not dominate the organization of class relations in nineteenth-century England. It was even less determinant in nineteenth-century France.

Skocpol's difficulties in *States and Social Revolution* with the ecological boundaries of the agrarian class system to which she traces the agrarian unrest in the Revolution show a similar mistake: attributing one common form of organizing agriculture, that of the northern plain, to French rural life. Skocpol does discuss regional variations, but then attributes the causes of the capacity of peasants to organize to features that really only characterized one ecological complex, open-field coordinated village agriculture with plentiful river and road transportation. Unrest was quite different in Brittany and in the Midi; it seems that very little is known about revolutionary activity in the Massif Central, the Alps, and the Pyrenees, presumably because the peasants there did not later join reactionary movements as western peasants did (see Charles Tilly, *The Vendée*). There was an ecological boundary around the mode of production that was involved in the agrarian unrest in the Revolution.

What then are the proper units of analysis, which can be described as having a "mode of production"? In the first instance it is clear that firms, agricultural holdings farmed as a unit, and herding families all exploit an ecological niche, have a technology, are unified by mutually dependent incentive systems, and have a definite population of people and of roles at any given time. The larger sets of human relations that we will want to call "modes of production" must therefore be made up of firms or "enterprises" that have similarities in the form of their transactions with nature, of their technologies, of their structure of property rights and worker incentives, and of their processes of role formation and recruitment.

Depending on one's purpose one may insist on more or less detailed analogies between firms for drawing the boundaries around a mode of production. For example, the trade union movement in the United States classifies together the oil, chemical, and nuclear industries. They all have continuous process production and their technologies require that half or so of the labor that goes into the final product is the labor of constructing the plants and pipelines (or to put it in commonsense terms, they have high capital–labor ratios and many accountants in their labor force), and all have technologies that involve many engineers and physical or biological scientists. The firms are almost all large corporations. Their markets are generally stable, so they provide careers for both their middle-class and the working-class employees. Their manual work force is made up of a great many maintenance men or responsible operators, most of whose skills are not readily transferrable to other firms. Thus there is an "internal labor market" with a high skill mix at both the manual and nonmanual levels. The work forces are heavily recruited from among the technical professions and semiprofessions, and except for the clerks are almost all male; they are disproportionately young because these industries have been expanding.

In short, the line drawn by the trade unions in the United States identifies a subsector of the economy within which firms show great analogies in technology, economic organization, and style of recruitment and reward in the labor market. We would therefore expect that the problems of class relations managed by the oil, chemical, and nuclear workers union would be similar in those industries.

A wider classification might also include the steel industry, but much of the technology here is batch production; productivity depends to some degree on how hard people work, so a people-driving line structure is in evidence; the market is much less stable; the role of engineers and physical scientists is somewhat reduced; and the manual worker skill level is perhaps somewhat lower. The broader category of highly capital-intensive, engineering-based, corporately organized manufacturing with highly paid career male labor forces thus generates sufficiently different problems of class relations in that its unions are separately organized. Steel workers are separate from oil, chemical, and nuclear workers, but both are clearly in the core of the core characterized by collective contract productivity bargains and other features of capital-intensive manufacturing.

For some other purposes one may want to distinguish a subsector of the chemical industry, for example, the drug manufacturers, because (1) the subsection is much more related to cohorts of biologically trained students (and consequently more female scientists), (2) its market has the peculiarity of "prescriptions" and advertising to physicians rather than consumers, and (3) the weight of the raw materials and product is small, so plant location is not as constrained by ecological factors as industrial chemicals and oil plants are.

In order to define a distinct mode of production, the more ecological, technological, economic organizational, and population details one requires to be similar, the fewer workers and firms the resulting mode will include. Obviously the choice of level of detail is a strategic one. If one is interested in the connection between advanced monopoly capitalism and labor market discrimination, a level of generality that includes the construction industry in the monopoly sector is too gross. The labor market discrimination in the construction industry has medieval roots, not advanced capitalist roots.

Similarly, if one is interested in the social bases of Bonapartism, as Marx was in the *18th Brumaire*, then perhaps one can lump all French peasants together, the northern plain with Brittany, the North with the Midi. (Actually when there were Bonapartist candidates in elections somewhat later, the peasantry of some regions was much more Bonapartist than the peasantry of other regions, so probably Marx chose the wrong level of generality.) But for Skocpol's problem one needs more detailed analogies between peasant holdings.

For a given purpose, the boundaries around a mode of production may be ecological, technological, economic organizational, or populational. For example, if one wants to analyze why in 1982 the market for MBA graduates from elite business schools is so soft, the relevant mode of production is large-scale bureaucratic corporations: "monopoly capitalism" narrowly defined. It is the role creation processes of these firms which have been creating positions for elite MBAs, so it must be some common response of such firms to the economic environment that is softening the MBA market. The boundary is populational. In contrast, the prosperity of Silicon Valley near Stanford University is clearly a phenomenon connected to applications of solid-state physics to computation and information processing. The boundary here is technological.

By and large modern Marxists are much more likely to make the mistake of too little industrial detail. The casual exclusion of retail trade from the "monopoly sector" of large bureaucratic corporate enterprise ignores the size of Sears, K Mart, Woolworth's, J. C. Penney, Safeway, and McDonald's (all among the 25 largest corporations ranked in terms of number of employees). This exclusion is no doubt partly to be explained by a vague feeling among Marxists that trade is not productive, so one cannot see why the integration of retail department and food stores with wholesaling would be technically efficient.

But further, since these firms all have low-paid, unskilled, dominantly female labor forces, that is, because the population and labor force boundary does not coincide with the economic organizational boundary, these extremely large firms are excluded from the "monopoly sector." But what this shows is that "monopoly sector" is too broad a characterization for the purpose of explaining the segmentation of the labor market, even though it might be just right for explaining the demand for new MBA graduates.

This reckless generality is encouraged by the fact that Marxists nowadays are rarely interested in class relations except as they are projected into the political arena. The distinctive class relations of very large retail department stores have small political implications. Radicalism has no home in the Sears labor force. While Marx himself was also inclined to forget the detail when analyzing politics, *Capital* is full of quotations about what happened in particular economic enterprises. Marx shifted level of detail depending on his purpose; most modern Marxism is stuck at the most general characterization of modes of production. So the massive destruction of small retail firms by chain stores in recent years goes almost unanalyzed.

CONCRETE SOCIAL FORMATIONS

The main way that the ecological, technological, economic organizational, and populational variety of modes of production gets into modern Marxist thought is implicitly, in the concept of "concrete social formation" (see Erik Olin Wright, *Class, Crisis and the State*). The basic imagery of this concept is very similar to sedimentary rock: while the most recent layer of sedimentary rock will reflect the sediments of modern history, the rock as a whole will have layers from ancient sediments as well. Similarly, the firms currently being formed are monopoly capitalist firms, but a layer of petty bourgeois farming reflects an earlier historical period.

The concept of concrete social formation therefore has a particular theory of the variety of modes of production in a particular society buried in it, an evolutionary theory. The implicit argument is that small family firms are on the way out. As we saw, two-thirds of all farms have in fact disappeared since World War II, which lends some credence to this view. But what that has meant is not corporate farming with wage workers, but family farms three times as big. The subcontracting system of small firms in the construction industry shows a similar survival capacity; a permanent feature of this system is that people who do not understand its technical virtues have always been predicting its demise, trying to destroy its unions, trying to manage a semiskilled labor force bureaucratically in housing tracts to increase efficiency. Subcontracting and skilled craftsmen have won out (except in the Soviet Union and some parts of Eastern Europe). The evolutionary drift in construction is not very fast.

The percentage of self-employed in the urban labor force was about 9% in 1965 and about 7% in 1978, probably reflecting mainly the bureaucratization of retail trade. The evolutionary disadvantage of small firms is thus specific to one or a few industries.

The difficulty with the stratigraphic image of concrete social formations is that it provides too easy an explanation of why industries differ in their mode of production. If the rapid growth of chain stores solves a technical problem in the distribution of complex inventories, one can predict the areas it is likely to invade next, and how far it is likely to spread. If one, however, imagines that all boutiques are mere feudal remnants, one will be surprised when luxury specialty stores keep springing up in suburban shopping centers next to the Sears store. Similarly, the medieval trappings, such as the initiation ceremonies of craft unions whose technical basis did not exist until the late nineteenth century (e.g., electricians, structural ironworkers, and elevator constructors) will be a mystery.

With a few exceptions, the archaic social forms that exist at a given time will be competitively viable in their niche. The exact boundaries of that niche may be defined by ecological factors (e.g., open-field agriculture in eighteenth-century France), by technical factors (e.g., the lack of mobility of field artillery defined by the weight of the cannon in early eighteenth-century armies), by institutional lack of a form of economic organization (e.g., the lack of cattle markets among the Karimojong), or by the supply of the relevant kind of labor (e.g., solid-stage physicists in the Silicon Valley near Stanford makes small high-technology manufacturing viable). Because these niches may not pass out of existence, and may even grow, the distinctive social life associated with an archaic social form may remain in the social formation long after it was the newest mode of production.

The idea of survivals of archaic social forms in an environment to which they are not adapted has turned the concept of concrete social formation into an untheoretical ad hoc method of bringing the theory of modes of production into congruence with obviously contradictory facts. The concept as it is used now is a hindrance to theoretical advance. It distracts analysts from the dynamics of the adaptation of particular social forms to their niche.

But that leaves us with the problem that the concept led us to avoid: how do the distinct varieties of modes of production add up to the class dynamics of a society as a whole? My own opinion is that this is a deep problem, because the answer is that they do not add up in any lawful way. Class unity in politics does not follow closely from common embedding of classes in relations of production. It follows instead from political processes proper. Class unity in concrete class relations in factories derives from class unity in politics, not the reverse.

This is shown by the fact that in all free societies, the units that actually bargain about the terms on which labor is exchanged for money—trade

unions—are more industrially differentiated than are the political organizations of the working class. Different industries have different organizations for dealing with class relations at work, but the same
organizations for dealing with the political problems of the working
class.

The same argument can be made historically. The times that class
unity is forged are times of political crisis, times of revolution. William
Sewell's account of the emergence of the working-class socialist movement in France in the nineteenth century (*Work and Revolution in France*)
discusses the worker organizations in different trades that were formed
after guilds were destroyed in the great Revolution. Chapter 9 of Sewell's
work is entitled "The July Revolution and the Emergence of Class Consciousness." It would similarly make sense to turn Marx on his head
and interpret the Great Revolution of 1789 as *the revolution in which the
bourgeoisie was formed as a political class*, rather than the revolution in
which an already–formed bourgeoisie finally won out. It is political
crises, not the evolution of forms of production, that forms unified
classes.

Cross-national comparisons support the same point. The English
working class is among the most politically unified; more of the working
class vote for the Labor Party, and fewer of the middle class support
Labor, than is true in most modern countries. Yet very many big industrial plants in England are not organized into a single trade union,
but instead into a large variety of crafts and shop groups, each with
relatively distinct bargains about the delivery of labor and the structure
of pay. The United States, with one of the lowest indexes of class political
unity, has a much larger number of industrial unions bargaining for a
variety of occupations within the plant on a unified basis. That is, unity
in class relations with concrete capitalists is higher in the United States
than in England, while class unity in politics is higher in England than
in the United States.

Thus, the political dynamics of the larger political system are related
to the class dynamics of the component parts of the economy in a con-
tingent way. The interests of construction workers are not, in concrete
terms, very much like those of automobile factory workers, as is shown
by the fact that in no free country do they belong to the same trade
union branch. But both construction and automobile factories create a
flow of grievances and interests, which *can be unified* into a common
political program. The unification is a political achievement, and that
achievement can be very successful in England and Germany, very precarious in the United States and Canada. The variety of class relations
in different parts of the economy are raw materials out of which political

systems and historical events can make very different political class conflicts and class accommodations. Thus, a concrete mixture of class relations from the different Marxian modes of production does not reliably produce a proportional mix of political currents.

The problem posed by the concept of concrete social formation, how to aggregate the variety of class relations in the part of society into overall class dynamics, is an impossible problem. Its answer depends on how the political system adds them up, not on how the economy adds them up.

AN EXCURSUS ON MODES OF DESTRUCTION

We saw in Chapter 3 that the organization of the eighteenth-century French army was much influenced by the character of military technology. It is also clear that terrain, military transport, and other ecological factors have an important role in military structure. But the concepts in military sociology that correspond to "relations of production" take quite a different form. The social relations in which military enterprises are embedded from late feudal times to the present day are systems of states. It is states that have armies or navies, and systems of states that have wars. Since Wallerstein is interested in the political economy of systems of states, and since Skocpol argues that military losses were central to the revolutions she studied, some comments on the economics of military forces may be in order.

Skocpol also emphasizes that the Royal Government was undermined by the effects of its military adventures. Although the military enterprises of the French state did not return a profit, they too have their economic dynamics. The existence of a state that can collect taxes in its own area depends on the existence of an army to put down rebellions, on the size and wealth of the area contolled, and on the administrative efficiency and deployability of the tax-collecting administration. (For the seventeenth-century background of the taxation and war-making system of eighteenth-century France, see Charles Tilly, "How One Kind of Struggle—War—Reshaped All Other Kinds of Struggles in Seventeenth Century France," Working Paper of the Center for Research in Social Organizations. No. 241.) A state has difficulty collecting taxes during civil war, or in desert or mountainous terrain, or when provincial tax collectors keep the money to build up their own armies. Much of the tax money of the Old Regime went into paying for the army, or to paying debts for past wars; and given the army's role in collecting taxes it is important to distinguish the economic balance of an army in the interior of France and on the borders.

In eighteenth century Europe, armies on the borders and abroad were losing propositions, those securing internal peace and tax collections were profit makers. The losses on the borders and abroad were, of course, higher during wartime. Even though in a certain sense the royal government won all the border wars in the eighteenth century and many of the colonial wars abroad, it was losing money overall on its military enterprises, so that something like half of the royal budget was being paid out in interest on the war debts.

In the countries Skocpol mainly studied, namely, late eighteenth-century France, early twentieth-century Russia, and early and mid-twentieth-century China, the overall military accounts had become unbalanced. Although the situation was complicated, the basic source of France's difficulty was a combination of Dutch–British wealth and sea power on her northwest, and an exceptional military and taxation organization under Frederick the Great in the east. The basic cause of Russian difficulty was the rapid industrialization and military modernization of Germany on the west and Japan on the east. The basic source of Chinese difficulty was a very low tax take of the civil apparatus for the Imperial government, combined with incursions along the coast by industrialized naval powers.

In all three societies the attempt to bring the national military accounts back into balance led to attempts to raise taxes, schemes for borrowing money at home and abroad, and pressure for technical innovation in the military itself and in industries supplying arms and war machines. The financial crunch also contributed some undetermined amount to erratic foreign policies, as when the French Royal Government compromised to stop an expensive war with the Dutch and English that France had almost won, or when Tsar Alexander stopped the Japanese war in 1905 to transfer troops to deal with rebellions in European Russia. Such "diplomatic" or "military" defeats undermine the legitimacy to raise taxes, so the stage is set for internal rebellions. This intertwining of diplomatic problems, military expenditures, and the legitimacy of tax increases (or of repayments of war loans, which means cutting government services while maintaining taxes) is what Skocpol refers to as French "involvement in the European state system," and by similar phrases for the other two countries. She does not deal explicitly with tax problems nor with the problem of balancing accounts of the military enterprises. Let us examine more carefully the forces behind the balances.

The return on taxes depends on two main sorts of forces: the productivity (net of subsistence for the population) of the economy, and the political capacity of the government to extract the surplus. For example, in Languedoc on the French Mediterranean coast near Spain, the traditional level of royal taxes in the sixteenth century was about 6% of total agricultural income (E. Le Roy Ladurie, *The Peasants of Languedoc*, pp. 121–122, and 320), while the tithe to the church amounted to 8–10% (p. 78). If the legitimacy of the French Royal Government depended on the church, legitimacy clearly came dear in Languedoc—around three-fifths of the surplus that could be extracted from Languedoc went to pay for legitimacy rather than warfare or debt service.

And even at that rate, by the eighteenth century at least, about half of the royal taxes went to local administration. So the capacity of the French government to extract resources for its military enterprises may have been as low as one-thirtieth of the total income of Languedoc. Wallerstein says that this rate was lower than the taxation rate in England or the Netherlands (*The Modern World System*, II, pp. 227 and 287) and probably lower than that in Prussia, while Austria–Hungary had a much lower rate of extraction. But the French government was the most powerful in Europe because even with this low extraction rate; it had easy access to one of the richest agricultural regions in the world of that time, the plains of northern France, and was the largest country in western Europe in terms of population.

What this all says is that the biggest enterprise in feudal empires of the sort Skocpol is analyzing was the state apparatus, sometimes including a state church. Just as agricultural enterprises have their ecological and technical side as well as their "political" or claims side, so also the state's revenues, expenditures, and military successes due to expenditures depend on the ecology and technology of social production (e.g., the tax base of northern France), on the technology of taxation and its social organization, and on the ecology and technology of military attack and defense, as well as on the politics of legitimate claims.

This means that Skocpol should have been analyzing regional variations in productivity, in taxation levels, in military vulnerability, and other aspects of the state as an enterprise, as well as the problems of legitimacy and rebellion she does analyze. An army or navy is expensive, and getting the expenses of participation in the world system out of reluctant citizens, especially when one is not doing too well in that world system, is the main source of political difficulties in these feudal empires. Again a theory of the enterprise, this time of state enterprises in military and taxation affairs, is needed to complete the theory. This argument supports both Skocpol and Wallerstein's arguments that the dynamics inside countries, at least in the last three or four centuries, depend on the system of states and on military contingencies. But it is easy to go broke fighting wars, and a much more detailed analysis of the ecological, technical, and economic and population basis of military enterprises is needed to understand how that world system works. To construct a complete analysis of a mode of destruction, then, the same components of ecology, technology, economic organization, and population dynamics are necessary.

ECONOMICS, INDIVIDUAL MOTIVATIONS, AND INSTITUTIONAL VARIETY

A main purpose of this book has been to give enough detail about the mechanisms of economic action in three societies so that one can recognize people acting on grounds we can understand under three very different institutional conditions. When a Karimojong herder follows a pattern of opportunistic exploitation of resources owned in common by the tribe, he is solving the same problem as an Idaho rancher trucking his cattle up to summer pastures. The fact that gasoline is cheaper in Idaho than is the cattle weight that would be walked off during the trek to the mountains clearly differentiates their technical levels, but they would recognize each other's rationality. Their ecological problems resemble each other. The adaptation of eighteenth-century infantry tactics to a gun that can fire about once a minute sounds much like the problem of reorganizing high-school schoolrooms with 30 students to a class to take advantage of televised lectures and demonstrations, or to use computers when the school cannot afford 30 terminals. Technical innovations often require social reorganization of purposive action and such reorganization often takes a long time.

The use of sharecropping in the more backward regions of eighteenth-century France is structurally the same as the incentive system of Burawoy's (1979) "Allied Corporation" in *Manufacturing Consent*, paying the worker a part of the marginal product. "Feudalism" looks a good deal like "monopoly capitalism." This incentive system is preferable to straight wages for the same reason in both places: supplying enough supervision on dispersed western French farms or on various complex machining tasks is too difficult; therefore one needs an incentive system that can substitute for supervision. Piece rates and sharecropping are such systems.

This last economic institutional analogy brings up the same problem of false consciousness. Just as Burawoy asked why workers did not focus on the total wage bill instead of on "making out," he could have asked why *metayers* were willing to be killed fighting for their landlords during the counterrevolution in the Vendée. The incentive systems in the backward *bocage* of the eighteenth century are thus sensible enough solutions to the problem of worker motivation and supervision to be viable in a medium-level technology Chicago factory.

The fact that people solve problems posed by their natural environment with the technical means at their disposal, to obtain the incentives built into their division of benefits, makes "mode of production" a variable across societies. That is, the structures of these three economies are made up of sensible, understandable actions. The reason they are understandable in a common way across societies at radically diverse levels is that economies have a common set of problems—ecological, technological, economic organizational (or incentive and property rights), and population allocation. The reason that economics has the fundamental tools that Marx needed to analyze this part of social structure is that structures have to elicit the behavior they need to keep themselves going, either by affecting people's possibilities or their incentives. Because ecology and technology are the structures that shape possibilities, they are central to the varieties of modes of production. Because economic organization shapes incentives, and population dynamics shapes those who enter a structure in which they are exposed to given incentives, different modes of production have different varieties of class relations.

The strategy of this book is based on the idea that only deep analysis of the way goods are produced and divided up in a society suffices for understanding its economic dynamics. Rather than locating eighteenth-century France along the diminsion from "feudal" to "modern," one has to understand how they fed the oxen and horses with which they plowed, and how many they needed. Otherwise one thinks the *araire* of the Midi and the mountainous areas was simply backward, rather than an adaptation to the terrain, and one is led in the wrong direction in interpreting regional differences. If one does not understand the ecological conditions, then the lighter, simpler plow is simply another indicator of backwardness along with fewer roads, less commercialization of grain crops, lower literacy rates, and less support of the Revolution.

The assumption that people are fairly sensible in arranging their affairs thus leads to a standard by which to judge comparative economic sociology, Marxist or otherwise. I argued in the introduction that Marx himself did better with economic determinism than many of his followers, because he was a better economist. He understood a great deal about how to run a spinning mill to make a profit, and how the overall organization of the market affected what one had to do to make that profit. I argued that this was because Marx firmly based his analysis on a theory of the capitalist enterprise. My argument here is that this virtue comes in part because so much of *Das Capital* is devoted to a detailed and differentiated picture of the English economy. Marx's accuracy in analyzing the factory mode of production came from knowing a great deal about a lot of factories. Modern Marxists would be wise to follow his example.

SOCIETAL VARIATIONS IN CLASS RELATIONS

When families are the dominant form of economic enterprise, then the total benefits of the economic activity form an incentive for the family. The age and sex norms of the family system determine how those total benefits are divided up. When the men of a given lineage live together after marriage and manage a family enterprise corporately, as in many herding societies, the intrafamilial power of men is maximized and that of women minimized (see Karen and Jeffery Paige, *The Politics of Reproductive Ritual*). Thus, one can expect that in societies like the Karimojong, the sexual inequality of benefits within the family would be maximized. When the Karimojong violate their "living off the interest" principles and sacrifice an animal, we will expect that the men get the tenderest pieces (see Neville Dyson-Hudson, *Karimojong Politics*, p. 94, and plate facing p. 212). The incentives for women are then expected to be below their marginal contribution to family welfare (Gary Becker, *A Treatise on the Family*, Chapter 2, to the contrary). The fact that a woman's contribution is more valuable to a family than what she takes out of the common larder is perhaps reflected in the fact that the bride price is paid *to the men of the bride's family of origin*, not, as in some societies, largely to the bride (e.g., see Mary Douglas, *The Lele of the Kasai*, pp. 130–133). Thus, the relation between husband and wives in patrilineal patrilocal herding societies has some of the formal elements of class relations and appropriation of surplus value. The "primitive" form of class relations is, to some degree, a relation between the sexes within the family.

The same is true of sons, both among the Karimojong and among the French peasantry. But sons ordinarily become herd owners or peasants (as small landowners or tenants), so their work for the benefit of the family headed by their fathers is balanced by succession to the headship of a family enterprise themselves. Nevertheless tensions between the generations on the division of benefits, such as the issue of when the son's bride price will be paid among the Karimojong or when the son can marry and start heading the farm among the French peasants, were common results of the structure.

Class relations between families are virtually unknown among the Karimojong: there is a class aspect to herding associations between families with too many cattle and families with too many sons, and in the situation of a man who has lost his herd in a raid, but these are normatively specifically exceptional, if statistically moderately frequent. There are great inequalities among Karimojong families, generally related to herd size, but the inequalities are not generally due to the exploitation of one family by another. The same was true (normally) of differences within French peasantry. A prosperous peasant in most parts of France did not usually hire members of a permanent proletariat.

But French society was riddled through with "exploitation," the use of the labor of people not in one's family for less than its full product. The labor was normally employed under tenancy arrangements, systems of division of the product in which the peasant collected part of the value of each unit produced. Provided such a contract is taken as given, it produces a common interest in higher productivity in both the landlord and the tenant. For most venal offices and land let in *fermage*, the rent or price of the office was fixed, and the tenant or venal officer's income increased directly with productivity. Tithe farming was sometimes arranged the same way (E. Le Roy Ladurie, *The Peasants of Languedoc*, p. 73), so that the last ounce of the tithe extracted went to the commercial tithe collector, while 85–89% went to the monastery as a fixed price paid for the right to collect the tithe. Much of the land was let in *metayage*, in which the landowner and the tenant divided each bushel (after the reserve for seed had been set aside).

Both of these create a peasant (or tithe farmer or venal official) interest in maximizing productivity of the resource, though *metayage* or sharecropping is less effective. While this creates a viable productive system with motivations for rational decision making on each farm, it also produces class divisions between families as well as within them. When the upper classes depend on land rent, it is common Marxist practice to call the mode of production "feudal," distorting somewhat the originally political meaning of that word.

But one does not understand a feudal system until one knows why it is rational for the peasant to work so hard even when the landlord (or the landlord's agent) is off in the city. If the peasant does not produce, there is no rent for the lord to *vivre noblement* on. The peasant, must, in fact, balance a rather delicate ecological intervention, without the help of herbicides or a gasoline tank to provide energy to plow and harvest with, in order to deliver an adequate rent. To understand how this class system works, then, one has to have enough detail to see how the incentive system for the peasant is set up.

We find that, as in modern society, "piece-rate" systems only require the exploiter to measure the total output. Hourly wage labor requires that one monitor the productivity of each hour of work. Thus, incentive and supervisory systems are closely related. One pays traveling salesmen or saleswomen on commission and dimestore salesmen or saleswomen a wage because the latter can be supervised. Reliable agents of the owner are a prerequisite of large-scale use of wage labor.

Similarly, if one looks at the modern corporation with crude surplus value theories for blinders, it is not clear why managers do not join the proletariat. But clearly, career incentive systems make salaries different from hourly wages without career structures. In fact, they supply that crucial missing element of reliable agents of the owners which was part of what kept French landlords from managing their large holdings as a unit with wage labor. Monopoly capitalism as we know it is impossible without bureaucratic management, which is impossible without career incentives.

This realization that the system of interdependent incentives and supervision is at the core of a system of class relations, and that one always has to go into enough detail to see that core, would have aided Paige in *Agrarian Revolution* in some of his more difficult distinctions. If indeed the landowners in the Mekong Delta were getting much of their income from performing transportation and trading services, just as the Grace Company was in coastal Peru, then it is not clear why the Vietnamese landowners should be intransigent and why the Grace Company was so easy to bargain with (*Agrarian Revolution*, p. 145, 319–20). It appears that probably the proportion of total profits in the rice business derived from processing and marketing are small compared to the profits from land rent, while the reverse is the case with Peruvian sugar. But the details of the owner's incentives are not clear enough to tell for sure. Since Paige's theory depends on the details of owner incentives in class conflict situations, this lack of detail is a strategic flaw.

In order to create any structural dynamics, a mode of production has to get all the necessary participants to do what is needed to produce the benefits. Without motivating a craftsman to get training in a difficult skill without a guaranteed career in a given firm, the construction industry cannot build up and tear down efficient site crews in an efficient way. Until one understands why a carpenter learns his trade and then remains available to a series of building contractors, the class relations of the construction industry are easily confused with those of the chemical industry, which also has skilled male workers (see my "Bureaucratic and Craft Administration of Production" *Administrative Science Quarterly*, 1959).

In our day, as in Marx's, the analysis of individual rationality in a setting that shapes the incentive system of the component roles is the subject of economic theory. But most economists are quite good at assuming what those incentive structures are and quite bad at investigating what they are in sufficient detail to see how specific modes of production work. This book has therefore been dedicated to two of Marx's basic postulates: first, that economic theory and its analysis of individual incentives tells us where the energy comes from that makes economic institutions go, and second, that detailed analysis of that actual physical and social setting is required to see exactly what those structural forces are that shape incentives. I have tried to provide an outline of what needs to be analyzed about these shapers of individual incentives in various modes of production in the substantive chapters. I have also tried to provide three examples of what the proper analysis of the mode of production of a society looks like.

In the introduction and conclusion I have argued that many problems in the work of those who draw some of their inspiration from Marx can be clarified by a more nuanced analysis of the economic structure. I would be glad to extend the argument to apply to non-Marxist macro-sociology as well, but a book has to end.

References

Aries, Phillippe
    1962 *Centuries of childhood.* New York: Vintage.
Bandois, Paul-M.
    1932 L'epizootie de 1763. *Revue d'histoire economique et sociale* **20**:354.
Becker, Gary
    1981 *A treatise on the family.* Cambridge, Mass: Harvard University Press.
Bell, Daniel
    1973 *The coming of post industrial society: A venture in social forecasting.* New York: Basic
           Books.
Blau, Peter, and O. D. Duncan
    1967 *The American occupational structure.* New York: Wiley.
Blum, Jerome
    1948 *Noble landowners and agriculture in Austria, 1814–1848: A study in the origins of the
           peasant emancipation of 1848.* Baltimore: Johns Hopkins.
Blumberg, Rae Lesser
    1978 *Stratification: Socioeconomic and sexual inequality.* Dubuque: Wm. C. Brown.
Bois, Paul
    1960 *Paysans de l'ouest: des structures économiques at sociales aux options politiques, depuis
           l' époque revolutionnaire, dans la Sarthe.* Paris: Flammarion.
Burawoy, Michael
    1979 *Manufacturing consent: Changes in the labor process under monopoly capitalism.* Chicago:
           University of Chicago Press.

Clark, Burton
   1960   The "cooling out" function in higher education. *American Journal of Sociology*
   May:569–76.
Cohen, Gerald
   1978   *Karl Marx's theory of history: A defense*. Oxford: Clarendon Press.
Cole, Robert, and Paul Siegel
   1979   *Work, mobility, and participation: A comparative study of American and Japanese industry*.
   Berkeley: University of California Press.
Delaspre, J.
   1952   La naissance d'un paysage rural au XVIIIᵉ siècle sur les hauts plateaux de l'est
   du Cantal et du nord de la Mageride. *Revue de geographie alpine* **4**:494.
Douglas, Mary
   1963   *The Lele of the Kasai*. London: Oxford University Press.
Dovring, Folke
   1960   *Land and labour in Europe, 1900–1950: A comparative survey of recent agrarian history*
   (2nd ed.). The Hague: M. Nijhoff.
Duby, Georges
   1968   *Rural economy and country life in the Medieval West*. Columbia: University of South
   Carolina Press.
Duby, Georges, Armand Wallon, and E. Le Roy Ladurie
   1975   *Histoire de la France rurale* (Volume 2). Paris: Seuil.
Duncan, Beverly
   1964   Variables in urban morphology. In *Contributions to Urban Sociology* edited by Ernest
   W. Burgess and Donald J. Bogue. Chicago: University of Chicago Press.
Duncan, Beverly, George Sabagh, and Maurice D. Van Arsdol, Jr.
   1962   Patterns of city growth. *American Journal of Sociology* **67** (4):418–429.
Duncan, Beverly, and Stanley Lieberson
   1970   *Metropolis and region in transition*. Beverley Hills, Calif.: Sage.
Duncan, Otis D., et al.
   1960   *Metropolis and region*. Baltimore: John Hopkins Press.
Dyson-Hudson, Neville
   1966   *Karimojong politics*. Oxford: Clarendon Press.
Edwards, Richard (editor)
   1973   *Labor market segmentation. Conference on labor market segmentation*. Cambridge,
   Mass.: Harvard University Press.
Elster, Jon
   1978   *Logic and society: Contradictions and possible worlds*. New York: Wiley.
Eyre, Samuel R.
   1968   *Vegetation and soils: A world picture*. Chicago: Aldine.
Festy, Octave
   1947   *Les conditions de production et de recolte des cerales: étude d'histoire économique,
   1789–1795*. Paris: Gallimard.
Forster, Robert
   1957   The noble as landlord in the region of Toulouse at the end of the old regime.
   Journal of Economic History **17**:224–244.
Fortune Magazine
   1981   May 4, The Fortune 500; August 24, The 50 Largest Exporters
Fussel, Georges
   1937   Animal husbandry in eighteenth century England. *Agricultural History* **11**:213, 114.

Galle, Omer
  1963   Occupational composition and the metropolitan hierarchy. *American Journal of Sociology* **69**:260–269.
Granick, David
  1967   *Soviet metal fabricating.* Madison: University of Wisconsin Press.
Hacker, Andrew
  1982   Farewell to the family? *New York Review,* March 18.
Hajnal, J.
  1965   European marriage patterns in perspective. In *Population in history,* edited by David V. Glass and D. E. C. Eversley. Chicago: Aldine.
Henry, Louis
  1965   The population of France in the 18th century. In *Population in history,* edited by D. V. Glass and D. E. C. Eversley. Chicago: Aldine.
  1972   Fécondité des mariages dan le quart sud-ouest de la France de 1720 à 1829. *Annales* Nos. 3, 4–5:612–639, 977–1023.
  1978   Fécondité des mariages dan le quart sud-est de la France de 1670 à 1829. *Population* No. 4–5:855–883.
Henry, Louis, and Claude Levy
  1962   Quelques donées sur la region autour de Paris au xviiie siècle. *Population* **17**:297–326.
Henry, Louis, and Jacques Houdaille
  1973   Fécondité des mariages dans le quart nord-ouest de la France de 1670 à 1829. *Population* No. 4–5:873–924.
Higham, John
  1970   *Strangers in the land: Patterns of American nativism, 1860–1925.* (2nd ed.) New York: Atheneum.
Hirst, L. F.
  1953   *The conquest of the plague: A study of the evolution of epidemiology.* Oxford: Clarendon Press.
Homans, George
  1941   *English villagers of the thirteenth century.* Cambridge, Mass.: Harvard University Press.
Houdaille, Jacques
  1976   Fécondité des mariages dans le quart nord-est de la France de 1670 à 1829. *Annales de démographie historique*:341–392.
Hutchinson, E. P.
  1956   *Immigrants and their children, 1850–1950.* New York: Wiley.
Jencks, Christopher *et al.*
  1972   *Inequality: A reassessment of the effect of family and schooling in America.* New York: Basic.
Kolko, Gabriel
  1962   *Wealth and power in America: An analysis of social class and income distribution.* New York: Praeger.
Latouche, R.
  1932   Le prix du blé à Grenoble du XVe au xviiie siècle. *Revue d'histoire economique et sociale* **20**:337–351.
Lefebvre, Georges
  1961   Urban society in the Orleanais in the late eighteenth century. *Past and Present* **19**:46–75.

Lenski, Gerhard E.
1966 *Power and privilege: A theory of social stratification.* New York: McGraw-Hill.
Le Roy Ladurie, Emmanuel
1974 *The peasants of Languedoc.* Urbana: University of Illinois Press.
Lizerand, Georges
1942 *Le regime rural de l'ancienne France.* Paris: Presses Universitaires.
McGirr, Nancy, and Charles Hirschman
1979 The two-generation urbanite hypothesis revisited. *Demography,* Feb.:27–35.
McKeown, Thomas, and R. G. Brown
1955 Medical evidence related to English population changes in the eighteenth century. *Population Studies* **9**(2):119–141.
Meuvret, J.
1965 Demographic crisis in France from the sixteenth to the eighteenth century. In *Population in History,* edited by D. V. Glass and D. E. C. Eversley. Chicago: Aldine. Pp. 517–518.
Mills, C. Wright, and H. H. Gerth
1952 A Marx for managers. In *Reader in bureaucracy,* edited by R.K. Merton *et al.* Glencoe, Illinois: Free Press.
Mols, Rodger
1954–1956 *Introduction á la demographie historique des villes d'Europe du xive au xviiie siècle.* Gembloux: J. Ducolot.
National Center for Educational Statistics
1981 *The Condition of Education, 1981.* Washington, D.C.: U.S. Government Printing Office.
Odum, E. P.
1963 *Ecology.* New York: Holt, Rinehart & Winston.
Paige, Jeffery
1975 *Agrarian revolution.* New York: Free Press.
Paige, Karen, and Jeffery Paige
1981 *The politics of reproductive ritual.* Berkeley: University of California Press.
Reinhard, Marcel
1968 *Histoire de la population mondiale.* Paris: Montchrestien.
Rothney, John
1969 *The Brittany affair and the crisis of the Ancien Regime.* New York: Oxford University Press.
Ryder, Norman
1973 Contraceptive failure in the United States. *Family Planning Perspectives* **5**:133–143.
Schumpeter, Joseph A.
1950 *Capitalism, socialism and democracy.* New York: Harper. (5th ed. 1976, London: Allen and Unwin.)
1951 *Imperialism and social classes,* translated by Heinz Norden, edited by Paul Sweezy. New York: A. M. Kelley. (Original in *Archiv für Sozialwissenschaft und Sozialpolitik.*)
Sée, Henri
1921 *Esquisse d'une histoire du regime agraire.* Paris: M. Girard. (Reprinted by Slatkine Reprints, 1980.)
Sewell, William, Jr.
1974 Etat, corps and ordre: some notes on the social vocabulary of the French old regime. In *Sozialgeschichte Heute: Festschrift für Hans Rosenberg zum 70 Geburtstag,* edited by Hans-Ulrich Wehler. Gottingen: Vandenhoek and Ruprecht.
1980 *Work and revolution in France.* New York: Cambridge University Press.

Siegfried, André
    1913   *Tableau politique de la France de l'ouest sous le troisième republique.* (Reproduced by
            Arno Press, 1975.)
Skocpol, Theda
    1979   *States and social revolutions.* New York: Cambridge University Press.
Slicher van Bath, B. H.
    1964   *The Agrarian History of Western Europe, A.D. 500–1850,* translated by Olive Ordish.
            New York: St. Martins Press.
Steward, Julian
    1955   *Theory of culture change.* Urbana: University of Illinois Press.
Stinchcombe, Arthur L.
    1959   Bureaucratic and craft administration of production. *Administrative Science Quar-
            terly* **4:**168–187.
    1970   Review symposium: On what is learned in school. *Sociology of Education,*
            43(2):218–222.
    1979   Social mobility in industrial labor markets. *Acta Sociologica* **22**(3):217–249.
    1982   On softheadedness on the future. *Ethics* October.
Thompson, James D.
    1967   *Organizations in action.* New York: McGraw-Hill.
Tilly, Charles
    1964   *The Vendée.* Cambridge, Mass.: Harvard University Press.
    1982   How one kind of struggle-war reshaped all other kinds of struggle in seventeenth
            century France. Working paper of the Center for Research in Social Organization
            No. 241.
Tolbert, Charles, *et al.*
    1980   The structure of economic segmentation. *American Journal of Sociology* **85:**1095–1116.
de Tocqueville, Alexis
    1856   *The Old Regime and the French Revolution.* (Translation published by Doubleday,
            1955.)
U.S. Bureau of the Census
            1940 Census of Population; U.S. Summary, Labor Force. Washington, D.C.: U.S.
            Government Printing Office.
    1949   *Historical statistics of the United States, 1789–1945.* Washington, D.C.: U.S. Gov-
            ernment Printing Office.
            1960 Census of Population, U.S. Summary 1-557-562. Washington, D.C.: U.S. Gov-
            ernment Printing Office.
            1960 Census of Population, Occupational Characteristics, Subject Report PC(2), &
            A. Washington, D.C.: U.S. Government Printing Office.
    1972   *Census of Population 1970,* Occupation by Industry, Final Report, PC(2)-7C. Wash-
            ington, D.C.: U.S. Government Printing Office.
    1979, 1980   *Statistical abstract.* Washington, D.C.: U.S. Government Printing Office.
    1980   *Current Population Reports,* Series P(2), No. 350, Population Profile 1979. Wash-
            ington, D.C.: U.S. Government Printing Office.
U.S. Bureau of Labor Statistics
            Occupational outlook handbook. Washington, D.C.: U.S. Government Printing
            Office.
Usher, Abbot Payton
    1930   The general course of wheat prices in France: 1350–1788. *Review of Economics and
            Statistics* **12:**159–169.

Veblen, Thorstein
1948   *The Portable Veblen.* New York: Viking.
Vilar, Pierre
1953   Geographie et histoire statistique, histoire sociale, et technique de production: quelques points sur l'histoire de la viticulture mediterranienne. In *Hommage à Lucien Febvre, (Vol 1).* Paris: Colin.
Wallerstein, Immanuel
1974   *The modern world system* (Vol. 1). New York: Academic Press.
1980   *The modern world system* (Vol. 2). New York: Academic Press.
White, Harrison
1970   *Chains of opportunity.* Cambridge, Mass.: Harvard.
Wildavsky, Aaron
1979   *The politics of the budgetary process* (3d ed.). Boston: Little, Brown.
Woodward, Joan
1980   *Industrial organization: Theory and practice.* New York: Oxford University Press.
Wright, Erik Olin
1979   *Class structure and income inequality.* New York: Academic Press.
Wright, Erik Olin
1978   *Class, crisis and the state.* London: New Left Books. (Distributed in the U.S. By Schocken Books.)

Index

STUDIES IN SOCIAL DISCONTINUITY

(*Continued from page ii*)

Lucile H. Brockway. Science and Colonial Expansion: The Role of the British Royal Botanic Gardens

James Lang. Portuguese Brazil: The King's Plantation

Elizabeth Hafkin Pleck. Black Migration and Poverty: Boston 1865-1900

Harvey J. Graff. The Literacy Myth: Literacy and Social Structure in the Nineteenth-Century City

Michael Haines. Fertility and Occupation: Population Patterns in Industrialization

Keith Wrightson and David Levine. Poverty and Piety in an English Village: Terling, 1525-1700

Henry A. Gemery and Jan S. Hogendorn (Eds.). The Uncommon Market: Essays in the Economic History of the Atlantic Slave Trade

Tamara K. Hareven (Ed.). Transitions: The Family and the Life Course in Historical Perspective

Randolph Trumbach. The Rise of the Egalitarian Family: Aristocratic Kinship and Domestic Relations in Eighteenth-Century England

Arthur L. Stinchcombe. Theoretical Methods in Social History

Juan G. Espinosa and Andrew S. Zimbalist. Economic Democracy: Workers' Participation in Chilean Industry 1970-1973

Richard Maxwell Brown and Don E. Fehrenbacher (Eds.). Tradition, Conflict, and Modernization: Perspectives on the American Revolution

Harry W. Pearson. The Livelihood of Man by Karl Polanyi

Frederic L. Pryor. The Origins of the Economy: A Comparative Study of Distribution in Primitive and Peasant Economies

Charles P. Cell. Revolution at Work: Mobilization Campaigns in China

Dirk Hoerder. Crowd Action in Revolutionary Massachusetts, 1765-1780

David Levine. Family Formations in an Age of Nascent Capitalism

Ronald Demos Lee (Ed.). Population Patterns in the Past

Michael Schwartz. Radical Protest and Social Structure: The Southern Farmers' Alliance and Cotton Tenancy, 1880-1890

Jane Schneider and Peter Schneider. Culture and Political Economy in Western Sicily

Daniel Chirot. Social Change in a Peripheral Society: The Creation of a Balkan Colony

Stanley H. Brandes. Migration, Kinship, and Community: Tradition and Transition in a Spanish Village

James Lang. Conquest and Commerce: Spain and England in the Americas

Kristian Hvidt. Flight to America: The Social Background of 300,000 Danish Emigrants

STUDIES IN SOCIAL DISCONTINUITY